MATERIAL HARM
archaeological studies of war and violence

MATERIAL HARM
archaeological studies of war and violence

edited by John Carman

1997

Glasgow

CRUITHNE PRESS

Cover illustration: Two earlier Acheulians kill an Austalopithecus in the Sterkfontein Valley about half a million years ago (from Revil Mason, *Prehistory of the Transvaal: a record of human activity*, reproduced with permission of Witwatersrand University Press, Johannesburg).

This horrific and disturbing image – of an event for which there is no evidence – serves to *naturalise* human violence by placing it in the deep human *past* and in the realm of *inter*-specific contralict rather than *intra*-specific conflict.

1997

© The authors

Cruithne Press
197 Great Western Road
St George's Cross
Glasgow G4 9EB

All rights reserved. No part of this publication may be reproduced, stored in a retrieval system, or transmitted in any form or by any means, whether electronic, telepathic, mechanical, photocopying, recording, or otherwise without the prior permission of the publisher.

British Library Cataloguing in Publication Data

A catalogue record for this book is available from the British Library.

ISBN 1-873448-10-4

Set in Palatino by JAZZ CORNETS
and printed and bound in Great Britain by Redwood, Trowbridge, Wiltshire

CONTENTS

Notes on Contributors   vi
Preface   vii
Introduction. Approaches to violence   1
John Carman

1. Identification and analysis of violent and non-violent head injuries in osteo-archaeological material   24
Jennifer Wakely

2. Ancient Egypt and Nubia as a source of information for violent cranial injuries   47
Joyce M. Filer

3. The Crow Creek Massacre, archaeology and prehistoric Plains warfare in contemporary perspective   75
Larry Zimmerman

4. Mightier than the pen? an edgewise look at Irish Bronze Age swords   95
Sue Bridgford

5. War in the Chalcolithic? the meaning of the West Mediterranean hillforts   116
Luiz Oosterbeek

6. The dread of something after death, violation and desecration on the Isle of Man in the tenth century   133
Sarah Tarlow

7. The victim or the crime, park focused conflict in Cambridgeshire and Huntingdonshire 1200–1556   143
Twigs Way

8. Violence and the face   167
Carmen Lange

9. The symbolism of violence in palatial societies of the late Bronze Age Aegean, a gender approach   174
Marianna Nikolaidou and Dimitra Kokkinidou

10. Fighters and foragers, warfare and the spread of agriculture in Borneo   198
Paul Beavitt

11. Giving archaeology a moral voice   220
John Carman

Index   241

NOTES ON CONTRIBUTORS

Paul Beavitt studied anthropology at the London School of Economics and the School of African and Oriental Studies. He carried out fieldwork in Sarawak between 1969 and 1991. He has taught in the Centre for South East Asian Studies at the University of Hull and is currently at the School of Archaeological Studies in the University of Leicester.

Sue Bridgford's first degree in mathematics at Somerville College, Oxford led to an investment management career but the lure of the Bronze Age finally proved too strong. Following distinctions achieved in the Diploma in Archaeology at Birkbeck College, London and the MA in Archaeology and Prehistory at the University of Sheffield, she is currently researching aspects of British Late Bronze Age weapons, warfare and society for her doctoral thesis.

John Carman is a Research Fellow at Clare Hall, University of Cambridge. After a professional career in commerce, he undertook post-graduate study and research in archaeological heritage management at Darwin College, Cambridge receiving his PhD in 1993. His research interests include the social valuation of archaeological material, its management under legal regimes, the history of archaeology, and approaches to writing archaeology – especially what he terms 'committed archaeology'.

After a career in audiology working with deaf people, *Joyce M. Filer* studied egyptology at University College, London. Following this she won a Wellcome Foundation Scholarship to study palaeopathology at post-graduate level. At present she is Special Assistant for Human and Animal Remains in the Department of Egyptian Antiquities at the British Museum, and is currently working on ancient skeletal material excavated in the Sudan.

Dimitra Kokkinidou studied archaeology and art history at the Aristotle University of Thessaloniki, Greece (1984). She received her MPhil (1986) and PhD (1989) in prehistoric archaeology from Birmingham University. She has participated in archaeological surveys and excavations in northern Greece and in Crete. She has published on Greek prehistory and on educational aspects of archaeology, and she is a co-author of *Archaeology and Gender: approaches to Aegean prehistory* (in Greek). She teaches archaeology and museum education at Thessaloniki University.

NOTES ON CONTRIBUTORS

Carmen Lange is pursuing research in archaeology at the University College London Institute of Archaeology.

Marianna Nikolaidou graduated from the Department of History and Archaeology, Aristotle University of Thessaloniki, Greece and did her graduate studies in Thessaloniki and in Cambridge, England. Recently she completed her PhD dissertation on Minoan religious symbolism, and she is a co-author of the book *Archaeology and Gender: approaches to Aegean prehistory* (in Greek). She has taken part in the excavation and study of Neolithic, Bronze Age and Iron Age sites in Crete and northern Greece. She is currently working as a research associate at the Institute of Archaeology, University of California, Los Angeles and as an intern at the Getty Museum in Malibu. She specialises in the Neolithic and Bronze Age of the Aegean and her recent research interests include pottery studies, religion and symbolism, and gender issues.

Luiz Miguel Oosterbeek graduated in History at Lisbon in 1982, and took his PhD at the Institute of Archaeology in London. He became assistant Lecturer of Archaeology at the Escola Superior de Tecnologia de Tomar (Portugal) in 1986 where he is now Joint Professor and head of the Department of Archaeology. His research has focussed on the Mesolithic to the Early Bronze Age in central Portugal, although he is also interested in the history of philosophy.

Sarah Tarlow gained her PhD in Archaeology at Cambridge University in 1995, her research having focused on metaphors of death in Orkney in the last four hundred years. She is also currently working on emotional and experiential aspects of the archaeology of death.

Jennifer Wakely BSc PhD (London) is a lecturer in the Department of Preclinical Sciences and the School of Archaeological Sciences at the University of Leicester. She teaches Human Anatomy to medical students and to students of other health professions and Physical Anthropology and Palaeopathology to undergraduate and postgraduate students in archaeology. Her research interests are in ancient disease and injury with particular reference to medieval England and the effect of urbanisation on health in the past.

Twigs Way is a field archaeologist and gained her PhD from the Department of Archaeology, University of Cambridge, in 1995.

Larry J. Zimmerman earned his PhD at the University of Kansas (1976). He is Distinguished Regents Professor of Anthropology at the University of South Dakota. As Executive Secretary of the World Archaeological Congress from 1990 to 1994 he has been editor of *Plains Anthropologist* and Associate Editor of *American Antiquity*. Research interests include Plains prehistory, computer applications, and the interactions of American Indians and archaeologists.

Preface

This book has a number of origins. Primarily, it is the result of the invitation from Ross Samson to edit a volume on the archaeology of violence and war. I am grateful to him for the opportunity and also for his immense patience in awaiting its arrival on his desk.

I was glad of the opportunity because it has given me the chance to indulge some ideas I have been developing over a few years. My main research interests concern what I call "vectors of moral change of archaeological material" – that is, processes and things that change our understanding of, attitudes towards and feelings about ancient remains. This in turn has led me to consider the role of emotional factors in archaeology – which resulted in a jointly organised session at the Annual Conference of the Theoretical Archaeology Group in Lampeter in 1990 on Emotion in Archaeology. One of the aspects of emotion which grew out of the discussions at that session was that of the moral dimensions of archaeological work, particularly in respect of excavations on former slave-sites in North America, where slavery is frequently relegated to something that happened only in the past, ignoring its modern forms (some of which are to be found only a few miles away from the excavation site). This particular revelation subsequently led to another project – an interdisciplinary conference on unfree labour past and present organised jointly with my wife Patricia in March 1994 which we called Confronting the Past, the aims of which were similar to those of this book. Quite apart from an individual stance on contemporary moral issues, what has emerged from all this is the understanding that the social sciences (including archaeology) are of relevance and value in engaging with the difficult and important concerns of our time. This book, then, aims to set out the beginnings of a specifically archaeological contribution to current debates surrounding the problem of human violence.

Like any edited volume, this book is very much a collaborative effort and I owe a debt of thanks to all those involved. Thanks are due in particular to all the contributors for their forbearance in dealing with a relatively inexperienced editor, and to all those who were invited to contribute and offered papers but were not, in the end, able to contribute for all the best possible reasons. These and others read my own contributions to the book and I am deeply grateful for their gentleness in not criticising them too harshly: this is especially kind of them, given my own tendency to interfere with the work of my contributors. Others yet showed enthusiasm for the project when my own belief that it was possible was waning, and for this I am especially thankful.

In addition to the contributors, then, and in various capacities I hereby thank Dr Dee De Roche, Dr James Gilligan, Professor John Keegan, Dr John Muke, Dr Alinah Kelo Segobye, and Sue Thomas. I am also grateful to my college, Clare Hall, for providing the technical facilities on which the book was put together and constituting a convivial and friendly interdisciplinary environment in which to work. The greatest thanks go to my wife Patricia for living with this project as long as anyone else (and far longer than many) and for regularly reminding me that books do not get published while contributed papers languish on shelves "to be sorted out tomorrow".

John Carman
Clare Hall, Cambridge
February 1996

INTRODUCTION

Approaches to Violence

John Carman

Glimpses of the experience of modern war . . .

An ugly man cradling his shattered hand [says] "Not much you can do, Doc. Cut it off." . . . The medics hide the severed hand under a carpet so the others won't see it. . . . [A colonel] wounded twice, sobbing with anguish, crawled on his hands and knees through the shattered trees, desperate to tell HQ about the slaughter taking place. . . . [Another colonel] wrung his hands together piteously when he heard the latest casualty figures – nearly twenty-five hundred killed and wounded out of a total of three thousand. . . . An ex-major of infantry, who after seeing the slaughter of his battalion . . . on Thanksgiving Day 1944 would never again eat a Thanksgiving Dinner. "I would get up and go to the backyard and cry like a baby. . . . I passed up a helluva lot of turkey dinners that way". . . . (Whiting 1990, ix).

. . . and its archaeological legacy

Here and there, the shell-pocked sides of an old house or a garden shed, which on closer inspection turns out to be made of steel plates marked "105mm howitzer" and dated 1944 . . . a line of foxholes, each one complete with pieces of rotting GI blanket . . . there is a length of Sherman tank track, rubber mounted in rusting steel. . . . Seven times a year . . . whitened skeletons are delivered [to the cemetery]. . . . They are found regularly by the search teams still looking for batches of ammunition... dating from the great slaughter of 1944–45. No-one knows anymore if they are German or [American] (Whiting 1990, 271–73).

Violence is an unpleasant subject to talk or write about, and it is even more unpleasant to encounter in life. It is something of which all human beings seem to be capable, and at the same time an attribute of humanity we would choose to deny. The present century is perhaps the most bloody in human history. At the same time, violence in all its forms has never been regarded as so abnormal and unacceptable as it is in modern societies. We live with violence, but are increasingly intolerant of it.

Archaeology is the long-term study of the human past through its material remains, from the beginnings of humanity to yesterday. Because of its deep time-dimension archaeology is uniquely placed to comment on the human condition. Human violence is a part of that condition. Archaeologists, however, have in general chosen not to comment on this aspect of humanity, preferring to leave the subject to other disciplines – closely related disciplines like anthropology and history, or more distant ones such as sociology and psychology. The aim of this collection of papers is to forge a specifically archaeological contribution to contemporary debates about human violence. In so doing, it is hoped to develop an appropriate language and mode of discourse by which archaeology can contribute to other debates on matters of contemporary ethical and moral concern.

The material remains of the past are mute and must be made to speak. That is the task of the archaeologist. Even such apparently powerful testimony to bloody slaughter as the remains of the Battle of the Hurtgen Forest quoted above (Whiting 1990) are nothing unless supported by a statement of what the experience of such slaughter consisted of and its effect on its human object. For large parts of the human past – even the quite recent past – no such additional testimony exists: there are no survivors' accounts, no official reports, no verbal record, no written transcripts. All that remains is the material record which is the domain of the student of past material culture – the archaeologist. It is one of the tasks of the archaeologist to turn this dead silence into an eloquent statement of experience.

This task is the reverse of that transformation identified by Bob Bushaway (1992) in his study of the monuments to the British casualties of the Great War. Between 1914 and 1919 the experiential material of the war underwent transformation: from lists of named casualties to the construction of monuments commemorating an anonymous "The Fallen" or "The Glorious Dead"; from previously unknown locations, via use as battlefields to places of pilgrimage as war cemeteries (thus becoming "Holy or Sacred Ground"); from military service or duty to a designation as "Sacrifice"; and from the soldier's day-to-day experience to an event akin to "Christ's crucifixion" (Bushaway 1992, 160). "Through the annual act of remembrance . . . the mass of British society was denied access to a political critique of the [Great] war by Kipling's universal motto 'lest we forget'" (Bushaway 1992, 161). To launch a critique of the war – to question its origins, its purpose, its consequences, to ask how people were persuaded willingly to take part – was to deny the dead or demean their sacrifice. To suggest that the war was immoral or unnecessary and that this was known at the time was to render the lives of its vast number of casualties meaningless.

To begin this reverse process of transformation – from material record back to experience – contributors to the book were invited to consider the following specific areas from the perspective of the analysis of material culture:

- the definition of – and archaeological correlates for – violence;
- the circumstances (including the extra-personal causes) of violence;
- sanctioned versus non-sanctioned violence;
- "levels" of violence – interpersonal, intra-societal, inter-societal – and the boundaries between them;
- moral versus physical violence;
- violence towards objects rather than people;
- the phenomenon of war (and its distinction – if valid – from warfare, the making of war);
- ethical and moral aspects of the uses of violence.

Violence and aggression

The book starts from the premise that while all human beings have a genetically programmed capability for violence, this is not necessarily something that is outside voluntary control or always acted upon. Acts of violence derive not from some innate drive but from specific culturally prescribed circumstances. Human beings have an equally strong and equally innate capacity for co-operation. Accordingly, human violence need not be considered or held to be perpetual, nor universal, nor in any circumstances inevitable.

This view of humanity is justified by Ashley Montagu, who set out in his book *The Nature of Human Aggression* (1976, 3–4):

> to refute the conclusions [of] writers who state that human beings are inescapably killers – that because of their animal heritage, they are genetically and instinctively aggressive, and cannot be otherwise. . . . [And] to present and to give evidence for the different view: that no specific human behaviour is genetically determined; that human beings are capable of any kind of behaviour, including aggressive behaviour, and also including kindness, cruelty, sensitiveness, selfishness, nobility, cowardice, playfulness; aggressive behaviour is but one in a long list . . . and that the kind of behaviour a human being displays in any circumstances is determined not by his genes . . . but largely by the experience he has undergone during his life in interaction with those genes.

Montagu's work examines in detail the evidence cited by those who hold that human beings are subject to genetic programming and "naturally" aggressive, together with the framework of thought in which such a depressing view of humanity can catch hold. Reviewing the simplicity of such a view as an explanation for complex behaviour – and the faulty logic underlying such simplicity (Montagu 1976, 52) – he shows how it fits into Judeo-Christian ideas of "original sin" and simplistic readings of the works of Freud and Darwin (pp. 31–39). Reviewing the arguments for the power of instinct and evolutionary adaptation in conditioning humans towards a violent response, he points out the rarity of war within species other than *Homo sapiens* and that (Montagu 1976, 59–60)

> There is nothing in the nature of war or in the nature of humanity that makes war inevitable. Human aggressive impulses can be canalized into other outlets. Political machinery can be designed to make war less likely. These things can be done. But they are most likely to be done when people understand that war is inimical to their personal and collective interests.

In addition, he questions the assumption that aggressive behaviour is the same in animals as it is in humans (Montagu 1976, 61–64), the rigid dichotomy between "innate" and "learned" behaviour patterns (pp. 68–72) and the idea that the human brain is "hard-wired" towards certain fixed propensities at birth (pp. 193–230). He reviews critically the relationship between instances of cannibalism and aggression (pp. 108–21), considers the palaeontological evidence for human violence in the distant past versus the effects of taphonomy (pp. 122–36; cf. Binford 1984) and the inborn "territorial imperative" (pp. 231–57) which leads to war. As alternatives, he quotes the results of research in the social sciences, identifying instances of non-violent co-operation (pp. 137–92), the many and complex causes of wars which cannot be reduced to an instinct towards violence (pp. 271–74) and the dangerous moral and ideological consequences of a belief in innate aggression (pp. 283–99). Montagu's (1976, 299) conclusion is that

> A genuinely healthy society is maintained and sustained not by the competitive struggle for existence to achieve a factitious success, but by a striving for that human cooperativeness which is the true dignity of man, and the respect that humans owe to each other.

Although the "innatist" position has an obvious appeal to the military (whose trade is killing, and for whom such a belief would act as a relief from guilt), it is evident from their reliance on techniques of training derived from psychology and other disciplines that theirs is not a total belief in the inevitability of human aggression and violence. Watson charts the many military uses of psychology, which include selection of personnel for "fighting spirit" (Watson 1978, 45–52); training for the more effective use of weapons individually (pp. 52–65) and in groups (pp. 120–27); and the development of techniques to seek out the "best killers" (pp. 249) and to encourage the "dehumanisation of the enemy" (pp. 250). If military authorities were truly convinced of the innate aggressiveness of the human species, much of this work would be redundant – particularly that related to atrocity research (Watson 1978, 242–50; Keegan 1976, 49–51).

It is for this reason – the specific and *a priori* rejection of the "innatist" or "territorial imperative" position, which regards violence as a genetically programmed inevitability in human affairs – that no contribution to this book is concerned with aggression in lower primates, evidence for prehistoric cannibalism, nor a consideration of the "nature" and incidence of aggressive tendencies. Instead, contributions focus on the search to identify, document and explain the conditions for specific acts of human violence by a reading of the material record.

THE STUDY OF VIOLENCE

In rejecting a purely biological explanation for aggression, the focus is shifted towards the social and cultural dimensions of violent acts.

Violent acts are directed by human beings against other human beings with the intention of doing those others harm. From this perspective, violence is a material event with material consequences. It thus falls within the purview of archaeology because archaeology is a "materialist" science – in the very simple and obvious sense that its object consists of material remains. These material consequences – the effect of violent acts upon material (frequently and all too often human flesh and bone) – are traceable in the archaeological record and are accordingly available for archaeological study. Archaeological study can locate violent acts in their context and thus arrive at a particular understanding of them. This understanding is part of the specifically archaeological contribution to the wider and continuing debate about human violence.

Violent acts can take place at a number of levels. The largest scale is called "war" – the largest of all "total" or "general" war, and at its extreme would see the end of all life on earth (save perhaps some microbes, cockroaches and scorpions which are immune to nuclear or other blast). Smaller scales operate at the interpersonal level – as criminal violence or as wife-beating (otherwise called "domestic" violence). The terminology of violence is interesting: "domestic violence" has the same relationship to violence in general as "civil war" does to war in general. A civil war – which divides a nation or community – is frequently more violent and leaves a more bitter legacy than other wars. Domestic violence – which divides a family – is frequently more intense, more personalised and does more harm to individuals than other forms of violence.

THE INSIGHTS AND FAILINGS OF ANTHROPOLOGY

Anthropologists turned their attention to a consideration of war and violence surprisingly late in the history of the discipline, and there has been much more interest shown by American anthropologists in this area than their British colleagues. Quite why this is the case is not clear, although it may have much to do with American attitudes to the wars in which they have been engaged this century.

The anthropology of war

It was during the period of the Second World War – at the same time as S. L. A. Marshall was carrying out his investigations among military personnel (Keegan 1976, 72–74; Marshall 1947) – that Harry Turney-High (1949) first considered war from an anthropological perspective.

His characterisation of "primitive war" as something distinctive from the "true war" fought by modern states (Turney-High 1949, 23) has had relatively little influence on his successors, although recently rediscovered by Keegan (1993; see below). This first step towards the kind of "materialist" approach advocated here was dismissed by Bohannan (1967, xiii) as merely "descriptive" but Bohannan's own edited volume focuses on law rather than war; out of twenty-three contributions, six are individual studies of warfare while seventeen concern law. Whereas Turney-High (1949) sees war as human beings engaged in actual fighting, Bohannan (1967) and his contributors are more concerned with war as a device for conflict resolution. This distinction may represent a difference in the kind of wars being waged: the Second World War was one of combat by United States forces, and Turney-High's focus on combat may reflect this; by contrast, its replacement – the "Cold" War – was one of threat and counter-threat and war by proxy, in which systems of conflict management came to the fore (Dupuy and Dupuy 1970, 1201–04).

The Cold War, with its threat of nuclear annihilation, seems in general, however, to have affected anthropologists very little in their professional sphere. Edmund Leach's (1965) contribution sought to focus on the reasons why humans kill each other, drawing on Freud to expound an argument – while not biologically based – similar in tone to that of the innate aggressionists. "Killing", he asserts, "is a classifying operation" (p. 175) which gives "psychological satisfaction in itself" (p. 180) and closely related to notions of sacrifice and marriage (p. 183):

> the moral of my story [is] that human society suffers from a kind of collective death wish [but this] does not mean we must respond to it. ... It is much too simple a formula that we kill ... because we are afraid of our own sexuality, but that is roughly the drift of my argument.

Like the innate aggressionists, Leach located the "drive" to war inside the individual human being. The response to his argument is similar to that against the notion of innate aggression: all forms of violence including war are too diverse in type and too complex to be explained simply in terms of a random desire to hurt or kill.

The American involvement in Vietnam – and especially its escalation in the later 1960s – caused American anthropologists in particular to take the subject of war much more seriously. Fried et al.'s symposium took place against a consciousness of the crisis of moral and political confidence the war engendered among academics (Fried et al. 1968, ix):

> the pressing period of intense and growing national unrest brought on by our Vietnam involvement has produced a crisis of conscience which has called into question the right of anthropologists to remain aloof from the great issues of our times.

Taking a generally oppositional and youth-oriented stance to the war – as suggested by the title of the book's foreword "Fink-out or teach-in?" (Fried et al. 1968, ix-xix) – their wide-ranging discussions covered such issues as the biological effects of war on populations (although not individual casualties), the nature of human aggression, the relationship between war and disease, the distinction between "primitive" and "modern" forms of war and their causes, the effects of war on social structure, the psychological dimensions of war (especially its effects), recruitment systems for war (including the draft and conscription) and the availability of alternatives to war. The immediate relevance of all these issues to the Vietnam experience would have been obvious to participants and observers at the symposium and to readers of the book.

The end of the Vietnam involvement led to another period of silence among anthropologists on the subject of war and violence. Partly, this was the period of dominance of innate aggressionist theories – and their popular success (Montagu 1976) – which rendered social explanations irrelevant. But this silence may also be a reflection of the general unwillingness of American institutions (including academic disciplines) to examine the causes and outcomes of the failure in Vietnam. By the 1980s, however, this unwillingness was beginning to be overcome, and a new American belligerence was in the air with an approaching end to the Cold War and American military activity in the Caribbean against governments in Grenada and Panama.

The rekindling of anthropological interest in war was marked by the holding of seminars dedicated to this subject in the 1980s. One of these – an Advanced Seminar held at the School of American Research in March 1986 – sought to "arrive at a better understanding of the causes of both war and peace in pre-state societies and the impact of war on the evolution of those societies" (Haas 1990, xi). The period of silence between Vietnam and the 1980s was marked by an explicit concern to compare the results of this seminar with that organised by Fried et al. in 1967, marking in particular the rise in importance of cultural and historical factors as explanatory mechanisms over biological ones (McCauley 1990).

Ferguson (1984b) and his contributors adopted what they termed a "materialist" approach somewhat different from the one advocated here. Their approach "focuses on war's relation to the practical problems of maintaining life and living standards" (Ferguson 1984a, 23). A review of the anthropological approaches representing this "materialist" approach to the study of war identified these as: considerations of economic causation, socio-cultural evolution, political explanations (Ferguson 1984a, 23–28), ecological studies (p. 28) including population growth models (pp. 33–34), and functionalist approaches (pp. 35–36). Ferguson's (1984a, 60–61) conclusion is that the results of other approaches have

> shown that humanity is doomed to war. . . . Anthropology could emphasise a different message . . . understanding war in state societies requires attention to the economic and political interests of those who decide military policy. . . . If the hidden stakes in modern wars were laid bare, stripped of convenient myths of human aggressiveness and of inevitability then perhaps those who are called to kill and to die will say "no more", and demand that conflicts be addressed through instruments of peace.

This approach is a valuable advance on innate aggressionism and it pays lip-service to the specificity of violent action by a focus on individual contexts for individual wars. Its totalising intent, however, belies the contextuality of individual studies, as summed up in Cohen's (1984, 353) contribution:

> Theories of warfare must develop . . . differing and related models of political process: (1) a model of conditions leading to war, (2) a model explaining the conduct of war and its relation to society, and (3) an explanation and predictive set of statements about the consequences of wars.

Ferguson's volume contains one specifically archaeological contribution which examines the Roman conquest of Britain (Goldberg and Findlow 1984). Its purposes are stated to be to (1) demonstrate the usefulness of archaeological data for the study of warfare, (2) delineate processes that promote or retard the concentration of political power by the application of military force, and (3) evaluate the utility of models derived from "the military sciences" (Goldberg and Findlow 1984, 374–75). In practice, this paper involves the extraction from a fairly eclectic reading-list of military texts "the basic principles of military science" (p. 360) and the construction of a mathematical model of the Roman military system (p. 361). In conclusion the authors assert the usefulness of (1) and (3) and on this basis list the consequences of (2) – all of which were factors included in their model. It is perhaps worth emphasising here that I do not doubt the usefulness of archaeological data in the study of warfare, which is what this volume is about, but I also believe that any form of ersatz wargaming which reduces the horror of human violence – including the actions of the killing machine that was the Roman imperial army – to abstract symbols is entirely inappropriate under the rubric of a "materialist" approach; "materialist" it most certainly is not!

Ferguson's interest in war is continued in a later collection of papers, the intention of which is "to inject history into the anthropology of war" (Ferguson and Whitehead 1992b, xi-xiv). The forms of conflict in which the editors are particularly interested – those on the fringes of large states and empires – are classified as: wars by indigenous peoples against the state; wars by indigenous peoples under state control; and wars between indigenous peoples in conditions created by the presence of the state (Ferguson and Whitehead 1992a, 18). They point out that "a tribal zone can be a very violent place. At its worst it can consume a population" (p. 27), a view which may reflect increasing concern among White Americans of their treatment of the native population. Ferguson and Whitehead's review of contemporary anthropological and ethnographic accounts of such warfare leads them to conclude that the effects of state presence in a "tribal" area generally precede descriptions of indigenous warfare and that the result of state infringement of "tribal" areas is to generate warfare and to transform it rather than to suppress it. Such wars, then, are – like colonialism generally – an appropriation of the "other" and like European "world" wars acts of totalisation (Young 1990, 13-15) and conquest. This theme is exemplified in Strathern's (1992) contribution, which concerns the role of the state in promoting the take-up of guns and the consequent escalation of killing in highland Papua New Guinea warfare. Like Ferguson's 1984 volume this book is totalising in tone and culminates in a series of generalising diagrams (Ferguson and Whitehead 1992b, 251-53).

The anthropology of small-scale violence

The anthropological concentration on war has tended to blunt any interest in violence at smaller scales. A rare exception to this is Riches' (1986a) volume which adopts an approach quite different from that of the materialism of Ferguson and his collaborators (Ferguson 1984b; Ferguson and Whitehead 1992b) by focusing on the symbolic power of violence. "Violence is very much a word of those who witness or who are victims of certain acts, rather than those who perform them" (Riches 1986b, 3). There is a tension in the triangular "performer/victim/witness" relationship of violence which adds to its potency because any act of violence is liable to have its legitimacy contended, while there will be minimal discrepancy between all involved (whether performer, victim or witness) as to a basic understanding that the act was violent since violent acts are highly visible to the senses and yet require little specialised knowledge or equipment to be effective (Riches 1986b, 11). These properties of violent acts make violence a relatively freely available resource which is "appropriate both for practical (instrumental) use and for symbolic (expressive) use" (p. 11). Violence is accordingly "a strategy which is basic to the experience of social interaction" (p. 26).

This view is very much shared by Nordstrom and Martin (1992b). "Violence is not a socio-culturally fragmented phenomenon that occurs 'outside' the arena of everyday life for those affected. It is part and parcel of everyday life for the millions of people who live under oppressive, repressive or explosive politico-military conditions. . . . Violence starts and stops with the people that constitute a society. . . . Violence is not inherent to power, to politics, or to human nature. The only biological reality of violence is that wounds bleed and people die" (Nordstrom and Martin 1992a, 13–14).

Nordstrom and Martin (1992a, 4) charge anthropology with avoiding an engagement with the experience of violence in favour of "a way of thinking that is enmeshed in structural and institutional frameworks" and which serves "the interests of their own country". Such a way of thinking derives at least in part from the tendency in anthropology to treat all subjects, including violence, "objectively" – the "experience-distant (comparative, or etic)" perspective, as Linger (1992, 15) puts it, rather than "experience-near (phenomenological, or emic)". This in turn derives from an early functionalist understanding of violence as one of two main ways of resolving conflict (Bohannan 1967).

Diverse approaches, diverse subjects

Serious anthropological interest in violence as a human phenomenon is clearly very recent – less than fifty years old. While the bulk of the literature concentrates on war, only in the past few years has any concerted interest been shown in violence at smaller scales. Verswijver (1992, 19–20) has usefully summarised the approaches taken, which break down into a concern with *causes* versus an interest in the *effects* of violence. Among those interested in causes, "naturalists" focus on the issue of innate aggression, Marxists have tended to focus on the scarcity of goods, and political exchange theorists on the relationship between warfare and exchange; Heelas (1983, 376) has attempted to reconcile both "innatist" and "culturalist" perspectives on the causes of violence through emphasising the institutions in a culture which encourage "coadapatation". Those interested in effects divide into the ecologically minded – concentrating on the ecologically adaptive functions of war – and the sociologically minded – concentrating on the symbolic attributes of violence. A further division is evident from the preceding discussion. Those interested in the symbolic attributes of violence concentrate on forms of violence other than war. Those interested in ecological and exchange theory have focused on war. Innate aggression, of course, has been used as an adequate explanation for both. Only very recently has the attention began to focus on the experience of violence (Nordstrom and Martin 1992b; Linger 1992) as opposed to a more "detached" approach.

From the perspective of the aims of this volume – the creation of a specifically materialist approach from archaeology, where materialist is defined simply in terms of a focus on physical remains which act as testimony to human experience – it is interesting that those anthropological texts which describe themselves as "materialist" are those which do not attempt to describe experience. Instead, they focus on war as an institution, distancing themselves from the human objects of violence in a search for totalising generalisations.

OTHER APPROACHES TO WAR

Large-scale inter-societal violence – and especially war – is *par excellence* the province of the student of politics and international relations, the strategic theorist and the military historian. For the sociologist it represents a problem remaining to be addressed, particularly since "the most fundamental problem facing us today is the seemingly implacable expansion of the means of violence in the hands of nation-states" (Giddens 1987, 182).

Non-materialist approaches

War has been defined from the political science perspective as "organised violence carried on by political units against each other [in which killing has] a vicarious and official character, [and is thus] the symbolic responsibility of the [political] unit whose agent the killer is" (Bull 1977, 184). There is a perceived need to distinguish between "war in the material sense, that is actual hostilities, and war in the legal or normative sense, a notional state of affairs brought into being by the satisfaction of certain legal or normative criteria" (Bull 1977, 185). For the strategic theorist, such "legal or normative" war is not in fact war since *"war is . . . an act of force to compel our enemy to do our will"* (Clausewitz 1976, 75; emphasis in original) – which requires actual violent action – and, because it has the purpose of compelling compliance, "war, therefore, is an act of policy" (Clausewitz 1976, 87). This view has been defended by Brodie (1973) who uses it as a starting point from which to conduct a critique of United States military policy in the twentieth century, culminating with a condemnation of the then current involvement in Vietnam and a compassionate but fierce critique of the exponents of the pre-emptive nuclear strike as the "solution" to the Cold War.

Such approaches derive from an entirely presentist perspective: their concern is war today and how to fight it if one must or how to avoid it if possible. They rarely, however, attempt to describe the experience of their subject: a rare example is from Clausewitz (1976, 113), who invites us to "accompany a novice to the battlefield" as he passes through "layers of increasing intensity of danger" – a passage clearly based upon his own battlefield experiences in the time of Napoleon.

In similar vein, military historians in general avoid a direct engagement with their subject-matter despite the fact that many – such as Montgomery, Fuller or the colonels Dupuy – have been, like Clausewitz before them, serving soldiers. Instead, they choose to focus on aspects which serve to de-emphasise the horrible experience of combat. Montgomery (1968, 5) claimed not to have "written [his] book to glorify war [but to] highlight the human endeavour . . . which is brought out in wartime" – but the human endeavour he focuses on is that of "GENERALSHIP [which] is a theme which will run like a golden thread throughout [his] book" (p. 15). Similarly, Fuller (1970) uses his work to explore what he sees as the irreconcilable difference between Western and Eastern modes of thought and systems of government; the frequent need to go to war becomes, for him, the fault of the influence of the imperialist ideal which "infects" Western democracy from time to time. The individual battles on which these books concentrate are seen from a detached, general's vantage-point – serving to reduce them to the level of academic problems rather than Clausewitzian provinces of danger.

Dupuy and Dupuy (1970, xi) take a broader view than Montgomery or Fuller although their *Encyclopedia* has the more limited aim of providing "a comprehensive survey of the history of war . . . and to provide a . . . reference work". The approach taken is necessarily dry, but it covers a wide range of concerns from the earliest evidence for war making (Dupuy and Dupuy 1970, 1) to 1965, taking in not only the great generals, but also developments in the fields of weaponry, tactics, military organisation, logistics and military law on land, sea and (latterly) in the air. All such works are in the end designed to improve military effectiveness by adding to the professional knowledge of military affairs. This aim is shared by, for example, Dupuy (1977) who sought to persuade the NATO military establishment of the value of a General Staff organised along the lines of that of Germany to 1945; and by Dixon's (1979) study of the psychological traits of senior commanders which caused them to fail as battlefield leaders.

The contribution of materialism

A recent trend among a few historians of war has been to adopt a more "materialist" approach in the sense used here, focusing on the experience of combat. The purpose has become (Keegan 1976, 78):

> to demonstrate, as exactly as possible, what the warfare, respectively, of hand, single-missile and multiple-missile weapons was (and is) like, and to suggest how and why the men who have had (and do have) to face these weapons control their fears, staunch their wounds, go to their deaths. It is a personal attempt to catch a glimpse of the face of battle.

In two key works – *The Face of Battle* and *The Price of Admiralty* – John Keegan has explored the experience of combat, on land since the fifteenth century and at sea since the eighteenth century. Hanson (1991) has extended this approach to the study of Ancient Greek hoplite warfare. Such an approach involves not only a consideration of the political and military context for individual battles (the "general's eye view" of conventional military historians such as Montgomery and Fuller), but a detailed consideration of the clash of individual types of arm and what actually happens to all concerned in, for instance, a cavalry charge against infantry (Keegan 1976, 94–97; 153–59), the types of wounds inflicted and their consequences (disfigurement, death), and what causes men to stand or flee (e.g. pp. 169–74). The charge of "squeamishness" which Keegan (1993) bestows upon his military historian colleagues is thus inapplicable to this approach, which has to engage with the full ghastliness of war "at the sharp end".

Keegan's (1993) "materialist" approach is maintained in his contribution to the theory of war – a refutation of Clausewitz's (1976, 87) dictum that "war is merely the continuation of policy by other means". Instead, he argues, war is a cultural phenomenon and over human history has become a habit. His examples are more representative of human history than is typically the case in military history texts: 60% of the book is read before one encounters any mention of classical Greek warfare, as compared with 10% for Montgomery (1968) and 1.5% for Dupuy and Dupuy (1970). There is throughout the book a strong focus on the physical material of war, such as weaponry, fortification, injuries to the human frame; on technology, from stone through iron to gunpowder, from the use of horses to motorised transport, the development of organisation in armies and logistics; and on the material conditions of war, including geographical and environmental limitations on war making. There is also an emphasis on action "not for the squeamish" (Keegan 1993, 160):

> the farmer lacks skills both as a butcher of slaughtered meat and as a killer of young, nimble animals likely to evade his lethal intentions. . . . Pastoralists, on the other hand, learn to kill, and to select for killing, as a matter of course. . . . Dealing the lethal blow, once, quickly, and neatly, was a principal pastoral skill, heightened no doubt by anatomical knowledge gained in regular butchery; the need to castrate most of the males in the flock taught another lesson in cutting flesh, as also did lambing and the rough veterinary surgery of flock management.
>
> It was flock management, as much as slaughter and butchery, which made the pastoralists so cold-bloodedly adept at confronting the sedentary agriculturalists in battle. . . . Working a herd . . . was the pastoralist's stock in trade. They knew how to break a flock up into manageable sections, how to cut off a line of retreat by circling to a flank, how to compress scattered beasts into a compact mass, how to isolate flock-leaders, how to dominate superior numbers by threat and menace, how to kill the chosen few while leaving the mass inert and subject to control.
>
> All the pastoralists' methods of battle . . . disclose such a pattern . . .

A crucial concept for Keegan is that of the "military horizon" – a concept derived from the anthropological work of Turney-High (1949), who distinguished "primitive" from modern war on this ground but who left the concept undefined. For Keegan (1993, 176), the military horizon is comprised of the combination of two key material elements: a technology of mass slaughter (originally located in the combination of the chariot, the composite bow and the horse with its trappings); and a technology of power and control allowing the emergence of the army as an institution (which he locates in the eighth century BC Assyrian state) (pp. 168–77). Communities who have yet to cross this horizon may fight wars, but they are characterised by "tentativeness of encounter and the association of ritual and ceremony with its aftermath" (p. 213), thus limiting its effect. In contrast, western war is "comprised of three elements . . . moral, intellectual and technological . . . the face-to-face battle to the death . . . the ethic of holy war . . . [and] forsaking arms control" by opening warfare up to technological innovation, especially gunpowder and high explosives (pp. 389–90). Many of Keegan's ideas derive from anthropological sources. He cites the Yanomamo "cult of ferocity" which is nurtured by inter-group and intra-family violence so as to be at the service of war-making (pp. 94–98), and the Maring whose limited ritualised fighting constitutes "war" but whose "raiding and routs" are forms of murder which derive from their wars (pp. 98–103). Keegan subscribes to the conventional view that war is derived from smaller-scale violence in the same way that large social groupings derive from agglomerations of nuclear families (pp. 115–16). If, however, we drop the assumption that societies are grounded in the family, and instead adopt as an alternative the notion that the family is a creation of cultural categorisation (Kropotkin 1972, 110–12), then Keegan's anthropological examples instead point to a different conclusion: that war does not arise out of small-scale violence, but that small-scale violence is a product of war-making by processes as yet unsought and therefore unrecognised.

Understanding Personal Violence

Legal anthropology recognises an opposition of "talking" to "fighting" (Roberts 1979, 154) which is equated with the difference between "law" and "war" (Bohannan 1967). Roberts sees in the anthropological literature a link between the "approved values" of a society and the actual incidence of interpersonal violence. Typically "societies where postures of independent, aggressive self-reliance are encouraged" are those where "disputes most often end in violent confrontation"

(Roberts 1979, 157). He also sees a link between levels of violence since "where private retaliatory violence is common inter-group fighting is also most frequently observed" (Roberts 1979, 157) although he is forced to admit that the linking mechanism is not clear.

This view is challenged by Campbell (1992, 239) in her discussion of wife-battering: "anthropologists have been unable to consistently demonstrate what, if any, forms of violent behaviour vary together." In attempting to find ways of dealing with wife-battering there is, she suggests, a need to consider (1) the general level of violence in a society, (2) the presence or absence of community intervention and (3) the degree of acceptance of definitions of masculinity which include the dominance of men over women and which sanction the use of violence against them (Campbell 1992, 240).

Much recent work, like Campbell's, concerns male violence directed against women. There are (Abercrombie and Warde 1992, 234)

> in sociology two strikingly different analyses of crimes of violence against women: one in which they are the infrequent consequence of a few mentally deranged men (which is supported by the low incidence of such crimes in the criminal statistics); and one in which they are an institutionalized set of practices which are part of an overarching system of gender inequality (in which the low number of convictions for such crimes is merely evidence for the state's collusion). The former, while fitting in with much of popular ideology, is contradicted by current sociological studies of men's violence; the latter is more consistent with the evidence of ... research.

Female violence is far less common than male violence. Out of 1,000 cases of domestic violence in 1979 only ten were instances of women attacking men (Morris 1987, 182). On the other hand, in a significant number of cases, wife battering by men is excused by laying blame on the woman's behaviour (Morris 1987, 185-87). Female violence is most often directed against members of the family but – to put this in context – a survey of 1967 indicated that of all violent offenders only 7% were women (Morris 1987, 28). In 1985, of all offenders, only 9% were women convicted of violence; the equivalent figure for men was 14% (Morris 1987, 206). Morris' (1987, 192) overall conclusion is that "men – and patriarchal social forces – are [responsible for rape, wife abuse and the sexual abuse of children]" – in other words, that women are the victims of violence, not its perpetrators. Keegan (1993), too, notes that war is an exclusively male activity without offering any explanation. In stressing the fact that men are more violent than women, Morris (1987, 35) notes that the increase in the violence of each over time is approximately the same. She points out that female violence is related to other factors, such as age, race and social class: violence is higher among adolescents than children or adults, among black women than white women, and among the working class than other groups (Morris 1987, 28).

This emphasis on the social context of violence is supported by Campbell (1992, 242), who points to cultural norms as a factor in the incidence of wife-battering. Vold (1979, 234) explains the higher murder rate in the United States over Europe in terms of the greater social acceptability of violence in the US. McKnight (1986) emphasises the effect of social stress as a context of violence in an Aboriginal camp and Dunning et al. (1986, 182) "the long-standing features of specific sections of the working class" as causal factors in relation to football hooliganism. A sophisticated approach marks Linger's (1992) identification of a culturally determined "script" which operates in the form of Brazilian street-fight called *briga*. Similarly, Jones (1980, 98) emphasises the need to distinguish between "an impromptu scrap [and] institutionalised combat". The difference he identifies is that the latter have rules which must be followed, since otherwise the participants lose rather than gain prestige (Jones 1980, 98). The duel (an example of institutionalised combat with rules to be followed, along with any aggressive competition of a social, economic or political kind) has, for Jones (p. 101), its roots in the "need, forced on participants by society, to maintain, and preferably to enhance their reputations". Forms of violence where there are no rules include, we are told, murder, assassination, ambush, street brawls (but see Linger 1992), terrorist activities and spectator violence at sports events (Jones 1980, 100).

It is evident that there is a concentration by some writers on the notion of personal honour as a causal factor – in Spanish insurrections (Corbin 1986), in the bullfighting culture (Marvin 1986) and in the attractions of the Japanese cinema genres of violence (Moeran 1986). Such a view can be well supported by the literature on the organised crime syndicate of the United States, where personal honour and the code of keeping silent (*omerta*) are enforced by the fear of extreme violence (Turkus and Feder 1974, 130; Maas 1968). As Vold (1979, 352–53) points out, however, the specifics of this highly organised and controlled form of criminal violence has less to do with psychopathology than with business practice:

the activities [of the syndicate] are illegal and undercover. . . . Competitors are brought into line by direct influence and intimidation. The goon squads of gunmen employed for this work are better understood as the enforcers of underworld decrees and decisions. . . . Uncertainties. . . are resolved through direct battle – gang war.

Once again – even where the individual psychology can be seen to be relevant through the notion of personal respect and honour – the social context is a crucial factor in understanding particular forms and instances of violence.

This point has direct implications for an archaeological contribution to understanding and documenting the phenomenon of human violence. Archaeological material is meaningless when divorced from its context. It is indeed the (re)creation of social context from the material remains of the past that is the concern of archaeology. The physical evidence of violence in the past is located in an archaeological context. That context provides the framework for its understanding.

ARCHAEOLOGY AND VIOLENCE

The preceding brief survey of some of the literature on war and violence has attempted to demonstrate the kinds of approaches taken in relevant fields and the need to take account of its context to understanding any act of violence. It is possible to recreate context from archaeology and it is here that archaeology can have value. This book, however, represents a beginning not an end. The papers collected together here were not written with the intention of demonstrating the effectiveness of the contextual archaeological approach to the study of violence, but with the idea that archaeology has a contribution to make and with the purpose of investigating the ways in which this can be done. The consideration of the specific forms such an archaeological contribution could make will be taken up in the conclusions which follow the individual papers.

In a collected volume such as this it is necessary to order the contributions in some way, and such ordering will always be arbitrary. No single order can do full justice to the varied themes represented by each individual paper, and these themes will be discussed in more detail in the conclusion. The aim in adopting this structure is to provide a greater sense of the coherence of the book than is normal in a collection as diverse as this; in effect, the idea is to create a single work out of many separate contributions. The papers that follow are grouped informally into sections representing various classes of evidence. The papers by Wakely, Filer and Zimmerman all concern the evidence of violence visible on human remains. Bridgford considers a particular class of object – the sword – while the papers by Oosterbeek, Tarlow and Way consider landscape monuments from different periods. The papers by Lange and by Nikolaidou and Kokkinidou concern the relationship between violence and symbolic representation in the ancient world. Finally, the paper by Beavitt takes an ethno-archaeological approach.

In addition to this grouping, the papers can be seen as moving along a rough continuum from a relatively un-socially contextualised approach to a more deeply socially contextualised approach. Having said this, it will be evident to readers that any such continuum that is visible here contains many loops, gaps, pauses and other disturbances and interruptions, so it is in no way a simple straight line. All the papers are concerned with social context in one way or another, and depending how you measure such contextuality each will be "more" or "less" socially "embedded" than either its predecessor or its successor.

There is no attempt to group the papers along a temporal continuum from more ancient to less recent, nor to group them geographically. Wakely, Bridgford, Oosterbeek, Tarlow, Way and Nikolaidou and Kokkinidou collectively consider material from various parts and periods of European prehistory and history. Filer covers Egypt while Zimmerman considers North America. Lange and Beavitt cover Asia. In all, the contributions range in time from the Bronze Age to the modern period.

Archaeology is – among other things – the study of long-term history and in one sense at least others have stolen a march on us in the field of the study of violence. We end this introduction where we began: with the experience of soldiers.

Keegan (1976, 320–24) charts the increasing difference from day-to-day life of the violence of battlefield experience. Soldiers are not unaware of this, and the increasing mechanisation of warfare is not lost on them. As Henry Ford pioneered mass production in industry, so the First World War pioneered mass slaughter on an industrial scale. In the Hurtgen Forest, where this chapter began, the industrialisation of war was noted with bitter but realistic humour: for those who were there, the Hurtgen Forest was and remains "The Death Factory" (Whiting 1990).

REFERENCES

Abercrombie, N. and Warde, A. 1992. *Contemporary British Society: a new introduction*. Cambridge, Polity Press.

Binford, L. 1984. *Bones: Ancient Men and Modern Myths*. London, Academic Press.

Bohannan, P. (ed.) 1967. *Law and Warfare*. New York, Natural History Press.

Brodie, B. 1973. *War and Politics*. London, Cassell.

Bull, H. 1977. *The Anarchical Society: a study of order in world politics*. London, MacMillan.

Bushaway, B. 1992. Name upon name: the Great War and Remembrance. In R. Porter (ed.), *Myths of the English*, 136–67. Cambridge, Polity Press.

Campbell, J. C. 1992. Wife-battering: cultural contexts versus social sciences. In D. A. Counts, J. K. Brown and J. C. Campbell (eds), *Sanctions and Society: Cultural Perspectives on the Beating of Wives*. Boulder, Co., Westview Press (Women in Cross-Cultural Perspective).

von Clausewitz, C. 1976 [1832]. *On War*. Edited and translated by M. Howard and P. Paret. Princeton, University Press.

Cohen, R. 1984. Warfare and state formation: wars make states and states make wars. In *Warfare, Culture and Environment. Studies in Anthropology*, 329–58. Orlando, Academic Press.

Corbin, J. 1986. Insurrections in Spain: Casas Viejas 1933 and Madrid 1981. In D. Riches (ed.), *The Anthropology of Violence*, 28–49. Oxford, Basil Blackwell.

Dixon, N. E. 1979. *On the Psychology of Military Incompetence*. London, Futura.

Dunning, E., Murphy, P. and Williams, J. 1986. "Casuals", "terrace crews" and "fighting firms": towards a sociological explanation for football hooligan behaviour. In D. Riches (ed.), *The Anthropology of Violence*, 164–83. Oxford, Basil Blackwell.

Dupuy, Col. T. N. 1977. *A Genius for War: the German army and General Staff 1807–1945*. London, Macdonald and Jane's.

Dupuy, R. E. and Dupuy, T. N. 1970. *The Encyclopedia of Military History from 3500 B.C. to the Present*. London, Macdonald and Jane's.

Ferguson, R. B. 1984a. Introduction: studying war. In R. B. Ferguson (ed.), *Warfare, Culture and Environment. Studies in Anthropology*, 1–81. Orlando, Academic Press.

Ferguson, R. B. (ed.) 1984b. *Warfare, Culture and Environment. Studies in Anthropology*. Orlando, Academic Press.

Ferguson, R. B. and Whitehead, N. L. 1992a. The violent edge of empire. In R. B. Ferguson and N. L. Whitehead (eds), *War in the Tribal Zone: expanding states and indigenous warfare*, 1–30. Santa Fe, School of American Research Press.

Ferguson, R. B. and Whitehead, N. L. (eds) 1992b. *War in the Tribal Zone: expanding states and indigenous warfare*. Santa Fe, School of American Research Press.

Fried, M., Harris, M. and Murphy, R. (eds) 1968. *War: the Anthropology of Armed Conflict and Aggression*. New York, Natural History Press.

Fuller, J. F. C. 1970. *The Decisive Battles of the Western World and their Effect upon History*, 2 vols. Edited by J. Terraine. London, Paladin.

Giddens, A. 1987. *Social Theory and Modern Sociology*. Cambridge, Polity Press.

Goldberg, N. J. and Findlow, F. J. 1984. A quantitative analysis of Roman military operations in Britain, circa AD 43 to 238. In R. B. Ferguson (ed.), *Warfare, Culture and Environment. Studies in Anthropology*, 359–85. Orlando, Academic Press.

Haas, J. (ed.) 1990. *The Anthropology of War*. Cambridge, University Press.

Hanson, V.D. (ed.) 1991. *Hoplites: the classical Greek battle experience*. London, Routledge.

Heelas, P. 1983. Anthropological perspectives on violence: universals and particulars. *Zygon* 18(4), 375–404.

Jones, S. Institutions of violence. In J. Cherfas and R. Lewin (eds), *Not Work Alone: a cross-cultural view of activities superfluous to survival*, 98–111. London, Temple Smith.

Keegan, J. 1976. *The Face of Battle*. London, Hutchinson.

Keegan, J. 1988. *The Price of Admiralty: war at sea from man of war to submarine*. London, Hutchinson.

Keegan, J. 1993. *A History of Warfare*. London, Hutchinson.

Kropotkin, P. 1972 [1902]. *Mutual Aid: a factor of evolution*. Edited by P. Avrich. New York, University Press.

Leach, E. 1965. The nature of war. *Disarmament and Arms Control* 3, 165–83.

Linger, D. T. 1992. *Dangerous Encounters: meanings of violence in a Brazilian city*. Stanford, Cal., Stanford University Press.

Maas, P. 1968. *The Valachi Papers*. New York, Putnam.

Marshall, S. L. A. 1947. *Men Under Fire*. New York, William Morrow.

Marvin, G. 1986. Honour, integrity and the problem of violence in the Spanish bullfight. In D. Riches (ed.), *The Anthropology of Violence*, 118–35. Oxford, Basil Blackwell.

McCauley, C. 1990. Conference overview. In J. Haas (ed.), *The Anthropology of War*, 1–25. Cambridge, University Press.

McKnight, D. 1986. Fighting in an Australian Aboriginal supercamp. In D. Riches (ed.), *The Anthropology of Violence*, 136–63. Oxford, Basil Blackwell.

Moeran, B. 1986. The beauty of violence: jidaigeki, yakuza and "eroduction" films in Japanese cinema. In D. Riches (ed.), *The Anthropology of Violence*, 103–17. Oxford, Basil Blackwell.

Montagu, A. 1976. *The Nature of Human Aggression*. Oxford, University Press.

Montgomery, Field Marshall Viscount, of Alamein. 1968. *A History of Warfare*. London, Collins.

Morris, A. 1987. *Women, Crime and Criminal Justice*. Oxford, Basil Blackwell.

Nordstrom, C. and Martin, J-A. 1992a. The culture of conflict: field reality and theory. In C. Nordstrom and J.-A. Martin (eds), *The Paths to Domination, Resistance and Terror*, 3–17. Berkeley, University of California Press.

Nordstrom, C. and Martin, J.-A. (eds) 1992b. *The Paths to Domination, Resistance and Terror*. Berkeley, University of California Press.

Riches, D. (ed.) 1986a. *The Anthropology of Violence*. Oxford, Basil Blackwell.

Riches, D. 1986b. The phenomenon of violence. In D. Riches (ed.), *The Anthropology of Violence*, 1–27. Oxford, Basil Blackwell.

Roberts, S. 1979. *Order and Dispute: an introduction to legal anthropology*. Harmondsworth, Penguin.

Strathern, A. 1992. Let the guns go down. In R. B. Ferguson and N. L. Whitehead (eds), *War in the Tribal Zone: expanding states and indigenous warfare*, 229–50. Santa Fe, School of American Research Press.

Turkus, B. B. and Feder, S. 1974 [1951]. *Murder Inc*. New York, Manor Press.

Turney-High, H. H. 1949. *Primitive War: its practice and concepts*. Columbia, University of South Carolina Press.

Verswijver, G. 1992. *The Club Fighters of the Amazon: warfare among the Kaiopo indians of central Brazil*. Gent, Rijksuniversitet.

Vold, G. B. 1979. *Theoretical Criminology*. 2nd edition, prepared by T. J. Bernard. Oxford, University Press.

Watson, P. 1978. *War on the Mind: the military uses and abuses of psychology*. London, Hutchinson.

Whiting, C. 1990. *The Battle of the Hurtgen Forest: the untold story of a disastrous campaign*. London, Mandarin.

Young, R. 1990. *White Mythologies: writing history and the West*. London, Routledge.

Identification and Analysis of Violent and Non-violent Head Injuries in Osteo-archaeological Material

Jennifer Wakely

It *is a commonly held* view that "human nature" is inherently violent, and that this tendency is a product of our genetic programming and evolutionary history. Evidence most commonly cited in support of this position is the frequent discovery of damaged skulls, particularly those of prehistoric date, by archaeologists.

To examine this material critically it is necessary to establish objective and repeatable criteria by which we can distinguish human-made trauma from taphonomic changes or disease processes that may cause skull damage. That is the intention in the first part of this chapter. In the second part human responses to head injury, in the form of attempts at treatment, will be examined. The literature in this field is vast, and it is not my intention to produce an exhaustive review of every reported example, but rather to use selected cases to illustrate the world-wide occurrence and long time-span over which head injuries and their treatment have been recorded archaeologically and to develop diagnostic criteria that can be cited to recognise the genuine ones. I will attempt throughout to interpret the motives of both combatants and healers whose activities are revealed to us in the marks they left on the skulls of their fellow humans.

An injury inflicted in formal or informal conflict is clearly violent in intent and performance. However, we will also see evidence of practices that, although they did damage to the skull and were physically

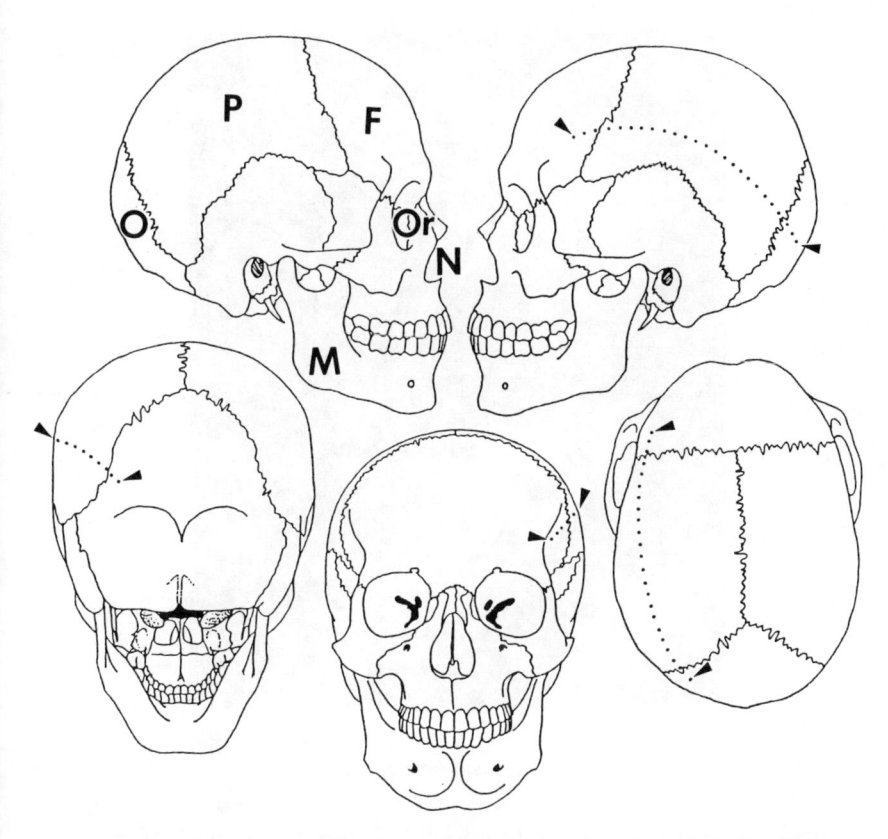

Figure 1. Location of sword cuts on an Anglo-Saxon skull from Eccles, Kent. Their position shows that they were inflicted by a right-handed opponent from in front. F = frontal bone; P = parietal bone; Or = orbit; N = nose; M = mandible; · · · · = cut (drawing courtesy of Dr S. J. Wenham).

traumatic to the recipient, were caused by an attempt to heal or as a result of deeply held tradition or belief. These I will describe as "non-violent head injuries".

THE VIOLENT INJURIES

Courville (1967) wrote that "man's inhumanity to man as manifested by wounds of the head is a heritage of his past." In support of his conclusion he describes a range of examples from the Lower, Middle and Upper Palaeolithic of Europe and Asia, from *Homo erectus* in Java and China to the Neanderthals and *Homo sapiens sapiens*. Most of the injuries he describes are depressed fractures, identified as in modern forensic science as a pond-like depression surrounded by radiating

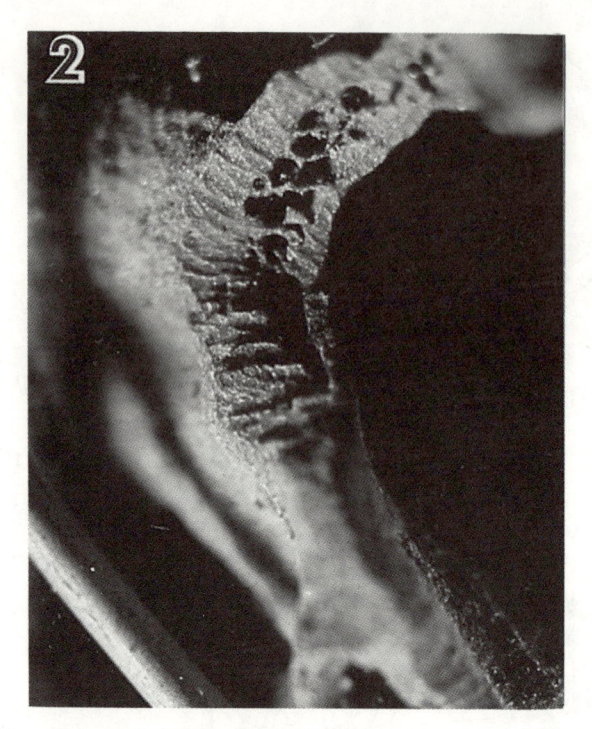

Figure 2. U-shaped grooves made by the teeth of gnawing rodents on an Iban trophy head from Borneo.

fissures, and on the left fronto-parietal region of the skull (Figure 1). This is the site at which an injury would be inflicted in hand-to-hand combat when facing a right-handed adversary. He also discusses the extensive destruction of the skull base, which is attributed to brain removal for cannibalism. In this he follows the position taken by Dart (1953), who explained the large number of damaged skulls in South African fossil deposits in emotive terms such as "blood lust". Later adherents to this viewpoint, such as Ardrey (1961; 1976), used the hypothesis of inherited violence, especially in males, to support his contention that the disappearance of the Neanderthalers from Europe was the result of systematic genocide by our own ancestors, *Homo sapiens sapiens*. How far do these often passionately held beliefs stand up to critical scrutiny? Leakey (1981) is of the opinion that they do not, holding that most can be explained as interactions between the pre-fossil bone and the burial environment, e.g. animal scavenging and soil or water damage; the sort of changes described by Wells (1967) as "pseudo-pathology".

Short acquaintance with any moderately sized non-fossilised skeletal collection soon teaches one that many of the skulls will be split, fragmented or show extensive erosion of the facial skeleton and the base. This is readily accepted as the result of natural decay processes and environmental conditions, or the effect of later human use of the site, such as agriculture or building works. It is not seized upon as evidence that the Christian citizens of London (White 1988) or York (Dawes and Magilton 1980) were in constant genetically determined strife. Animal damage is also common on bodies left unburied for any length of time (Figure 2). It most often affects long bones because they are most easily chewed but is also seen on skulls. Whether the animals are large, like a hyena (Horowitz and Smith 1988), or small, like rats or mice (Brothwell 1981) they favour places on the skull which they can bite easily, such as holes or protrusions. Since these occur predominantly on the face or skull-base the front and base of the skull is the most often attacked. The burden of proof rests on those who would attribute these natural events to human violence or ritual (Wells 1967; Fulchieri et al. 1986).

Criteria for the identification of head injuries inflicted in vivo or around the time of death (perimortem) fall into two groups – the location and the appearance (naked-eye or microscopical) of the damaged skull. Within the classification of genuine trauma we also have to distinguish between injuries due to personal conflict and those occurring accidentally. According to Lovejoy and Heiple (1981) a population in which fractures mainly affect the post-cranial skeleton, such as the Native Americans of Libben County Ohio, and where men, women and children are equally affected is one where most trauma is accidental. Studies on non-human primates (Jurmain 1989) show that both accidents and aggression contribute to the overall frequency of cranial and post-cranial injury within a population. So too with ourselves.

There can be no disputing that the location of the damage is a strong indicator of deliberate intent in inflicting it. Modern forensic science and ethnography as well as the archaeological record agree that injuries to the left fronto-parietal region of the skull are caused by a fairly "formal" style of fighting, face-to-face with a right handed opponent (Manchester 1983; Wenham 1989). However, this is far from saying that all injuries in this part of the skull are purposefully inflicted (Figure 1).

A good example of a large collection of human skeletons showing violent cranial and post-cranial injuries is that of the Scandinavian medieval battlefield cemetery of Wisby, described by Inglemark

(1939). Three mass graves were excavated. In the first, twenty-four out of thirty skulls showed sword or axe wounds on the left side or front, in the second, the figure was twenty-six out of forty-five and in the third and smallest grave, three out of eight.

From an entirely different time and culture Martin et al. (n.d.) showed that thirty out of four hundred and twenty-nine skulls from the prehispanic Guanche people of the Canary Islands showed head wounds. Sixteen fell on the frontal bone (R-9 L-7) and fourteen (L-8 R-2 both-4) on the parietal bone, indicating perhaps a less structured fighting style than in medieval Europe. Out of the four hundred and eighty-six skeletons recovered from the ossuary at Crow Creek, South Dakota, forty-two per cent showed depressed fractures of the skull, predominantly on the front at the top. These Plains Indians had been the victims of a massacre in AD 1325 (Willey 1982; and see Zimmerman, this volume). Webb (1989) examined a large sample of Australian prehistoric skulls, using conflict levels as an indicator of social and biological stress. He discovered some interesting regional differences in the location of skull fractures. In skeletons obtained from desert environments depressed fractures in males were most common on the front and left. In females however they occurred mainly on the right and the back, suggesting an attack from behind, perhaps better described as murder than combat. Walker (1989) studied skeletons from a pre-European contact Native American community from the coast of Southern California. The majority of depressed fractures were found in men on the front and top of the skull. He quotes historical accounts of these people settling disputes between men by exchanging blow for blow, face-to-face until blood was drawn, when the combat would stop.

Although this appears to be a male activity it should not be used to support the contention that the human male has some sort of genetically determined mystical affinity for weapons and warfare (Ardrey 1961). Rose et al. (1989) in their critique of biological determinism argue that male aggression is socially not biologically conditioned. We should not forget either that hunting, low-technology agriculture and moving about in caves or forests will all take their toll of human heads.

Another "grey area" is that of self-inflicted injuries. Walker (1989) describes examples from Australia, Morocco and the Americas in which women in particular cut and strike their heads repeatedly often causing serious damage during mourning rituals. Archaeologically it would be impossible to tell self-inflicted from other-inflicted wounds.

Figure 3. A healed depressed fracture on the skull of an adult male from the medieval cemetery at Abingdon. Note its round shape and, in the centre, an area of newly deposited bone, indicating healing.

Ethnography is an invaluable guide to means and motives.

After examining the location of an injury the next task is to consider its appearance, which can give many clues to the inflicting weapon, and to whether or not the blow was fatal. Much of this information can be obtained by naked-eye examination of the injured bone, but modern microscopical techniques have much to offer, particularly in weapon identification. Two broad categories of injury can be recognised; those made with a blunt instrument, producing a crushing blow; and those where the weapon has a sharp cutting edge.

In the "blunt" category the weapon may be relatively small, such as a sling-shot or small club, or some implement more normally used as a tool such as a digging stick (Courville 1948; Courville and Kade 1964; Martin et al. n.d.; Walker 1989; Webb 1989). Small weapons will produce a depressed fracture if the point of impact is small and round, seen as a dimple in the bone sometimes with radiating fissures (Figure 3) (Brothwell 1981; Walker 1989; Bloom and Smith 1991). An elongated weapon will cause a linear fracture, that is, a simple crack with no separation of the bones (Martin et al. n.d.). Large weapons such as clubs or maces simply smash the skull like an eggshell.

Sharp weapons produce a penetrating injury if the impact on the bone is from a point, such as an arrow, bullet, spear or lance-point (Wilson 1901; Inglemark 1939; Courville 1948; Manchester 1980; Wenham 1989). A long straight-edged weapon such as a knife or sword will make a sharp cut in the bone and overlying soft-tissues. An axe because of its thickness and weight will combine its cutting qualities with those of a blunt instrument (Manchester 1983; Pahl 1985; Wenham 1989; Martin et al. n.d.). Wells (1982), discussing the cranial injuries, including decapitations, from the Romano-British cemetery at Cirencester, Glos., remarked that the sharply incised wound is that least likely to be received accidentally, and almost diagnostic of a combat injury. For this reason, clear and consistent criteria for the identification of edged-weapon injuries are particularly important.

A cut made into bone that is still "fresh", i.e. with its organic matrix intact because the victim was alive or recently dead, looks different even to a superficial view from a cut or break in long-dead bone, for example excavation damage. The latter lacks the colour or patina of bone exposed before burial and has a "crumbly" appearance like a broken biscuit. A cut made in fresh bone shows the following features, whether it be a battle wound (Wenham 1989) or a decapitation (Wells 1981; Wakely and Bruce 1989):

1. linearity;
2. well-defined clean-cut edges;
3. one flat, often polished surface and one flaked-up one, representing bone lying behind and in front of the blade respectively as it entered the bone;
4. macroscopic and microscopically visible striations running in the direction of cut.

These features are illustrated in Figures 4, 5, 6, and 7.

Sharp-weapon injuries are most easily investigated by modern techniques such as scanning electron microscopy. This method produces high-resolution detailed three-dimensional images of surfaces. Use of scanning electron microscope technology does not destroy the bone. Epoxy resin replicas are prepared from the original bone surface using a non-destructive method and will faithfully reproduce surface features small enough to need one thousand times magnification or more to see them (Shipman 1981; Bromage and Boyde 1984; Wenham 1989).

Figure 4. A linear cut across the frontal and parietal bones of an Anglo-Saxon skull from Eccles, Kent (photograph courtesy of Dr S. J. Wenham).

It has been successfully applied to problems such as taphonomic processes (Shipman 1981; Bromage 1984) and human behaviour including butchery (Olsen and Shipman 1988) and the disposal of the dead (Wakely 1993). It enables the observer to distinguish between known human-made marks experimentally created on modern bone and marks suspected of being of human origin on archaeological bone. It can in some cases even reveal the type of implement by which the marks were inflicted, whether stone, metal or seashell for example (Cook 1986; Stevens and Wakely 1993).

The theoretical basis of experimental/archaeological comparisons is what Shipman (1988) has termed an "actualistic argument". That is, if cutmark A (ancient) resembles cutmark M (modern), which has been made in a known way with a known tool or weapon, then cutmark A was probably made in a similar manner to cutmark M. Unlike physical or biomedical scientists who can do an experiment and then record the results knowing what they have done, in archaeology we are often faced with situations, like that of identifying human-made cutmarks, where we have the "results" but must reconstruct the natural or human "experiment" that made them. Microscopical criteria are, as for the large-scale investigations, based on location and structure.

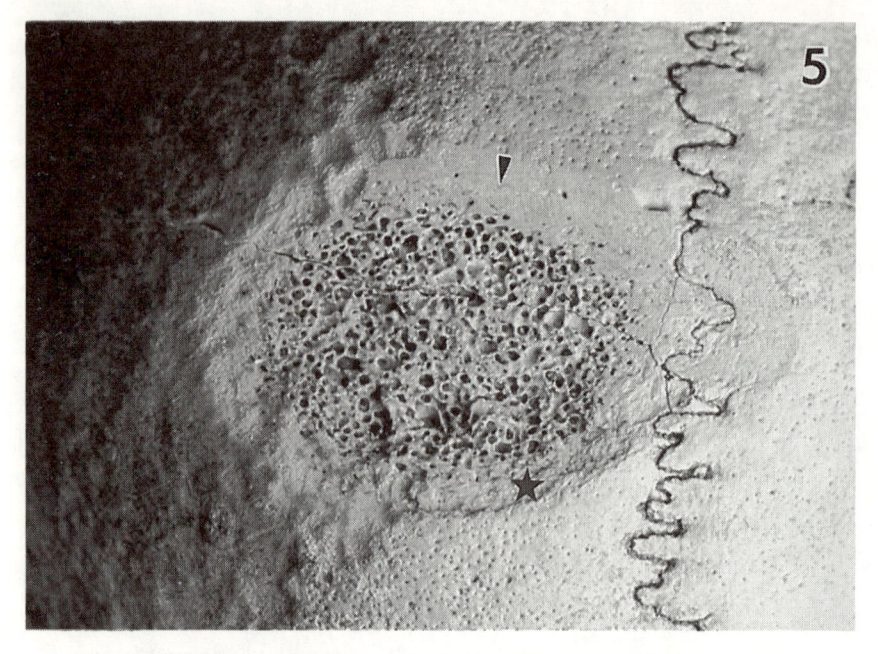

Figure 5. A slicing would on the skull vault of an Anglo-Saxon skull from Eccles, Kent. Note the smooth side (arrow) behind the blade and the flaked side (*) in front (photograph courtesy of Dr S. J. Wenham).

Olsen and Shipman (1988) use the term "intentionality" to indicate that the cuts are not randomly distributed over the bone but clustered in functionally or anatomically meaningful sites, for example at tendon attachments in suspected cases of meat processing or funerary dismemberment (Fulchieri et al. 1986). A wound category of particular interest here is that of scalping, confined to the native peoples of North America. Removal of the central portion of the scalp from a dead or dying enemy as a trophy generates a circular pattern of clearly defined short cuts on the bone, along with short cuts within the circle caused by undercutting the skin (Hamperl 1967; Willey 1982; see also Zimmerman, this volume).

Directionality, i.e. a common orientation, is a feature of deliberately made cuts, as is a tendency to asymmetry, possibly caused by the tendency to rotate the hand towards the ulnar (little-finger) side in cutting (Bromage and Boyde 1984). Individual cutmarks are U- or V-shaped in cross section, with fine parallel striations on the sides, caused by minute irregularities in the edge of the cutting tool (Shipman 1981; Bromage and Boyde 1984; Stevens and Wakely 1993).

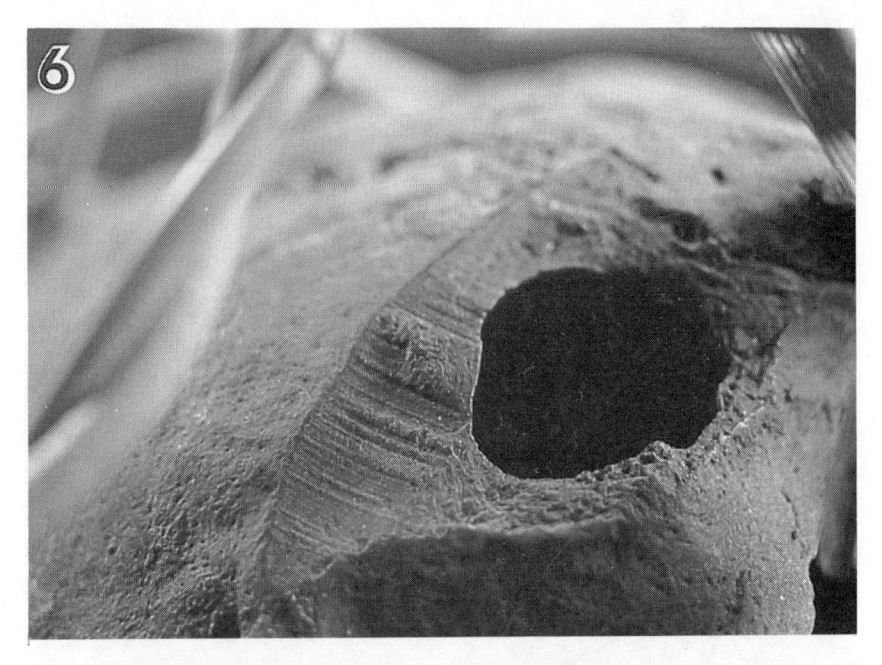

Figure 6. Ploughed field appearance of a slicing cut on the base of an Iban trophy head from Borneo (from a specimen in the collection of Mr P. Beavitt).

All of these criteria were developed to deal with individual cutmarks as created in activities such as butchery. However they can be extrapolated to the broad cuts and slices made by sharp-edged weapons, or to surgical incisions on bone. A slicing cut is simply a wide area bearing many small cuts each due to an irregularity on the cutting edge. A single cut from a sword for example causes a pattern of parallel scratches like a ploughed field (see Figures 6 and 7; and Wenham 1989). No overlapping occurs because the blade only passes through the bone once. Repetitive scraping on the other hand generates a complex criss-crossing of cuts and scratches (Wakely and Duhig 1990).

Any cutmarks inflicted on living bone are obliterated by natural repair processes if the victim survives for more than a few days after the incident. Bone-forming cells are activated, and begin to round off the edges of the opening, later to fill it in. It is a natural sequence of events, not dependent on what type of weapon or other implement inflicted the wound, or whether the intention was violent or non-violent, e.g. surgical intervention (see below). This is the feature used to distinguish fatal from non-fatal trauma, on skeletons. If, during the

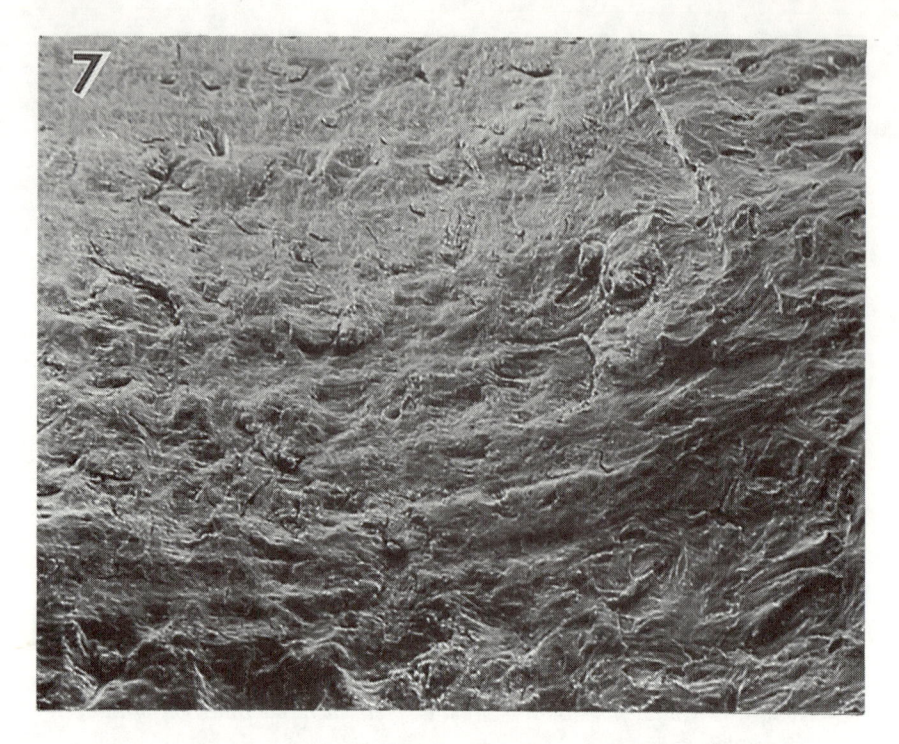

Figure 7. High magnification scanning electron micrograph (x 1200) of parallel striations made by a replica sword in cutting bone from fresh meat. The direction of the cut is shown by an arrow (photograph courtesy of Dr S. J. Wenham).

survival period, the wound becomes infected there may be a bony reaction on the surface (periostitis) or a deeper penetration into the bone, known as osteomyelitis (Ortner and Putschar 1985, 117-18).

A variety of non-traumatic disease processes, and even normal anatomical variations (Stewart 1976), can be mistaken for injuries or attempts to treat them. A recurring example from normal anatomy is that of the vascular grooves on the sides of the skull, made by the superficial temporal artery. These are frequently, and mistakenly, reported as incised wounds (Saul and Saul 1992) and not the normal features that they are.

A genetic variation known as biparietal thinning (Brothwell 1967) or the Catlin Mark (Goldsmith 1945) produces two large holes (foramina) on the skull roof, sometimes mistaken for holes deliberately produced for medical or ritual reasons, called trephinations (see below). Cranial dysraphism, a congenital defect (Stewart 1975), can be similarly misidentified.

Diseases such as cysts or tumours can also produce holes in the face or skull bones that can be easily mistaken for healed injuries because of their rounded edges (Cardenas-Arroyo and Huertas-Motta 1991).

Before leaving the topic of head injuries inflicted in anger and passing on to look at treatment it is worth pausing to consider the extent to which the people of the past were aware of how especially lethal cranial wounds are. Courville (1948) comments on the preponderance of "skull-bashing" weapons among the military equipment of people who did not have the use of firearms, a fact also noted by Willey (1982). Courville (1953) believed that this does indicate a knowledge of the effectiveness of skull wounds in killing people, and that the knowledge was derived from the experiences of hunting. The types of injuries seen will depend on the weapons available. For instance, Jurmain (1991) comments on the frequency of bites in chimpanzees compared to their rarity in human fighting, our dentition being relatively feeble in comparison to the massive jaws and teeth of the great apes.

TREATMENT, AND NON-VIOLENT INJURIES

Along with humanity's awareness of how to kill there has developed an awareness of how to protect with armour (Stendahl and Courville 1954) and how to cure (Courville 1959). In humans, as in animals, even severe injuries can heal naturally given time and rest, provided that immediate risks like pain, shock and blood loss, and later complications such as infection and brain damage, can be controlled. Evidence of healing is not in itself proof of actual treatment being carried out (Roberts 1991).

Skulls showing healing of quite severe cranial wounds are frequently found (Figure 8). They are of particular interest when the remains are those of a named, even historically important person, as in the case of Philip II of Macedonia, the father of Alexander the Great (Musgrave et al. 1984). His skull shows distortion of the right orbit and maxilla, associated with healed bony injuries, as well as facial asymmetries that may have been congenital. These findings are confirmed by forensic methods of facial reconstruction, and corroborate historical accounts of the king having received an arrow in his right eye at the siege of Methone, eighteen years before his death by murder in 336 BC. The eye was reportedly removed after the incident. Contemporary coins and portraits of Philip also show facial damage. It is not recorded whether there were any behavioural changes due to brain damage, im-

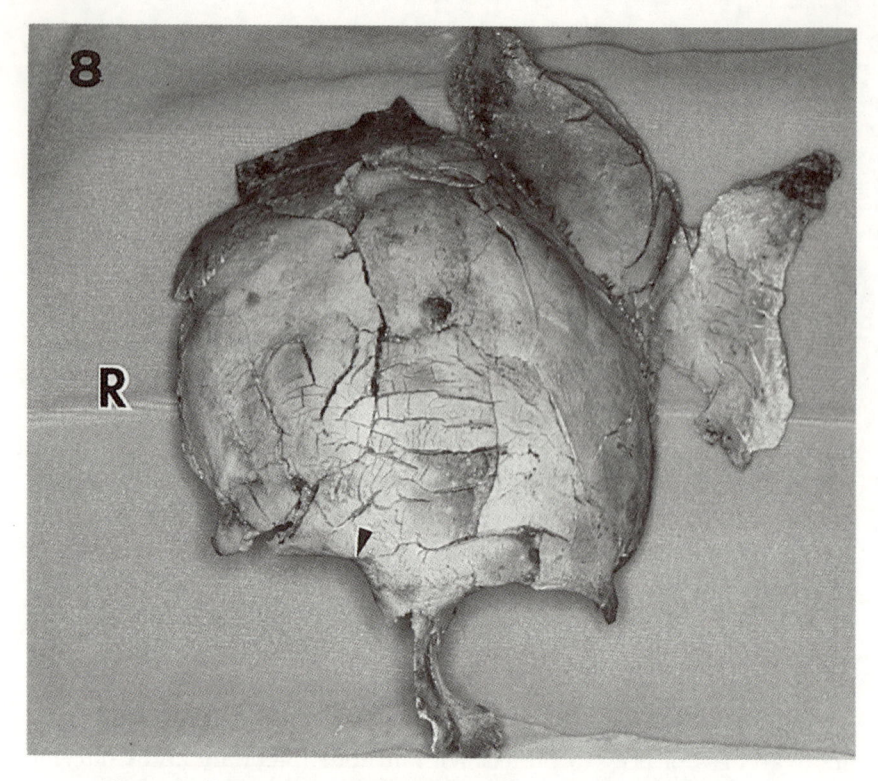

Figure 8. Frontal bone and adjacent portions of the parietal, nasal, and squamous temporal bones of Philip II. Evidence of a healed wound is seen as a notch in the right (R) orbital margin (arrow). A similarly placed crack on the left is due to cremation damage. The injury has resulted in an asymmetry between the shapes of left and right orbits (photograph and permission to publish by courtesy of Dr J. H. Musgrave).

mediate or long-term, because physical deformities and disabilities were regarded as irrelevant in Greek literature and drama (Figure 8).

One is most likely to obtain evidence for active treatment if it takes the form of surgical intervention that leaves visible traces on the bones. Rösing (1989) discussed the historical and palaeopathological findings associated with the skeletons of two prominent citizens of Worb, Switzerland who suffered from gout; Christoph von Gottfried "the uncle" (1661–1743) and Christoph von Gottfried "the nephew" (1663–1719). While the older man led an active public life the younger man was quiet and private in his behaviour. Rösing used their different lives as an illustration of two contrary reactions to illness or disability – ignore it and continue as normal or accept it and live within its limitations. A third response by individuals or groups, which can be combined with either of the first two strategies, is to try to bring about a cure. Evidence of treatment therefore speaks to us of the human need to explain and control the world, whether outside us or in our own bodies. It has led to the variety of medical and surgical technologies evolved at different times and places, including that of "western scientific medicine". Western medicine is based on the Cartesian dualistic outlook that sees the body as a machine and draws a clear distinction between the tangible world of the natural and the immaterial world of the supernatural, which it summarily rejects. In other cultures a non-materialist concept of health and disease, cause and effect may prevail, yet the final result, whether experienced by the patient or seen in the archaeological record may be very similar, so that one cannot easily deduce the underlying metaphysics from the skeletal findings. Ethnography can often produce useful guidance in resolving this dilemma, which to one writing from a contemporary scientific viewpoint may be summarised as "surgery or sorcery?". The practice of trephination is a good example to choose, because of its long history and widespread geographical distribution, leading one to expect that methods and motives will show great diversity.

Trephination is an obvious case of a non-violent head injury. There is no ethnographic evidence that it is practised in violent circumstances such as combat or punishment. Trephination or trepanation is the deliberate opening of the skull to expose the brain in its covering layers (meninges). It has given rise to a century of medical, archaeological and anthropological research, generating a wealth of literature on the techniques and the reasons for doing it.

If we consider Europe alone it has been detected in the Neolithic (Piggott 1940; Parker et al. 1986; Wakely and Duhig 1990), the Bronze and Iron Ages (Parker et al. 1986) and in Romano-British material (Wells 1977; Parker et al. 1986). It was practised in Anglo-Saxon England (Wells 1974), in medieval Europe, including France (Giot and Laurent 1977), Czechoslovakia (Thurzo et al. 1991), Minorca (Campillo and Mercadal 1988) and England (McKenzie 1936), and in the post-medieval period (England 1962; Martin 1989; Siraisi 1990). Of course it continues today, with sophisticated technology in modern neurosurgery.

World-wide it is particularly commonly recorded, archaeologically and ethnographically, from the Americas, especially in the Andean region (Stewart 1957; Oakley et al. 1959). In Africa it existed, perhaps still exists, as part of traditional medical systems (Hilton-Simpson

1913; Margetts 1967; Imperato 1977). Isolated cases are recorded from Australia (Webb 1989) and it was widespread within living memory among the peoples of the Pacific Islands (Crump 1901; Ford 1937; Brothwell 1981; Stevens and Wakely 1993). Mainland Asia alone lacks clear examples of trephination in the skeletal remains of its dead.

Techniques of trephination vary from culture to culture. Basically there are four methods that can be used to make a hole in a skull – leaving out the use of a specialised instrument, the trephine, to cut a circular opening, as in modern practice. The trephine was first recorded from classical Greece (Toole 1964) and from Roman Britain (Brothwell 1974). Methods involving non-specific tools of stone, metal, glass or shell include scraping, grooving, sawing, and drilling (Wilson-Parry 1914; 1923; Lisowski 1967). Scraping and grooving, which give a slow penetration of the skull with controlled entry into the cranial cavity appear to carry the lowest mortality. Microscopical analysis of toolmarks on unhealed skulls give evidence of the method of use (Wakely and Duhig 1990) and even the nature of the material from which the tool was made (Stevens and Wakely 1993). As with incised and other wounds of violent injury the criteria for survival and healing are rounding of the edges of the opening and an encircling halo of reactive spongy bone (periostitis).

To gain insight into the reasons for which trephination was practised we have to rely on historical and ethnographic material. Fortunately, missionaries, explorers and the bureaucratic apparatus of colonialism have recorded and published an abundance of accounts of trephination around the world.

Imperato (1977) described it as a widespread procedure among native healers in West and East Africa, particularly among people whose weaponry is of the crushing type, such as clubs, rather than sharp, so that many depressed fractures are inflicted. They are treated by cutting out damaged bone and extraneous material. British and German colonial rulers made trephination in its traditional form illegal, but it continued covertly until the present day. It now only reaches the public eye when the operation is a failure and the relatives of the deceased and the unsuccessful healer resort to litigation. Cases like those described by Imperato are recognisably rational, i.e. "surgery" rather than "sorcery" from a Western standpoint, as are the skulls observed by Stewart (1957) from South America, where trephinations often coexist with depressed fractures or other wounds on the opposite side of the head. Prunières (1874), Burton (1920), Krogman (1940), Piggott (1940), Stewart (1957), Lisowski (1967) and

Mann (1991) have all emphasised the medical appropriateness of opening the skull to relieve dangerous intracranial pressure levels after head injury. The examples described by Burton (1920) and Mann (1991), where trephination appears to be used to treat chronic ear disease, can also be seen as reasonable extrapolations from its success in dealing with fractures. Actual opening of the skull may be an extension of less drastic treatments such as scarification or cauterising the skull, sometimes in a T-shape (syncypital-T) to relieve chronic head pain, whether or not it resulted from head injury, or to "cure" epilepsy, as is recorded in medieval Europe (Ortner and Putschar 1985, 102–03).

Slightly harder to understand from a contemporary position, more "sorcery" than "surgery" is the suggestion made by Broca (1876), Horsley (1888) and Wilson-Parry (1916) of trephination as a treatment for conditions such as migraine, epilepsy or mental illness by letting malevolent spirits out of the skull by making a hole (Margetts 1967).

Broca (1876) dismissed all therapeutically rational motives, claiming that prehistoric people were incapable of logical deductive thought, only of ritual and superstition, unlike the self-perceived civilised elite of the heyday of scientific rationalism. Wilson-Parry (1916) also arrogantly diminished the humanity of our ancestors by attributing motives of self-aggrandisement to those already marked as "special" by their seizures or psychiatric disorders. He suggested that they further enhanced their status by submitting to ritual opening of the skull. Piggott (1940) viewed Neolithic trephination as a purely ritual act intended to procure skull roundels from the dead as amulets. The most recent suggestion, by Prioreschi (1991), is that Neolithic trephination of the dead was part of a funeral rite intended to ensure a material or spiritual resurrection of the corpse.

Ackerknecht (1967) surveyed a wide range of ethnographic data in order to determine whether the practice of surgery, including trephination, is a universal response to injury or deformation or whether it existed in some non-industrial societies and not in others. He found that while most societies that he categorised as "primitive" were very good at treating wounds and some fractures not all went beyond this to actual operative procedures. This is in spite of the fact that in many societies where there is no surgery, bodily deformation for ritual, judicial or aesthetic reasons may be the norm. Perhaps in these societies where processes such as ritual scarring are used as badges of identity it is unacceptable to render an individual different by further use of the knife. Where mutilation is punitive, post-operative patients would run the risk of being mistaken for criminals. A similar stigma attached to post-mortems and dissection in eighteenth and early nineteenth century Britain, where anatomists were forced to do business with the public hangman and the likes of Burke and Hare to obtain material for teaching and medical research (Richardson 1988). Above all modern Western surgery is rooted in a detailed knowledge of the normal structure and function of the body. Was such knowledge available to or deemed necessary by the trephiners of the past? Krogman (1940) argued that activities such as hunting, butchery and warfare would have led to an empirical body of knowledge that could have been the basis for trephination and other forms of surgery. However, this knowledge would have had to coexist or compete with other belief systems about the body, health and disease. These other beliefs could have prevented observational knowledge being assimilated into the society's contemporary body of information. Ackerknecht (1967) cites medieval Europe as an example. The practice of dissection did not eliminate erroneous Galenic concepts of anatomy until the Renaissance freed the minds of the medical profession from the constraints of blind obedience to classical authority.

In the rationalistic climate of classical Greek thought there was certainly a reliance on observation rather than tradition (Toole 1964; Phillips 1973). They knew that there were certain places where one did not incise the scalp because of the risk of catastrophic bleeding from superficial temporal arteries. On the other hand there are examples from Anglo-Saxon England of trephinations placed where even a mediocre junior medical student would hesitate to cut a hole because of the presence of very large venous channels inside the skull (Wells 1974; Wakely and Duhig 1990). Interestingly, none of these skeletons show signs of healing.

The Egyptian author(s) of the Edwin Smith Surgical Papyrus drew a distinction between treatable and non-treatable head injuries on the basis of a careful examination of the wound. If the skull is split but not smashed and its contents are undamaged the injury is classified as "An ailment with which I will contend" (Breasted 1930, 148). "An ailment not to be treated" (p. 159) is one in which the skull is comminuted and the brain and its coverings exposed and damaged (see also Filer, this volume).

So, surgery or sorcery? Perhaps the question itself is a product of a culture which sees them as different and opposing concepts. If the hole is seen as a door to let "something" out of the skull, be it sling-shot or a demon, it is easy to understand how the two concepts may merge.

Griffith (1990) described an analogous conceptual problem for local health workers in the Maldive Islands, trying to reconcile their traditional belief that babies come according to the will of God with the scientific belief taught to them in their training that conception requires an egg and a sperm to meet at the right place at the right time. In the traditional medical texts of Tibet (Kumzang 1976) personality changes and disabilities after head injury are described. It is recognised that movement disorders occur on the side of the body opposite to the brain damage. However the text also describes a vigorous debate over whether these effects are physiological or demonological in origin.

There is a painting by Breughel, done in 1559 – the Witch of Magellen – which beautifully illustrates the ambiguous relationship between material and non-material ideas of medicine, particularly in relation to the head, where many of the long-term effects of injury may be seen in behaviour (Klein 1963, 167–68). It shows a travelling healer, surrounded by assistants, some eagerly collecting money. She is seen cutting holes in the heads of patients brought by their relatives to have their insanity cured by "removing" large stones, discreetly handed to her by an assistant under the table. This picture is not too far removed from the modern New Age phenomenon of "spirit surgery" – a little cutting, a lot of sleight of hand, a similar portion of faith, and a nice big fee!

Before the invention of effective control of pain, bleeding, and infection, any surgical intervention must have been a method of last resort, especially one as dramatic as trephination. Unfortunately, non-surgical treatments leave no marks on the skeleton to be studied in modern laboratories. Occasional glimpses can be obtained from literate cultures such as the Greeks (Toole 1964; Phillips 1973), the Egyptians (Breasted 1930) and medieval and Renaissance Europe (Payne 1904; Bowser 1963; Siraisi 1990). For instance, the Anglo-Saxon treatment for "broken head" was to wash the wound with an infusion of the herb Betony (*Betonica officinalis*) and then dress it with egg yolk and honey (an excellent antiseptic also used in Egyptian treatment of head injury [Breasted 1930]) "if the brain protrude". The site was then bound with tow, left for three days and then cleaned. A red ring around the wound, i.e. infection, after three days was a sign that "thou mayst not heal it" (Bowser 1963; Payne 1904).

Accounts such as these from so many different times and places remind us that the urge to care for the sick and wounded is as much a feature of human behaviour as that to compete and fight. How interesting that it has not attracted the attention of those who would reduce us to biologically programmed machines, inexorably proceeding towards mutual destruction. The evidence of the bones suggests otherwise.

Faced with a skull bearing holes, clearly not made in the heat of combat but with deliberate care, sometimes healed, one cannot fail to be moved by the expertise of the toolmaker, the skill and confidence of the operator and the courage and faith of the subject, whether willing or coerced, and the complex social bonds that bound them together in the act of healing.

Acknowledgements

I am pleased to thank Miss D. Meecham and Mr G. L. C. McTurk for technical assistance and Mrs J. d'Lacey for typing the manuscript. I am also grateful to Mr P. Beavitt, Miss M. Harrison, Dr J. H. Musgrave, Dr G. C. Stevens, and Dr S. J. Wenham for access to specimens and photographs.

References

- Ackerknecht, E. H. 1967. Primitive surgery. In D. R. Brothwell and A. T. Sandison (eds), *Diseases in Antiquity*, 635–50. Springfield Ill., Charles C. Thomas.
- Ardrey, R. 1976. *The Hunting Hypothesis*. London, Fontana.
- Ardrey, R. 1961. *African Genesis*. London. Collins.
- Bloom, R. A. and Smith, P. 1991. A healed depressed frontal bone fracture in an early Samaritan (the Goliath injury). *Journal of Palaeopathology* 3(3), 167–70.
- Bowser, W. 1963. *The Medical Background of Anglo Saxon England*. London, Wellcome Historical Medical Library.
- Breasted, J. H. 1930. *The Edwin Smith Surgical Papyrus*. Chicago, University of Chicago Press.
- Broca, P. 1876. Sur les trépanations préhistoriques. *Bulletin de la Société d'anthropologie* 11, 236.
- Bromage, T. G. 1984. Interpretation of S.E.M. images of abraded forming bone surfaces. *American Journal of Physical Anthropology* 64, 161–78.
- Bromage, T. G. and Boyde, A. 1984. Microscopical criteria for the determination of directionality of cutmarks on bone. *American Journal of Physical Anthropology* 65, 359–66.
- Brothwell, D. R. 1967. Biparietal thinning in early Britain. In D. R. Brothwell and A. T. Sandison (eds), *Diseases in Antiquity*, 413–16. Springfield, Ill., Charles C. Thomas.
- Brothwell, D. R. 1971. Forensic aspects of so-called Neolithic skeleton Q1 from Maiden Castle Dorset. *World Archaeology* 3, 233–41.
- Brothwell, D. R. 1974. Osteological evidence of the use of a surgical modiolus in a Romano-British population: an aspect of primitive technology.

Journal of Archaeological Science 1, 209–11.
Brothwell, D. R. 1981. *Digging Up Bones*. London and Oxford, British Museum and Oxford University Press.
Burton, F. A. 1920. Prehistoric trephining of the frontal sinus. *California State Journal of Medicine* 18, 321–24.
Campillo, D. and Mercadal, O. 1988. New trephined skulls in Minorca. In L. Capasso (ed.), *Advances in Palaeopathology*, 15–20. Chieti, Marino Solfanelli.
Cardenas-Arroyo, F. and Huertas-Motta, R. 1991. A frontal sinus mucocoele from Prehispanic Colombia. *Palaeopathology Newsletter* 74, 8–10.
Cook, J. 1986. The application of scanning electron microscopy to taphonomic and archaeological problems. In D. A. Roe (ed.), *Studies in the Upper Palaeolithic of North West Europe*, 143–162. Oxford, British Archaeological Reports (International Series 296).
Courville, C. B. 1948. War weapons as an index of contemporary knowledge of the nature and significance of cranio cerebral trauma. *Medical Arts and Sciences* 3, 85–111.
Courville, C. B. 1950. Cranial injuries in prehistoric man. *Bulletin of the Los Angeles Neurological Society* 15(1), 1–21.
Courville, C. B. 1953. Cranial injuries in prehistoric animals. *Bulletin of the Los Angeles Neurological Society* 18, 117–26.
Courville, C. B. 1959. Cranioplasty in prehistoric times. *Bulletin of the Los Angeles Neurological Society* 24, 1–8.
Courville, C. B. 1962. Cranial injuries in the goldrush period of California. *Bulletin of the Los Angeles Neurological Society* 27, 91–94.
Courville, C. B. 1967. Cranial injuries in prehistoric man. In D. R. Brothwell and A. T. Sandison (eds), *Diseases in Antiquity*, 606–22. Springfield Ill., Charles C. Thomas.
Courville, C. B. and Kade, H. 1964. Split fractures of the skull produced by edged weapons and their accompanying brain wounds. *Bulletin of the Los Angeles Neurological Society* 22, 32–39.
Crump, J. A. 1901. Trephining in the South Seas. *Journal of the Royal Anthropological Institute* 31, 167–72.
Dart, R. 1953. The predatory transition from ape to man. *International Anthropological and Linguistic Review* 1(4), 201–13.
Dawes, J. and Magilton, J. R. 1980. *The Cemetery of St Helen-on-the-Walls, Aldwark*. York, York Archaeological Trust.
England, I. A. 1962. Trephining through the ages. *Radiography* 28, 301–14.
Ford, E. 1937. Trephining in Melanesia. *Medical Journal of Australia* 2, 471–77.
Fulchieri, E., Rabino-Massa, E. and Do Caretto, T. 1986. Differential diagnosis between palaeopathological and non pathological environmental factors in ancient human bone. *Journal of Human Evolution* 15, 71–75.
Giot, P.-R. and Laurent, J.-L. 1977. Le cimetière des anciens Bretons de Saint-Uriel ou Saint-Saturnin en Plomeur (Finistère). *Gallia* 35, 141–71.
Goldsmith, W. M. 1945. Trepanation and the "Catlin Mark". *American Antiquity* 10, 413–16.
Griffith, G. 1990. Shariyani nights. *Current Anthropology* 6, 4–5.
Hamperl, H. 1967. The osteoarchaeological consequences of scalping. In D. R. Brothwell and A. T. Sandison (eds), *Diseases in Antiquity*, 630–37. Springfield Ill., Charles C. Thomas.
Hilton-Simpson, M. W. 1913. Some Arab and Shawia remedies and notes on

the trepanning of the skull in Algeria. *Journal of the Royal Anthropological Institute* 43, 715–21.

Horowitz, L. K. and Smith, P. 1988. The effects of striped hyena activity on human remains. *Journal of Archaeological Science* 15, 471–81.

Horsley, V. 1888. Trephining in the Neolithic period. *Journal of the Royal Anthropological Institute* 17, 100–06.

Imperato, P. J. 1977. *African Folk Medicine*. Baltimore, York Press Inc.

Inglemark, B. E. 1939. The skeletons. In B. Thordeman (ed.), *Arms and Armour from the Battle of Wisby, 1361*, 149–209. Stockholm.

Janssens, P. A. 1987. Étude palaeopathologique de neuf crânes de l'abbaye Cistercienne de Coxyde (Belgique). *Helinium* 27, 109–27.

Jurmain, R. 1989. Trauma, degenerative disease and other pathologies among the Gombe chimpanzees. *American Journal of Physical Anthropology* 80(2), 229–37.

Jurmain, R. 1991. Patterns of trauma in humans and chimpanzees. *Palaeopathology Newsletter* 74 (supplement), 3.

Klein, H. A. 1963. *Graphic Worlds of Peter Breughel the Elder*. New York, Dover Publications Inc.

Krogman, W. M. 1940. The medical and surgical practices of pre and protohistoric Man. *Ciba Symposium*, 444–52.

Kumzang, Ven. R. R. J. 1976. *Tibetan Medicine*. Berkeley and Los Angeles, University of California Press.

Leakey, R. E. 1981. *The Making of Mankind*. London, Book Club Associates.

Lisowski, F. P. 1967. Prehistoric and early historic trepanation. In D. R. Brothwell and A. T. Sandison (eds), *Diseases in Antiquity*, 651–72. Springfield Ill., Charles C. Thomas.

Lovejoy, C. O. and Heiple, K. G. 1981. An analysis of fractures in skeletal populations with an example from the Libben site, Ottawa County, Ohio. *American Journal of Physical Anthropology* 55, 529–41.

Manchester, K. 1980. Forensic aspects of an Anglo-Saxon injury. *Ossa* 7, 179–88.

Manchester, K. 1983. *The Archaeology of Disease*. Bradford, Bradford University Press.

Mann, G. 1991. Chronic ear disease as a motive for trephination. *International Journal of Osteoarchaeology* 1, 165–68.

Margetts, E. L. 1967. Trepanation of the skull by the medicine-men of primitive cultures, with particular reference to present-day native East African practice. In D. R. Brothwell and A. T. Sandison (eds), *Diseases in Antiquity*, 673–701. Springfield Ill., Charles C. Thomas.

Martin, G. 1989. Successful drainage of an extradural abscess in 1667: Prince Rupert's Trephination. *British Journal of Neurosurgery* 3, 211–16.

Martin, C., Gonzales, A. and Estevez Gonzales, F. n.d. Cranial Injuries in the Guanche Population of Tenerife (Canary Islands): a Biocultural Interpretation. Unpublished MS.

McKenzie, D. 1936. Surgical perforation in a medieval skull with reference to Neolithic holing. *Proceedings of the Royal Society of Medicine* 29, 895–902.

Musgrave, J. H. Neave, R. A. H. and Prag, A. J. N. W, 1984. The skull from tomb II at Vergina, King Philip II of Macedon. *Journal of Hellenic Studies* 101, 60–78.

Oakley, K. P., Brooke, W. M. A., Akester, R. and Brothwell, D. R. 1959. Contributions on trepanning or trephination in ancient and modern times. *Man* 133, 93–96.

Olsen, S. L. 1989. On distinguishing natural from cultural damage on archaeological antler. *Journal of Archaeological Science* 16, 125–35.

Olsen, S. L. and Shipman, P. 1988. Surface modifications on bone: trampling v. butchery. *Journal of Archaeological Science* 15, 535–53.

Ortner, D. J. and Putschar, W. G. J. 1985. *Identification of Pathological Conditions in Human Skeletal Remains.* Washington DC, Smithsonian Institution Press.

Pahl, W. M. 1985. Schädel-Hirn-Traumata im alten Aegypten und ihre Therapie nach dem "Wundenbuch' des Papyrus E. Smith (ca. 1500 v. chr.). *Ossa* 12, 93–122.

Parker, S., Roberts, C. and Manchester, K. 1986. A review of British trepanations with reports on two new cases. *Ossa* 12, 141–57.

Payne, J. F. 1904. *English Medicine in Anglo Saxon Times.* Oxford, Clarendon Press.

Phillips, E. D. 1973. *Aspects of Greek Medicine.* London, Croom Helm.

Piggott, S. 1940. A trepanned skull of the Beaker period from Dorset and the practice of trepanning in prehistoric Europe. *Proceedings of the Prehistoric Society* 3, 112–32.

Popham, R. E. 1954. Trepanation as a rational procedure in primitive surgery. *University of Toronto Medical Journal* 31, 204–11.

Potts, R. and Shipman, P. 1981. Cutmarks made by stone tools on bones from Olduvai Gorge Tanzania. *Nature* 291, 577–80.

Prioreschi, P. 1991. Possible reasons for Neolithic skull trepanning. *Perspectives in Biology and Medicine* 34, 296–303.

Prunières, de M. 1874. Sur les crânes artificiellement perforés à l'époque des dolmens. *Bulletin de la Société d'anthropologie Paris* 9, 185–205.

Roberts, C. A. 1991. Trauma and treatment in the British Isles: a design for multidisciplinary research. In D. J. Ortner and A. C. Aufterheide (eds), *Human Palaeopathology: Current Syntheses and Future Options,* 225–40. Washington, Smithsonian Institution Press.

Rose, S. Kamin, L. J. and Lewontin, R. C. *Not in Our Genes.* London, Penguin Books.

Rösing, F. 1989. Ancient disease and coping strategies: future options of palaeopathology. *Journal of Palaeopathology* 3, 5–6.

Richardson, R. 1988. *Death, Dissection and the Destitute.* London, Penguin Books.

Saul, F. P. and Saul, J. M. 1992. Vascular impressions and pseudo-pathology revisited. *Palaeopathology Newsletter* 80, 7–8.

Shipman, P. 1981. Application of scanning electron microscopy to taphonomic problems. *Annals of the New York Academy of Science* 276, 357–85.

Shipman, P. 1988. Actualistic studies of animal resources and hominid activities. In S. L. Olsen (ed.), *Scanning Electron Microscopy in Archaeology,* 261–85. Oxford, British Archaeological Reports (British Series 452).

Siraisi, N. G. 1990. *Medieval and Early Renaissance Medicine.* Chicago, University of Chicago Press.

Stendahl, A. and Courville, C. B. 1954. Development and use of helmets as a means of protection against craniocerebral injury. *Bulletin of the Los Angeles Neurological Society* 19, 1–17.

Stevens, G. C. and Wakely, J. 1993. Diagnostic criteria for the identification of seashell as a trephination implement. *International Journal of Osteoarchaeology* 3, 167–76.

Stewart, T. D. 1957. Stone Age skull surgery: a general review with emphasis on the New World. *Smithsonian Institution Special Reports* 1957, 469–91.

Stewart, T. D. 1975. Cranial dysraphism mistaken for trephination. *American Journal of Physical Anthropology* 42, 435–37.

Stewart, T. D. 1976. Are supra-inion depressions evidence of prophylactic trephination? *Bulletin of the History of Medicine* 50, 414–34.

Thurzo, M., Lietava, J. and Vondrakova, M. 1991. A case of an unusually large neurocranial trauma with marks of partial trephination from West Slovakia (10th century AD). *Journal of Palaeopathology* 4, 37–45.

Toole, H. 1964. Fractures of the skull, diagnosis and treatment in Ancient Greece. *Journal of the International College of Surgeons* 42, 89–94.

Wakely, J. and Bruce, M. F. 1989. Interpreting signs of trauma on a human axis vertebra. *Journal of Anatomy* 167, 265.

Wakely, J. and Duhig, C. 1990. A comparative microscopical study of three European trephined skulls. *Journal of Palaeopathology* 3, 75–87.

Wakely, J. 1993. The uses of scanning electron microscopy in the interpretation of some examples of trauma in human skeletal remains. In G. Grupe and A. N. Garland (eds), *Histology of Ancient Human Bone*, 205–18. Berlin and Heidelberg, Springer-Verlag.

Walker, P. I. 1989. Cranial injuries as evidence of violence in Prehistoric Southern California. *American Journal of Physical Anthropology* 80, 313–23.

Webb, S. G. 1988. Two possible cases of trephination from Australia. *American Journal of Physical Anthropology* 75, 541–48.

Webb, S. 1989. *Prehistoric Stress in Australian Aborigines*. Oxford, British Archaeological Reports (International Series 490).

Wells, C. 1967. Pseudopathology. In D. R. Brothwell and A. T. Sandison (eds), *Diseases in Antiquity*, 5–19. Springfield Ill., Charles C. Thomas.

Wells, C. 1974. Probable trepanation of five early Anglo-Saxon skulls. *Antiquity* 48, 298–300.

Wells, C. 1977. Une curieuse blessure dans un squelette du deuxième siècle AD. *Travaux et documents du centre palaeoanthropologie et de palaeopatologie* 4, 9–13.

Wells, C. 1982. The human bones. In A. McWhirr, L. Viner and C. Wells, *Romano-British Cemeteries at Cirencester*, 135–201. Cirencester, Cirencester Excavation Committee.

Wenham, S. J. 1989. Anatomical interpretations of Anglo-Saxon weapon injuries. In S. J. Hawkes (ed.), *Weapons and Warfare in Anglo-Saxon England*. Oxford, 123–29. Oxford, Oxford University Committee for Archaeology (Monograph no. 21).

White, W. 1988. *The Cemetery of St Nicholas Shambles*. London, London and Middlesex Archaeological Society.

Willey, P. S. 1982. Osteology of the Crow Creek Massacre. PhD Thesis, University of Tennessee, Knoxville.

Wilson, T. 1901. Arrow wounds. *American Anthropologist* 3, 513–31.

Wilson-Parry, T. 1914. Prehistoric man and his efforts to combat disease. *Lancet* 1, 1699–703.

Wilson-Parry, T. 1916. The art of trephining among pre-historic and primitive peoples. *Journal of the British Archaeological Association* 22, 33–69.

Wilson-Parry, T. 1923. Trephination of the living human skull in prehistoric times. *British Medical Journal* 1, 457–61.

Ancient Egypt and Nubia as a Source of Information for Cranial Injuries

Joyce M. Filer

Violence *has been described* as an intractable phenomena in contemporary society (Riches 1986, vii), yet were acts of violence any less refractory in earlier human societies? As the incidence of intentional violence will vary from skeletal sample to skeletal sample (Manchester 1983, 59) so will the causes vary. There are a myriad reasons for violent and traumatic injury: military activities, civilian disputes and accidents in the home or workplace may account for many of them. It is important to note that it cannot be assumed that all injuries are incurred on the battlefield. Underlying these more physical causes there may also be psychological factors which may be less easily understood. These two levels of comprehension are difficult enough to fathom in modern societies and so in trying to come to terms with violence in ancient societies we need recourse to examine as wide a range of sources of information as possible.

Human remains and the lesions they present are good sources of information because bone can record any violence committed upon it. Traumatic lesions, particularly fractures, are frequently found in ancient skeletal and mummified remains. Studies of the different types of fractures may give some insight into the behaviour of ancient peoples and in some cases may indicate the types of occupations they engaged in. Cranial injuries are particularly useful in understanding human behaviour for, whereas the causative factors leading to fractures of the post-cranial skeleton may or may not be accidental, there is less doubt about cranial injuries, which are more likely (but not exclusively) the result of intentional violence.

Whilst human remains provide the best source of information for cranial injuries the value of other categories of information should not be overlooked. An examination of ancient texts may give access to the attitudes towards cranial injuries as experienced by the society or culture concerned. Naturally, such depth of thought would not be apparent from the actual human remains. Artistic representations may serve to show reality or may act as symbols of an ideal or preferred state. Together, textual and artistic sources, if available, will add greatly to the knowledge gained from an examination of any biological material.

A fracture may be defined simply as "a structural break in the continuity of bone" (Manchester 1983, 55). Studies have shown that in antiquity skull injuries were more frequent than injuries to any individual bones of the post-cranial skeleton (Alexandersen 1967, 623–29). The head is a complex piece of apparatus and the violences to which it is subjected are variable in magnitude, direction and in area of application (Rowbotham 1964, 56), and these physical forces may act upon the cranium to produce deformation, acceleration or deceleration (Bagchi 1980, 22). Bone possesses the property of elasticity and so will bend when sufficient force is applied to it. Any resulting fracture will depend upon the amount of force it is subjected to. The faster the blow the greater the likelihood of depressed fractures or even penetration of the skull taking place. Alternatively a blow may be of sufficient force to break the skull but may be low in velocity. This would then produce a linear fracture, a pattern of fracture which is very common in archaeological material. Healing and recovery will depend upon several factors. For example, whether or not the fracture is "open" or "closed" will certainly affect the healing process. In ancient contexts open fractures were a ready passage for infection through bacteria and may have had fatal consequences. That many individuals from early societies survived the most severe head injuries without the aid of the type of antibiotics we take for granted is only to be marvelled at. Normally a bone begins its healing process by the deposition of new bone between the fractured ends thus forming a callus or a raised bony cuff.

Head injuries are common to most societies and have been reported from widely separated areas of the world. The people of Pecos Pueblo

(Wells 1964, 55) revealed a high proportion of head injuries; Peruvian skulls from Bilboa Park were peppered with sling-shot wounds which showed little evidence of infection (Wells 1964, 56), and in the Guanche population of Tenerife a variety of head injuries were found (Martin et al. 1993, 130–35). Ancient Egypt and Nubia, of course, provide a vast sample of such injuries. Really, it is likely that head injuries are as old as, and as widely dispersed as, humanity itself.

Although this discussion is primarily concerned with Egypt and Nubia, there are several points of interest that have emerged to show that there are some factors about head injuries common to ancient populations of the world. Generally in most cultures there is a noticeable sex difference with regard to head injuries, with men sustaining more lesions than women. This point is discussed in more detail below in connection with skulls from Kerma. Even widely differing cultures sustain injuries to the same parts of the skull. Whilst injury does occur on the occipital bone, the frontal and parietal bones are the more usual sites of injury. The majority of these latter injuries occur on the left side of the skull, which may suggest a frontal assault by a right-handed attacker. Fractures to the right side of the skull do occur, of course, but are less frequent. This situation is the same whether the injuries occur on Egyptian or Nubian skulls or on skulls from other parts of the world.

In the absence of direct communication with those Egyptians and Nubians who sustained cranial injuries, we can only guess at the extent of their suffering. Many of the ancient skulls examined show evidence of healing and it is likely that some individuals concerned may have suffered little more than minor discomfort at the time of the assault. Yet remarkably, some individuals survived horrific head and facial injuries and the examples discussed below will show that some of the variable consequences of these injuries may have been: loss of hearing or eyesight; speech or eating difficulties; headaches; paralysis and breathing problems. For some of the very badly injured the ultimate consequence was, of course, death.

Sometimes archaeological excavations reveal only one source of information – human remains or texts or artistic representations. Whilst even one aspect is informative, a more rounded picture of the events leading to a cranial injury is more desirable. We are fortunate that ancient Egypt and Nubia are particularly rich in sources of information about cranial injuries and these will be described and commented upon below.

It should be noted that the conventions in transliterating Egyptian names varies due to the nature of the hieroglyphic script.

TEXTUAL SOURCES

Ancient Egyptian texts offer diverse information on injury, especially cranial injuries. They can be divided into medical and non-medical (literary) texts. Examples of each type will show the diversity of information revealed and in particular the Egyptian attitude towards such injuries.

With regard to medical texts, the best and most important source for cranial injury is the Edwin Smith Surgical Papyrus. Purchased by Edwin Smith in 1862, the text was translated from the hieratic form of the Egyptian language by James Breasted in 1930. The papyrus dates from the New Kingdom (c. 1700 BC) but is likely to be a copy of a much earlier document because the text contains glosses (or comments) explaining "old fashioned" vocabulary to the "modern" reader of New Kingdom Egypt. A text of such a great age would testify to the antiquity of the ancient Egyptian experience of cranial injuries. The document contains nine cases which deal specifically with injury to the skull and brain and eighteen other cases dealing with injury (wounds and/or fractures) to the brow, temple, nose and the face and so on. Throughout history the battlefield has provided practical experience for medical practitioners (Aker et al., 1984, 921) and it is possible that the author of the Edwin Smith Papyrus was a surgeon who had encountered these injuries to the face and skull when attending the wounded on the battlefield or whilst healing the injured in civilian life. The text, which contains forty-eight surgical cases altogether, obviously intended to deal with injury to all parts of the body in topographical order, i.e. beginning with the head and working downwards. Unfortunately, after finishing the cases of injury to the thorax, the author (or a scribe) stopped in the middle of a sentence in the first case of treatment to the spine. That the cases in the Edwin Smith Papyrus begin with the skull may well be a commonsense way of approaching a set of descriptive surgical procedures. This way of dealing with material fits in well with the ancient Egyptians' love of order and abhorrence of disorder. Also their positioning in the text reflects the urgency of dealing with such potentially fatal injuries.

Each case, discussed in a systematic order of topics and materials, begins with a title. The title consists of the words *ss'.w* (Figure 1a) meaning "instructions" which is then followed by an identification of the injury with an indication of the part of the body affected. Next, the words *ir'.k sn* (Figure 1b) ("if thou examinest a man") denotes the "examination". The form of the examination is that of a teacher in-

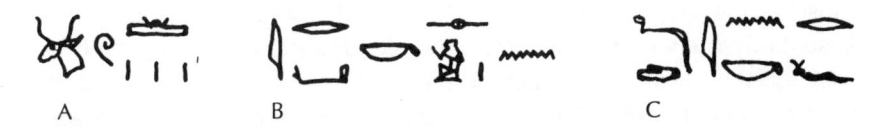

Figure 1. Hieroglyphs, meaning instructions (A), examination (B) and diagnosis (C), dating from the New Kingdom, from the Edwin Smith Surgical Papyrus (drawing by Carol A. Randle).

structing a student (or a second party) with such instruc-tions as "thou shouldst probe his wound" or "thou shouldst place thy hand upon him" and so on. Gurdjian (1974, 157) notes that the ancient Egyptians palpated the interior of open or gaping head wounds. At this point in the investigation the patient may be questioned and the examiner may take ocular, olfactory and tactile observations. The words *dd in.k r.f* (Figure 1c) ("thou shouldst say concerning him [the patient]") introduces the "diagnosis". This could entail one of three possible outcomes:

1. an ailment which I will treat (i.e. certainly successful);
2. an ailment with which I will contend (i.e. possibly curable);
3. an ailment not to be treated (i.e. untreatable).

The next section outlines the "treatment" for that particular case. The surgeon (or author) does not always decide to treat the injury in every case and in several cases no treatment is suggested. The treatment when given may be one of three types:

1. purely mechanical or surgical, which may also involve bandages, adhesive plasters, splints or braces, cauterisation or surgical stitching;
2. a combination of surgical treatment and the external use of medicaments;
3. use of externally applied medicaments only – as in the case of sprains, abscesses and flesh wounds, etc.

In order to illustrate the extent to which the ancient Egyptian surgeon could deal with injuries to the face and head, it would be useful to look at one or two of these surgical cases in more detail, but the work by Breasted (1930) should be consulted particularly with respect to his comments on the difficulties in translating the Egyptian language. The title of case 6 (Breasted 1930, 164–74) is "Instructions concerning a gaping wound in his head, penetrating to the bone, smashing his skull, (and) rending open the brain of his skull." This is one of the most serious head injury cases dealt with by the surgeon/author. Essentially the wound is a compound, comminuted fracture which has opened the skull to the extent that the brain is exposed and the meninges are broken and issuing fluid. In the diagnosis the surgeon/author decides it is "an ailment not to be treated" (Breasted 1930, 170) for the outcome is not hopeful. Despite the unfavourable outcome some treatment is suggested in order to alleviate the patient's sufferings. The particular importance of this case is that it contains the first reference in antiquity to the brain. Interestingly, in trying to explain some of the difficult terminology the surgeon/author clarifies it by comparing the object's attributes with more familiar objects. Thus in describing the brain he likens the convolutions of the surface to the corrugations of metallic slag. Similarly, the pulsations of the brain felt by the surgeon's palpating finger are likened to the weak place (or fontanelle) of the infant's skull.

An injury of opposite extremes is case 11 (Breasted 1930, 234–44): "a broken nose", which presents little difficulty for our ancient surgeon. Here the injury described is a depression in the column of the nose which has also been disfigured. Blood has issued from each nostril but the patient is obviously expected to make a good recovery because the surgeon's confident diagnosis deems it "an ailment which I will treat" (Breasted 1930, 236). After cleaning the wound, two plugs of linen saturated with grease were to be put (one into each nostril) with the external parts supported by two rolls of stiffened linen. Broken noses were probably fairly common in the ancient world, but it should be noted that evidence of such injuries will remain in the archaeological record only if the nasal bones were broken and ill-set and not if only the muscular portions were injured for these would heal and after death they would decompose. Further reference to broken noses can be found in the section on human remains below.

The Edwin Smith Surgical Papyrus is an immensely valuable source of information for head injuries. Apart from providing the earliest references to certain anatomical, physiological and pathological descriptions, the document also informs us as to the types of treatment the Egyptian surgeon deemed appropriate for each type of head injury. We are especially privileged to have some insight also into the workings of the Egyptian mind regarding their attitudes to injuries and their prognoses.

Turning to some non-medical (literary) texts we read that the might and power of the pharaoh was equated with his ability to inflict cranial injury. For example, a tale from the Middle Kingdom, "The Story of

Sinuhe" (Lichtheim 1973, 225) is told in the form of an autobiography composed for the tomb. In the story Sinuhe tells how he fled to a foreign land after overhearing a conspiratorial plot following the death of King Amenemhet I. The ruler of the foreign land questions Sinuhe about the condition (or well-being) of Egypt now that the king is dead. Sinuhe replies that the dead king's son (Sesostris) has inherited his father's throne and that he is "the smiter of foreign lands" and that (Lichtheim 1973, 225),

> Keen-sighted he smashes foreheads,
> None can withstand his presence,
> Wide-striding he smites the fleeing.

Here the image of the king smiting and clubbing craniums is a political statement designed to ensure that the ruler of the foreign land fully understands that Egypt has lost none of its power whilst undergoing a change of leadership.

Two monumental texts, commemorating the triumphs of Amenhotep II following his return from Asiatic campaigning, seem to echo the action depicted on the Narmer Palette (see below) and on wall reliefs – that of Pharaoh smiting the enemy. In the "Memphis and Karnak Stelae" (Pritchard 1955, 247) we are told that Amenhotep II kept watch alone over prisoners and booty with his battle-axe in his right hand. Although it may be suggested that this scene is a deliberate attempt to create a powerful persona for the king, nevertheless the image chosen – that of the ruler with battle-axe in hand – is one implying strength and victory and the implicit right to rule and inflict injury because of that strength. The second monumental text – the "Amada and Elephantine Stelae" – presents the same king, Amenhotep II, in an even more active role. We are told that Amenhotep "returned in joy of heart to his father Amon, when he had slain with his own mace the seven princes who had been in the district of Takhshi" (Pritchard 1955, 248) (Takshi was in the area of Damascus).

This image of the king ties in very closely with the royal image represented on Egyptian monuments: that of the victorious smiting ruler with a mace, sickle-sword or battle-axe (for further discussion see "artistic sources" below).

Some royal texts intimate that the king not only led his troops into battle but fully participated in the fighting as well. In the "Annals of Thutmose III" (in his first campaign in the Battle of Megiddo) we are told that (Lichtheim 1976, 32)

> Then his majesty overwhelmed them (i.e. the enemy) at the head of his army. When they saw his majesty overwhelming them, they fled headlong (to) Megiddo with faces of fear.

In the "Boundary Stela of Sesostris III" (Lichtheim 1973, 119) the king outlines his military strategies and lists his activities in defending his boundary between Egypt and Nubia. Of himself he says (Lichtheim 1973, 119)

> I am a king who speaks and acts,
> What my heart plans is done by my arm.

The reference to the king's arm taking action is strongly reminiscent of the iconographic image of the king's arm upraised and ready to strike his enemy on the head.

In turning to some non-royal examples of head injury in ancient Egyptian literature, nothing could describe a head injury in context better than the following (Caminos 1954, 169):

> What is this that you say, so it is reported "The soldier's calling is pleasanter than the scribes?" Come, let me describe to you the condition of the soldier, that much tormented one. He is taken when yet a child to be imprisoned in a barracks. A searing [?] blow is dealt his body, a rending blow is dealt his eyebrows. His head is split open with a wound. He is laid down and beaten like papyrus and battered with castigation.

Here one scribe is informing another (possibly a student) that their chosen profession is far superior to that of the professional soldier's. From his observation it is obvious to the scribe that head injury was a very real danger in the soldier's life and so it was a career to be avoided.

From this short review of some Egyptian medical and literary texts, it can be understood that cranial injury was seen as part of life and it had to be dealt with. From the royal point of view, in particular, cranial injury was a symbol of the king's prowess and his ability to protect his land and his people.

ARTISTIC SOURCES

Egyptian monuments often record events of political importance pictorially and, not infrequently, scenes of battles and fighting are depicted. As well as revealing historical information they are a valuable source of information on injuries, especially head injuries, and the

Figure 2. Part of a battle scene from the tomb of Inti at Deshasheh showing head injuries being inflicted, Fifth Dynasty (drawing by Neville Parker).

types of weapons used to inflict those injuries. A selection of such scenes together with some non-military ones will illustrate their contribution to our knowledge of head injuries.

A Fifth Dynasty scene from Deshasheh shows a spirited and dramatic battle in progress (Petrie, 1898, pl. iv). This scene in the tomb of Inti depicts a battle between Egyptians and a people of northern Arabia or southern Palestine. In four registers we see progressive stages of the action. First, some Egyptian archers advance towards a walled town. Then, the two groups of enemies engage in fighting: the Egyptians armed with shallow battle-axes, their opponents with clubs. Meanwhile, inside the walled town women are helping the wounded. Finally we see Egyptians leading their captives away. The whole scene teems with action: one man puts up his arm to ward off a blow to his head, another man falls with arrows piercing all parts of his body and the back of his skull. Yet another man, arrows jutting out of his eye socket and skull, breaks his bow as a sign of defeat whilst an Egyptian delivers the final cutting blow to his left shoulder (Figure 2).

From the Middle Kingdom tomb of Baqt (no. 15) (Newberry 1893, pl. v, rows 7–9) we see soldiers storming a fortress, with foot-soldiers attacking one another. In row 8 a kneeling soldier is assaulted by an opponent with a stick. The stance of the attacker is somewhat reminiscent of the image of the smiting pharaoh, as discussed below and alluded to above.

Part of a wall relief from the Major Temple at Abu Simbel (c. 1296 BC) described by Curto (1971, 9) shows a Syrian castle under attack by Ramesses II. The Syrian defenders on the castle ramparts (and one of their number outside the castle) have been hit by arrows either in the eye or the skull. Such, we are to understand, is the precision of Egyptian archers in inflicting head wounds but more importantly the iconography stresses that battles can be won through the maiming (and sometimes fatal) effects of such injuries.

Other scenes, of a non-militaristic nature, also provide us with information about potential head injuries in more peaceful and civilian settings. As is well known the ancient Egyptians were fond of depicting scenes from daily life on the walls of their tomb. Aspects depicted included feasting, sporting, and the types of work people engaged in. It is this last category which provides another situation in which head injuries could be sustained. A scene from the tomb-chapel of Senbi's son Ukh-Hotp (Blackman 1915, pl. iv) shows two groups of boatmen on the river. Whilst some men are punting the boats along, their companions are having a mock fight and even though the fight is a pretence it is easy to see how an accidental injury could occur. With their punting poles the men playfully knock each other about. One man is lying supine with his head over the side of his boat as another man from the opposing boat pins him down at the neck. The first man is in danger of receiving a very real and fatal head injury for beneath his reclining head a crocodile lurks expectantly. Mock fights were also encouraged in other sections of ancient Egyptian society. These, together with wrestling, cudgelling and other feats of physical strength, were considered beneficial to the training of soldiers (Wilkinson 1937, 286).

One of the most dominant images in Egyptian iconography is that of the king with arm upraised in the act of smiting his enemies whom he grasps firmly by the hair. Such an image has already been alluded to in a literary context, but it is essential to review this image of the king as represented pictorially. Smiting scenes can be demonstrated from the very early periods of Egyptian history. The scene of smiting, "so

Figure 3. A ceremonial slate palette of King Narmer, showing the king smiting an enemy, Predynastic period (from a cast at the British Museum).

familiar as to become an adjunct to the decorative arts on the one hand, a formula for temple walls on the other" (Hall 1986, 48), can be seen on a variety of media. An early smiting scene was recorded at Hierakonpolis, an early southern capital of Upper Egypt, on the walls of a tomb dating to the Late Gerzean period (i.e. before 3000 BC). In this scene a large man raises a weapon in one hand while his other hand grasps a rope attached to three bound and kneeling prisoners. The ceremonial slate palette of King Narmer (Figure 3) from the "main

Figure 4. King Den smiting an enemy with a mace, First Dynasty (drawing by Richard Parkinson).

deposit" at Hierakonpolis has been widely discussed as a scene recording the actual unification of the two lands – Upper Egypt and Lower Egypt – into one country. A preferred view is that the unification of Egypt was achieved through a steady progression of events and was unlikely to have been the result of one mighty battle (Spencer 1993, 53). Thus, it may be suggested that the scenes on the palette represent a single event, possibly a local conflict (Davis 1992, 164) in the period leading to unification. On one side of the palette, Narmer can be seen clutching a mace in his raised right hand while his left hand grasps a kneeling captive by the hair. This is the first formal statement of an Egyptian king smiting his enemy. This powerful image of the king occurs time and again throughout the Pharaonic period and continued into the Ptolemaic and Roman periods and was a constant reminder of the potential use of such threats to subdue or control enemies.

Several examples of smiting scenes from different periods will suffice to show the continuity of this image in Egyptian iconography. From the First Dynasty, a carved ivory label from Abydos shows King

Den smiting an enemy (Figure 4). A Third Dynasty cliff relief at Wadi Maghara (Sinai) shows King Sekhemhet also smiting an enemy with a mace (Davis 1992, fig. 49). Much later during the Nineteenth Dynasty father and son, Seti I (The Epigraphic Survey 1986, pls 15A and 15B) and Ramesses II (Desroches-Noblecourt and Kuntz 1968, pls xxxii, xxxiii and xxxv) were also depicted in the same victorious pose. The image is a persistent one and could be exemplified from many periods in Egyptian history.

It is important to briefly explore the levels of information these royal smiting scenes offer. Firstly, it should be noted that the king is not struggling with his enemy, for essentially the king has already conquered him (Hall 1986, 3). Secondly, an interesting comment by Parkin (1986, 210–11) suggests that any immoral act committed by a divine king would affect the qualities of his rulership because he is both the moral and political leader of his people. This view of the Egyptian king as divine ruler and moral leader of his people and as a "smasher of skulls", makes it clear that he was committing what would be seen as a moral or "legal" act when inflicting cranial injury. Whether the act depicted is real or symbolic (we do not know how many kings actually partook in such activities) is immaterial; the smiting act is viewed by the populace as a part of his divine right of rule.[1] This was reinforced by the king's expected (or implied) actions in battle (see below).

At a third level the image of the king smiting (i.e. defeating) his enemies may also be viewed as a rhetorical threat of violence. Such an image demonstrates to any future and potential enemies the king's (and by implication, his country's) capacity to inflict real cranial injury, thereby hinting at an act of which the enemy may have had experience and of which the full implications are understood.

Another strong image frequently presented in Egyptian scenes is that of the king commanding his forces in the field and thereby exposing himself to injury. That some kings did lead their troops into battle is suggested in some texts and reliefs and, of course, the badly damaged skull of King Seqenenre Tao of the Seventeenth Dynasty, discussed in detail in the next section, strongly suggests that this king actively fought in a battle (against the Hyksos in about 1580 BC) and incurred injuries as a result.

On a more practical level these images of the king as a battle leader and more importantly as a "smasher of skulls" or a "smiter of foreheads" serve to show that the ancient Egyptians fully understood the potentially lethal nature of cranial injuries. This sometimes fatal characteristic of such injuries was obviously witnessed upon the battlefield (as the aforementioned battle scenes show) and again during surgical treatment (where appropriate) as demonstrated above in the Edwin Smith Papyrus. Although the incidence of actual king-inflicted head injuries was unlikely to have been high, the iconography of the king in such a pose serves to stress the importance the Egyptians attached to both actual cranial assault and the threat of it.

BIOLOGICAL SOURCES

The most revealing source of information for cranial injuries, of course, is the human skull itself. Due to both natural mummification and the artificial mummification techniques practised by the ancient Egyptians, there are many preserved bodies which provide us with actual examples of injuries to the face and cranium.

A powerful influence on the development of Egyptian civilisation was a belief in an existence after death, which was expressed in the provision of funerary gifts and by the preservation of the corpse. The importance of mummification cannot be stressed too strongly. During the Predynastic period (before 3000 BC) most graves were pits into which the corpse was introduced. In consequence of this the body was in direct contact with the hot desert sands which quickly dehydrated the body and prevented further decay. Later, attempts were made to provide the body with better grave goods and protection, but, ironically, these protective superstructures, of firstly wood then of stone, led to the separation of the body from the desiccating effects of the sand. During the Dynastic period coffins were increasingly used and this also served to intensify the decomposition of the body (Spencer 1982, 34). The first attempts at mummification consisted of wrapping the body in layers of linen bandages. Throughout the Dynastic period the technique of mummification improved reaching its zenith during the Twenty-first Dynasty (c. 1000 BC) when artificial eyes and subcutaneous packing gave a more life-like appearance to the corpse. As a result of these particular skills in preserving bodies any pathological lesions (fractures and certain diseases) evident on the bodies were also preserved.

The following section will describe and discuss a selection of head and facial injuries evident on mummies and skeletons from both ancient Egypt and Nubia. Where possible some assessment of the effects of those injuries upon the individual's quality of life will be made.

The body of a Predynastic female is part of the collection of human remains in the Department of Egyptian Antiquities, British Museum. The body, from Gebelein, lies in a flexed position with the hands held near the face. An X-ray examination (Dawson and Gray 1968, 1) of this desiccated, naturally preserved body has revealed a grossly comminuted fracture of the skull. Whether this injury was received as the result of an accident (e.g. a fall) or through violent assault there is no indication. Two interesting skull injuries from Predynastic Naga-ed-Der have been described by Podzorski (1990, 21). One, an adult, probably male, may have acquired his lesion through violence. Podzorski cites Lythgoe's description of the lesion, as he recorded it in the field, as a healed left-sided wound as if made by an axe or similar weapon. Yet, interestingly, Podzorski comments that this lesion was not noted by G. Elliot Smith after his previous examination of the skull. The second case, another male, of about thirty years of age, is less mysterious. The lesion, again on the left side, was the result of a blow to the zygomatic arch (cheek area). As before, the fracture had healed, but an accidental or intentional cause for the injury could not be determined.

Moving into the Dynastic period we return once more to the British Museum to an adult male skull, which is of particular interest because he is from an early date in Egyptian history and because his name and occupation are known. Meri-Re-Hashetef lived during the mid-Sixth Dynasty and, from information found with his remains, during life he had been a gardener (Petrie and Brunton 1924, 3). His skull has two linear fractures running across the left parietal which join at the mid-coronal suture area to form a triangular-shaped lesion. The lesion shows no sign of healing and, whilst it may be too convenient to suggest he was hit by a gardening implement, this may be an example of an occupationally related injury.

Excavations in 1923 on the hillside at Deir-el-Bahari near the Valley of the Kings, Upper Egypt, brought to light a group of bodies in a roughly hewn catacomb (Winlock 1945). The remains were not fully examined until 1926, and then it was realised that the bodies, of about sixty men in number,[2] were from the Eleventh Dynasty, an important period in Egyptian history when the country was reunited after a period of political unrest. That the remains were those of soldiers was apparent from the types of wounds on the bodies, their accompanying weapons and equipment and observations about their ages at death. Based upon the developmental stage of their teeth (i.e. adult) and the amount of wear on them it was judged that all the men were between thirty to forty years of age at death. None of these men fall into the elderly or immature age groups and so were of the optimum age for military service. Four of the men had evidence of well-healed fractures (to the left side of the skull) suggesting that they were veterans of earlier skirmishes and had received these injuries in a frontal assault. Two other men had archer's wrist guards still in situ and these, together with other wrist guards lying amongst the torn bandages, bow tips with twisted gut bow cord still attached and remnants of arrows, would support the notion that these remains were the corpses of military men. Most pertinent to this discussion is the fact that many of these sixty soldiers showed evidence of injuries received just before death. The bodies had extensive cranial and post-cranial injuries, but for the purposes of this discussion only the injuries to the skull and face will be commented upon. Fourteen of the soldiers had eighteen different types of cranial wounds. It is possible that these were caused by arrows or by stones hurled with some force from a height. Body no. 63 (Winlock 1945, 13) has a small (c. 1 cm in diameter) irregularly circular puncture-like wound at the mid-point of the left half of the coronal suture. It is most probable that only the sharp point of an arrow could have made such a wound in the suture serrations. There can be no doubt as to the weapon which caused the injury to body no. 21 (Winlock 1945, 12) for the ebony tip of an arrow was still in situ in the left eye socket after penetrating some 5.5 cm into the head. This injury may be usefully compared with the eye injury described by Homer in the *Iliad* (book XIV, 487). Had this soldier lived longer no doubt the sight of that eye would have been lost.

Other wounds likely to have been caused by rocks and stones being hurled down onto the men were: fractures to the supra-orbital ridges, fractures to the jaw and the maxilla, fractures to the nasal bones and a variety of oval and circular depressions to the frontal and left parietal bones. All of these suggest a frontal assault and this picture of arrows, stones and other missiles raining down onto these soldiers strongly echoes scenes from monuments showing soldiers storming fortresses as we saw above in the scene of soldiers storming a Syrian fortress. Although it cannot be stated that soldiers are more likely to suffer head injuries than other kinds of injuries, these soldiers do seem to offer the opportunity to compare actual physical injuries with those depicted in battle scenes.

The horrific injuries to another fifteen of the soldiers would suggest they had been clubbed repeatedly about the skull and face. Several of these men showed signs of having received other incapacitating wounds before being clubbed to death. This image again brings to mind the Egyptian scenes discussed earlier of the king smiting or

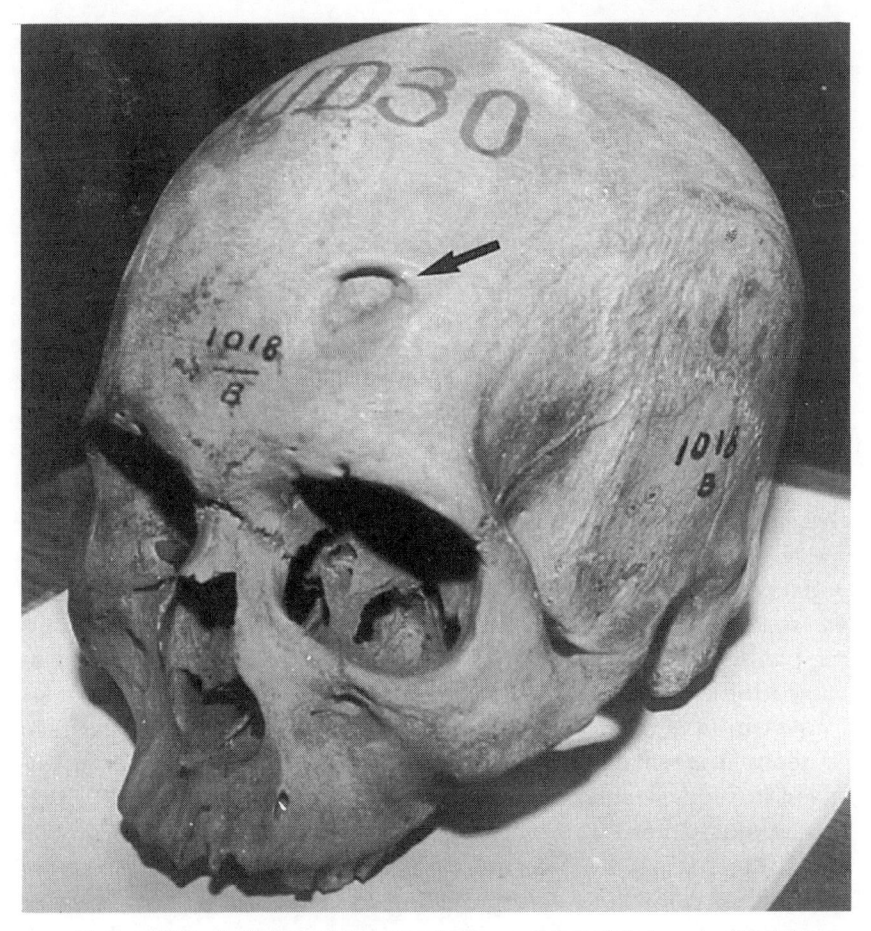

Figure 5. A skull from Kerma with an oval-shaped injury to the left frontal bone.

clubbing his enemy whom he has grasped by the hair. Again this type of crushing injury can be compared with Homer's *Iliad* (book XVI, 575) where Hector splits open a man's skull with a rock.

These sixty soldiers of the Eleventh Dynasty are an important source for the history of head injury for not only do they represent a variety of lesions they also show evidence of some of the weapons which made them and the context in which they occurred.

During 1913–14 and 1915–16, G. A. Reisner excavated a series of skeletons from the "eastern cemetery" at Kerma (Reisner 1923, 59–528). Kerma lies just south of the Third Cataract and north of the Dongola area in the Sudan. A group of skulls from Kerma (numbered SUD 1 to SUD 309), some with post-cranial remains, are now part of the Duckworth Collection in the Department of Biological Anthropology, University of Cambridge. These skulls, of a Middle Kingdom date, were examined and found to have a high percentage of head injuries (Filer 1992, 281–85). Thirty-four skulls (i.e. 11%) had injuries mainly on the left parietal and frontal bones, again suggesting they had met with face-to-face assault and again may indicate a right-handed attacker. Although the Kerma skulls had a variety of types of injury, by far the most frequently occurring lesion was the depression: a hollowed area sunk below the horizontal plane of the skull. Thirty out of thirty-four skulls (i.e. 88.2%) exhibited one or more of three forms of depression: oval, round and kidney-shaped with the oval (or pear-shaped) being the most commonly seen. Unusually, in this sample both sexes were well represented. It has been suggested that in most cultures more males than females sustain traumatic injuries and that the sex difference is especially noticeable with regard to cranial injuries (Manchester 1983, 59). In the Kerma group, however, seventeen males/probable males and thirteen females/probable females had a depressed injury (Figure 5). Whilst militaristic activities may be postulated as the causes of the depressions on the male skulls, this is less likely for the injuries on the female skulls. Whilst it is not unknown for women to take arms (e.g. in the English Civil War) there is no firm evidence that females (of the Middle Kingdom period) in Kerma engaged in military action, although Shinnie (1967, 19–20 and 47 citing Dio Cassius) notes that a Meroitic queen titled Candace led her troops into battle c. 25–21 BC. It is more probable that the women of Kerma were either camp followers providing food for the fighting men or were caring for the wounded, as seen in the battle scene from the tomb of Anta above, and so were caught in the melée. A comparison can be made with the skeletons from the "Belgic war cemetery" at Maiden Castle, Dorset, England, where 50% of the female skeletons showed injuries to the skull (Wheeler 1943). It was suggested that the mutilations were a result of the massacring of a total population (by the invading Roman army) rather than an indication of female participation in battle. An alternative situation for both sexes in the Kerma group might be that the depressed injuries were sustained during civil or domestic disputes involving clubs, stones or sticks and may indicate a quarrelsome community. Whatever the reason for these injuries they were not the cause of death for most of the individuals showed a smooth well-healed lesion. It is possible that the victims suffered little more than a severe headache or bouts of dizziness.

One of the Kerma skulls had a nicked cut to the lower edge of the left orbit and may be usefully compared to the injury found in one of the slain soldiers of the Eleventh Dynasty described above, where an arrow tip was found still in the left eye socket. In the Kerma case, it seems possible that this individual suffered some eye defect as a result of the injury. Another skull from Kerma may have had a fractured mandible, but as the left ramus is absent the diagnosis must remain tentative. From an examination of the extant part of the mandible the (probably) fractured part had set badly aligned (Filer 1992, 284). It may be suggested tentatively that in life this individual may have had a somewhat deformed jaw which could have interfered with eating and speaking. Again, this example may be usefully compared with a young female described by Nielson (1970, 116 and pl. 16) as having a face deformed due to a badly set fracture of the temporo-mandibular joint sustained during childhood.

A final example from Kerma leaves us with an intriguing conundrum. Subsidiary Nubian graves, excavated by Reisner in 1915–16 and not included in his 1923 publication, *Excavations at Kerma*, were described by Dunham (1982). The skeleton in grave K3718 (Dunham 1982, 9 and fig. 17) was that of an adult woman lying in a partially contracted position on her right side. She appears to have a pre-mortem wound to the left vertex of the skull. Dunham questions whether the woman may have been pregnant. It is likely he based his comment on the position of the woman's right hand which, in the published photograph, seems to be placed in a rather protective position around the abdomen. Whether the woman had indeed been pregnant and whether the seemingly unhealed head injury was inflicted in connection with her condition will remain a mystery.

Possibly the most famous case of head injury from ancient Egypt is that of King Seqenenre Tao of the late Seventeenth Dynasty. It is essential to view his injuries in the context of the politics of his time. During the Twelfth Dynasty Egypt successfully prevented invasion by Asiatics from the Palestine area, however, due to later internal problems which weakened the country during the Thirteenth Dynasty, groups of Asiatics (known as the "Hyksos") infiltrated firstly the delta area of Egypt, eventually taking over the whole country. Seqenenre too played an important role in ridding Egypt of these invaders. In the sections above, the role of the king as represented artistically and textually was discussed. This image of the king leading his military forces into battle seems to be borne out by the remains of Seqenenre Tao, for the condition of his body strongly suggests some violent injuries were incurred upon the battlefield. The results of an examination of his body, now in the Cairo Museum, reveal that Seqenenre was about thirty years old when he died (Harris and Weeks 1973, 122). His skull and face present five lesions: a long wide gash along the mid-line of the frontal bone; a broad gaping wound above the right brow ridge; a punctured and depressed wound to the right zygomatic area near the right eye; a large circular depression at the glabella and a long gash on the left cheek running obliquely from under the left eye and over and into the cheek bone (Fleming et al. 1980, 27). The German scientist, Metzel, (cited in Fleming et al. 1980, 27) has shown that there had been some bone re-growth around the long horizontal mid-frontal gash indicating that Seqenenre had received this injury several months before sustaining the other head injuries which led to his death. It has been suggested that the partial paralysis evident in one of the king's arms is a direct consequence of this earlier injury and that the actual blow which killed the king was a sixth wound, a spear-thrust, entering deeply into the skull behind the left ear (Fleming et al. 1980, 27). The alternative suggestion that the king was assassinated by some of his courtiers at Thebes (Harris and Weeks 1973, 122) is possible but the size and shape of the wounds are concurrent with those made by a battle-axe. That Seqenenre's mummy "is the worst preserved of all the royal mummies in the Egyptian Museum" (Harris and Weeks 1973, 122) suggests to some researchers that the body was hastily embalmed and wrapped far away from the proper facilities of his Theban home, possibly lending support to the idea of his death on the battlefield. However, the situation remains unresolved.

In the early part of this century, W. M. F. Petrie excavated a group of 1,726 skulls at Giza, which was then given to Karl Pearson, a biometrician at University College, London. Pearson was undertaking a study of the variability in a large series of skulls and this group, known as the "E" Series, formed part of that study. The material is believed to date from the Twenty-sixth to Thirtieth Dynasties but, unfortunately, little information is known about this series.[3] This group of skulls, however, is extremely pertinent to this discussion because it presents a wide and informative range of head injuries. Of the 1,726 skulls, twenty-one (i.e. 1.2%) had injuries ranging from cuts and depressions to pierced lesions and severe gashes (Filer 1992, 281–85). As with the group of skulls from Kerma, the depressed lesions found on five of the Giza skulls were probably the result of stones being hurled with some force. Two Giza skulls show healed and possibly untreated fractures of the left nasal bones suggesting blows from a right-handed frontal facing attacker. A militaristic attack or a civilian "punch on the nose"

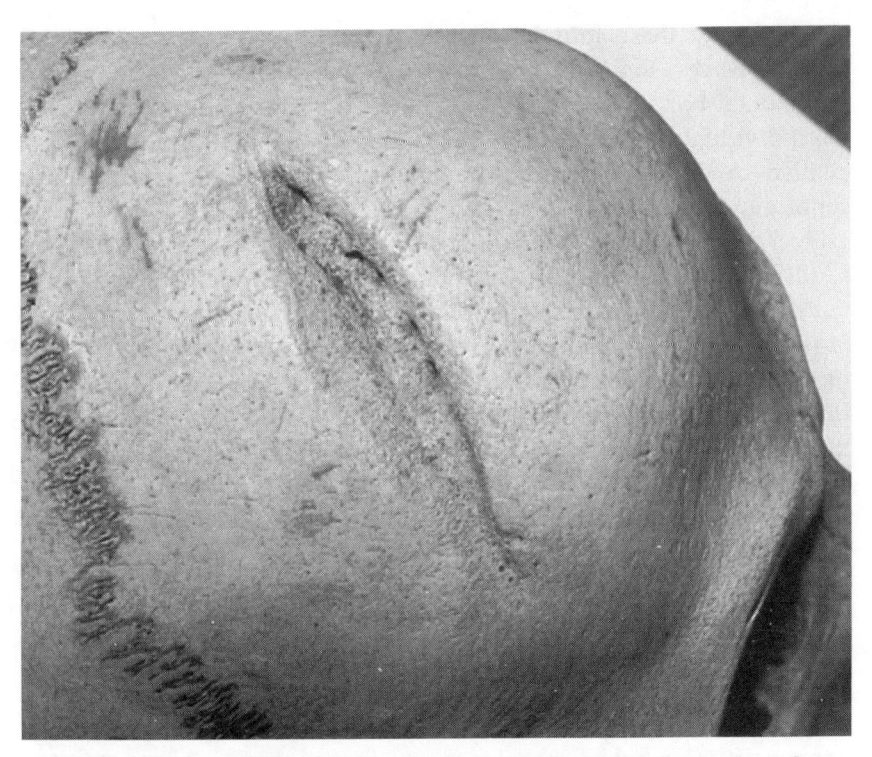

Figure 6. A skull from Giza showing a cleft-like injury to the frontal bone.

may be equally to blame for these wounds which were long standing and which were unlikely to have affected the quality of life apart from a slightly crooked nose.

One injury in particular, however, is likely to have had some effect on the recipient's quality of life. This individual, a mature male, had a sliced lesion running from the vertex of the skull down the mid-left parietal bone through the temporal area and into the auditory meatus. Although the injury had healed well, it is probable that this man suffered a hearing loss afterwards, for one of two types of deafness – conductive or sensori-neural or a combination of both – may have been acquired under these traumatic conditions (Filer 1987). This injury was probably made by the sharp edge of a sword as were several more injuries observed on other Giza skulls. Five other skulls had severe gashes: long and deep clefts of uniform or undulating depth. Four of these individuals are male and it is difficult to suggest a cause other than a military one, the wounds being made by a heavy sharp implement smashing down onto the skull (Figure 6). Despite their severity these four lesions showed signs of healing. The fifth skull, however, showed no sign of re-growth around the lesion to the mid-frontal bone indicating it was made shortly before death and, as the individual is a female, the gash was more likely inflicted during a civilian or domestic altercation, but her being a victim of military action cannot be ruled out.

Overall, the mainly more serious nature of the injuries to the Giza skulls reflects the types of weapons available to ancient Egyptians at that time. During the New Kingdom period the techniques of processing iron became known to the Egyptians, thus changing the development of weapons. Iron, an extremely durable metal, could inflict horrific injuries time after time without the necessity of re-sharpening. Metals used prior to iron – namely copper and bronze – whilst able to administer fairly serious wounds, blunted easily and were, in comparison, more restricted in use. Iron battle-axes and swords were extremely effective in inflicting injuries during short-range combat.

The final group of human remains to consider is an important series collected during the excavations of the archaeological survey of Nubia directed firstly by Reisner (during the 1907–08 season) and then by Firth for the next three seasons (1908–09; 1909–10; 1910–11). The excavations were instigated in order to record the historical material in danger of being submerged by the waters of the newly constructed Aswan Dam. This included cemeteries from the Predynastic period to the Coptic period. Thus over 6,000 bodies from cemeteries of many periods were excavated and recorded. Anatomical reports on the bodies were undertaken by Grafton Elliot Smith, firstly with the assistance of F. Wood Jones and then with D. E. Derry, and these reports (see bibliography) should be consulted in their entirety for the rich source of information they contain. The information recorded for each body included: age, sex, race and any externally observed pathology. Generally, the pathology included examples of gout, arthritis, dental abscesses, a variety of inflammatory conditions and, of course, fractures. Some of these Nubian remains showing external pathology are now housed at the Natural History Museum, London, and are the subject of a concise and informative report by Molleson (1993, 136–43).

Wonder and astonishment was expressed at the remarkable recovery made by some of these ancient Nubians from their often severe head injuries. From the cemetery at Hesa an adult woman of the Byzantine period showed "one of the most remarkable of the healed fractures of the skull" (Elliot Smith and Wood Jones 1910, 298). The fracture extended from the right nasal bone up and across the frontal bone, up to and across the coronal suture and down to an area above the right ear. Apparently the lesion had healed without any inflammatory reaction or adverse effects as far as can be judged. Several cases of injury made by a sharp implement were noted as were many concurrent with being made by maces or other blunt instruments. Among the facial injuries observed it was suggested that broken noses were "a somewhat common accident in ancient Nubia and the deformity that it produced seems in most cases to have passed untreated" (Elliot Smith and Wood Jones 1910, 300), a situation noted elsewhere in this discussion. Yet, according to the Edwin Smith Papyrus (see above) such injuries were easily treated. Seven cases of nasal depressions were noted, one of which involved the left and right nasal bones and four of which involved the left side only. Again these examples support the notion that the majority of injuries were sustained to the left part of the skull and face as noted in other series, namely the Kerma and Giza series and so on. Finally, a young man of the Byzantine period (between the second and fourth centuries AD) seems to have been a walking catalogue of cranial lesions. He had three exceptionally serious wounds (Elliot Smith and Derry 1910, 13–15). One extensive lesion, from an axe or sword, had penetrated the left area of the frontal bone above the brow ridge and this had forced open a wide gaping wound from the glabella across to the sphenoid. Parts of the frontal bone had been cracked into several pieces some of which had become rejoined by callus formation. In the words of Elliot Smith and Derry (1910, 14) "it is astounding that this man could have lived, as this man certainly did, for long afterwards with this gaping chasm in his forehead and a large part of his brain destroyed". The second lesion was a slicing wound some 42 cm in diameter on the left parietal and, as with the first, the man had survived the injury. The third lesion, a slicing cut across a large part of the mid areas of the left and right parietals, showed no signs of healing and must be assumed to have been the *coup de grâce*.

At this point it would seem useful to compare the incidence of cranial injury with post-cranial injury yet, as early as 1910, Wood Jones (in Elliot Smith and Wood Jones) suggested that a tabulation of how many times particular bones in the skeleton are broken is of little value as such baldly stated facts would do little to indicate the causes of those fractures. Wood Jones suggested, however, that a comparison of ancient fractures with those occurring in modern populations might better indicate causative factors. In his comparison of fractures in ancient Nubian populations with those of modern (1907) cases of fractures from hospitals in London and New York, Wood Jones found marked differences in the forms of fractures between the ancient and modern populations. With regard to fractures of the lower leg these were found to be more numerous in the two modern populations and Wood Jones put this down to particular circumstances of modern life such as street traffic accidents and slips on pavements which were not a feature of ancient life. The numbers of fractures to the humerus were roughly equally recurring in both the ancient and modern populations. It was suggested that the causative events for these fractures are not dependent on any particular environmental factors. Fractures of the forearm, femur and skull and face, however, were more numerous in the ancient Nubian populations and led Wood Jones to postulate intentional violence as the motivating force. Wood Jones (in Elliot Smith and Wood Jones 1910, 297) considered forearm fractures to be "common out of all proportion in these early Nubian cemeteries" and were viewed as "parry" or defence fractures sustained as the forearm (more commonly the left than the right) was raised to ward off an assault to the face or skull. Fractures to the femur were considered "the outcome of very considerable violence" whilst injuries to the head and face were viewed as the probable "result of homicidally inflicted blows and were not the results of falls and accidents" (p. 296).

In her discussion of the predynastic human skeletons from Naga-ed-Der in Egypt, Podzorski (1990, 20) noted in her sample that the overall frequency of fractures to the various bones in the skeleton was similar to the Nubian sample reported by Wood Jones above. Skull and facial fractures were represented by only 5% of the sample but as in the Nubian sample fractures to the ulna were common (31% in the Nubian sample, 35% at Naga-ed-Der) strongly suggesting the forearm was used as a defence against potential head injury.

A comparison of head injuries with post-cranial injuries seems to indicate that the former (together with associated parry fractures of the forearm) did occur more frequently in ancient populations and that intentional violence accounted for many of them. Thus the iconographic and literary focus on cranial injury is reflected in the actual incidence of violent injury.

The list of bodies from ancient Egypt and Nubia which exhibit cranial injuries could continue for the length of this volume, but it is hoped that the examples chosen show that, from Predynastic times onwards, the populace of Egypt and Nubia were no strangers to cranial assault and that a range of the types of head injury has been successfully demonstrated.

CONCLUSIONS

The wide variety of human remains exhibiting lesions on the head together with contemporary texts and artistic representations indeed show that ancient Egypt and Nubia provide a wealth of information about cranial injuries. In the introduction to this volume it was stressed that archaeology can make a valuable contribution towards an understanding of the phenomenon of human violence but that this can only be achieved if the archaeological material is assessed within its own social context. From this standpoint ancient Egypt and Nubia are in a unique position in the types of information they proffer and in the sheer volume of material available. Few other ancient cultures have left such a rich legacy of knowledge.

At the beginning of this discussion the desirability of having more than one source of information on a subject was indicated and with regard to cranial injury Egypt and Nubia fulfil this wish. Egyptian texts provide information from the medical point of view where the need for ordered observations of, and treatment for, injuries is deemed essential. From the literary or non-medical textual point of view, royal power is expressed through the dominant image of the smiting king, whilst at another social level the actual pain involved at the receiving end of a cranial injury is often poignantly described. Iconographically, there is a strong and traditional image of the Egyptian king in the victorious pose of smiting (and thereby subduing) enemies through cranial violence which parallels that expressed in Egyptian texts. The image is a strong statement of the significance of both the portend of physical harm and its actual occurrence within the ancient Egyptian mind. On a more practical level, military and non-military scenes show the less symbolic and more practical aspect of violence to the head. The biological evidence shows the results of the intentions implied in the texts and the artistic scenes and the outcome of any accidental trauma. Information from human remains from Egypt and Nubia testify to the continued use of cranial violence in one form or another throughout their recorded histories, for indeed bone itself is a chronicler of information. Ancient human remains demonstrate whether or not a person survived often the most grievous of injuries. Sometimes we can make an assessment of the surviving person's quality of life and empathise with his or her suffering.

ACKNOWLEDGEMENTS

Thanks are due to the following: Neville Parker for drawing the battle scene from the tomb of Inti; Richard Parkinson for the drawing of King Den smiting; Carol A. Randle for drawing the hieroglyphs. To A. J. Spencer for advice and Pat Terry and Jenny May for typing the original manuscript. I am grateful to Dr R. Foley, Director of the Department of Biological Anthropology, University of Cambridge, for the opportunity to study the skulls from Kerma and Giza.

NOTES

1. A particularly interesting aspect of the image of smiting is discussed by Robert Morkot 1986, 1–9, who notes that whilst the role of smiter is usually performed by a male – the king – attention should be drawn to Nefertiti, queen of Akhenaten/ Amenophis IV, who is depicted, scimitar in hand, smiting enemies. Morkot also points out that the queens of Meroe (Sudan) are also shown in the same smiting role as the king. He suggests this to be a reflection of their particular role within their own society.
2. Winlock 1945, 7: states that only fifty-nine skulls and fifty-two right femurs were identified. The actual record numbers went up to ninety-six but because tomb robbers had thoroughly scattered the bones it was difficult to determine with any assurance the exact number of bodies. Thus the number arrived at – sixty – is an estimate.
3. This information was obtained from handwritten notes which accompanied the Pearson Collection when it was moved from University College, London, to the Duckworth Biological Anthropology Laboratory, Cambridge. The series is mentioned briefly in Petrie (1907, 29) where the material is dated to about 600–300 BC.

REFERENCES

Aker, Frank, Schroeder, Dawn C. and Baycar, Robert S. 1983. Cause and prevention of maxillofacial war wounds; a historical review. The Society of the Federal Health Agencies Annual Meeting, 4 to 7 November 1984, San Diego. *Military Medicine* 148 (December 1983): 921–27.

Alexandersen, V. 1967. The evidence for injuries to the jaws. In D. R. Brothwell and A. Sandison (eds), *Diseases in Antiquity*, 623–29. Springfield, Ill., Charles C. Thomas.

Bagchi, Asokek 1980. *An Introduction to Head Injuries*. Oxford, Oxford University Press.

Blackman, Aylward M. 1915. The tomb-chapel of Senbis son Ukh-Hotp (B, no. 2). In *The Rock Tombs of Meir*, part 2. London, Egypt Exploration Fund.

Breasted, James Henry 1930. *The Edwin Smith Surgical Papyrus*, vol. 1. Chicago, University of Chicago Press.

Caminos, Ricardo A. 1954. *Late Egyptian Miscellanies*. Oxford, Oxford University Press.

Curto, Silvio 1971. *The Military Art of the Ancient Egyptians*. Turin, Egyptian Museum of Turin (Pamphlet no. 3 of the Egyptian Museum of Turin).

Davis, Whitney 1992. *Masking the Blow: The Scene of Representation in Late Prehistoric Egyptian Art*. Berkeley, University of California Press.

Dawson, Warren R. and Gray, P. H. K. 1968. *Catalogue of Egyptian Antiquities in the British Museum*, vol. 1, *Mummies and Human Remains*. London, Trustees of the British Museum.

Decker, Wolfgang 1992. *Sports and Games of Ancient Egypt*. New Haven, Yale University Press.

Desroches-Noblecourt, Chr. and Kuentz, Ch. 1968. *Le Petit Temple dAbou Simbel*, vol. 2, *Planches*. Cairo, Ministère de la Culture (Centre de Documentation et d'Étude sur l'Ancienne Egypte – Mémoires, tome II, Le Caire).

Dunham, Dows 1982. *Excavations at Kerma*, part 6. Boston, Museum of Fine Arts.

Elliot Smith, G. and Derry, D. E. 1910. Anatomical report. In *The Archaeological Survey of Nubia. Bulletin no. 5: work from 1 November to 21 December 1909*, 11–25. Cairo.

Elliot Smith, G. and Wood Jones, F. 1910. *The Archaeological Survey of Nubia report for 1907–1908*, vol. 2, *Report on the Human Remains*. Cairo.

Epigraphic Survey. 1986. *The Battle Reliefs of King Sety I: Reliefs and inscriptions at Karnak*, vol. 4. Chicago, Oriental Institute of the University of Chicago.

Filer, Joyce M. 1987. Spelling and the Hearing-Impaired. Unpublished MSc thesis. London, The City University.

Filer, Joyce M. 1992. Head injuries in Egypt and Nubia: a comparison of skulls from Giza and Kerma. *Journal of Egyptian Archaeology* 78: 281–85.

Firth, C. M. 1912. *The Archaeological Survey of Nubia Report for 1908–1909*, vol. 2. Cairo.

Firth, C. M. 1915. *The Archaeological Survey of Nubia Report for 1909–1910*. Cairo.

Firth, C. M. 1927. *The Archaeological Survey of Nubia Report for 1910–1911*. Cairo.

Fleming, Stuart, Fishman, Bernard, OConnor, David and Silverman, David 1980. *The Egyptian Mummy, Secrets and Science*. Philadelphia.

Ghalioungui, Paul 1963. *Magic and Medical Science in Ancient Egypt*. Hodder and Stoughton, London.

Gurdjian, E. Stephen 1974. The treatment of penetrating wounds of the brain sustained in warfare. *Journal of Neurosurgery* 39, 157–67.

Hall, Emma Susan 1986. *The Pharaoh Smites his Enemies: A Comparative Study*. Munich, Deutscher Kunstverlag (Münchner ägyptologische Studien 44).

Harris, James E. and Weeks, Kent R. 1973. *X-Raying the Pharaohs*. London.

Homer, *The Iliad* (translated by E. V. Rieu). 1985. Harmondsworth, Penguin.

Lichtheim, Miriam 1973. *Ancient Egyptian Literature*, vol. 1, *The Old and Middle Kingdoms*. Berkeley, University of California Press.

Lichtheim, Miriam 1976. *Ancient Egyptian Literature*, vol. 2, *The New Kingdom*. Berkeley, University of California Press.

Manchester, Keith 1983. *The Archaeology of Disease*. Bradford, University of Bradford.

Martin, Conrado Rodrigues, Anton, Rafael Gonzalez and Gonzalez, Fernando Estevez 1993. Cranial injuries in the Guanche population of Tenerife (Canary Islands); a biocultural interpretation. In W. Vivian Davies and Roxie Walker (eds), *Biological Anthropology and the Study of Ancient Egypt*, 130–35. London, British Museum Press.

Molleson, Theya I. 1993. The Nubian pathological collection in the Natural History Museum, London. In W. Vivian Davies and Roxie Walker (eds), *Biological Anthropology and the Study of Ancient Egypt*, 136–43. London, British Museum Press.

Morkot, Robert 1986. Violent images of queenship and the royal cult in Wepwawet. In M. Collier and M. Kamish (eds), *Wepwawet*, 1–9. London, University College London (Papers in Egyptology, vol. 2).

Newberry, Percy E. 1893. *Beni Hasan Part II*. London, Egypt Exploration Fund.

Nielson, O. V. 1970. *The Scandinavian Joint Expedition to Sudanese Nubia, 9, The Human Remains*. Uppsala.

Parkin, David 1986. Violence and will. In David Riches (ed), *The Anthropology of Violence*. Oxford, Basil Blackwell.

Petrie, W. M. Flinders, 1898. *Tomb of Anta in Deshasheh (1897)*. London, Egypt Exploration Fund.

Petrie, W. M. Flinders 1907. *Gizeh and Rifeh*. London.

Petrie, W. M. Flinders and Brunton, Guy 1924. *Sedment I*. London, British School of Archaeology in Egypt.

Podzorski, Patricia V. 1990. *Their Bones Shall Not Perish: An Examination of Predynastic Human Skeletal Remains from Naga-ed-Dêr in Egypt*. New Malden, SIA Publishing.

Pritchard, James B. 1955. *Ancient and Near Eastern Texts Relating to the Old Testament*. 2nd edition. Princeton, Princeton University Press.

Reisner, G. A. 1910. *The Archaeological Report for 1907–1908*, vol. I. Cairo.

Reisner, G. A. 1923. *Excavations at Kerma I-III*. Harvard African Studies V.

Riches, David 1986. The phenomenon of violence. In David Riches (ed.), *The Anthropology of Violence*, 1–27. Oxford, Basil Blackwell.

Rowbotham, G. F. 1964. *Acute Injuries of the Head: Their Diagnosis, Treatment, Complications and Sequels*. 4th edition. Edinburgh, E. and S. Livingstone Ltd.

Shinnie, P. L. 1967. *Meroe. A Civilisation of the Sudan*. London, Thames and Hudson.

Spencer, A. J. 1982. *Death in Ancient Egypt*. Harmondsworth., Penguin.

Spencer, A. J. 1993. *Early Egypt: The Rise of Civilisation in the Nile Valley*. London, British Museum Press.

Wells, Calvin 1964. *Bones, Bodies and Disease*. London, Thames and Hudson.

Wheeler, R. E. M. 1943. *Maiden Castle, Dorset*. London, Society of Antiquaries (Reports of the Research Committee of the Society of Antiquaries 12).

Wilkinson, J. G. 1937. *Manners and Customs of the Ancient Egyptians*, vol. 1. London, John Murray.

Winlock, H. E. 1945. *The Slain Soldiers of Neb-Hepet-Re Montu-Hotpe*. New York, Metropolitan Museum of Art.

The Crow Creek Massacre: Archaeology and Prehistoric Plains Warfare in Contemporary Contexts

Larry J. Zimmerman

The *fourteenth century* Crow Creek Massacre near the Missouri River in South Dakota, USA, is the largest known prehistoric massacre in the Americas. Discovery, excavation and analysis of the skeletal remains of at least 486 individuals, summarised in this paper, have changed the way prehistoric warfare on the Great Plains is viewed by archaeologists. The pattern of conflict was intense, with mutilations such as scalping commonplace. At the same time, the politics surrounding the discovery and the interpretations have demonstrated the dilemma facing archaeologists in terms of responsibility to the accurate presentation of data and to its impact on contemporary American Indians. Stereotypes of American Indian warfare abound. Countless novels and films about the American West focus on the archetypical Plains Indian, with horseback-riding, bow-and-arrow shooting, war-bonneted warriors attacking a fort or an encircled wagon train of European American settlers. But truth is often lost in these created images. The truth is also lost in the politics of the contemporary period where consciousness raising among American Indians has challenged stereotypes, particularly those relating to warfare and mutilation that are used by members of the dominant culture to dehumanise Indian people.

Reliable ethnographic works help to combat the stereotypes, showing a more complex pattern. Smith's (1938) *The War Complex of the Plains Indians*, Secoy's (1953) *Changing Military Patterns on the Great*

Plains and Mishkin's (1940) *Rank and Warfare among the Plains Indians* document the vastly more complex horse-and-gun warfare patterns common on the Great Plains after European American contact. They report everything from "coup counting" to scalping and body mutilations, but within a complex social structure and belief system.

Exactly how access to European American technology changed the pattern from before contact is difficult to ascertain, but certainly the increased mobility provided by the horse and the firepower of the gun must have had an impact. However, we actually know little of the prehistoric pattern.

Sites like the Sully site (Dietrick 1980) in Larson County, South Dakota, have produced evidence of violent inter-tribal conflict at a time immediately prior to white contact. Earlier sites, like the Initial Middle Missouri tradition Fay Tolton site (39ST11) in Stanley County, South Dakota, recount episodes of small-scale raiding, violent death, and mutilation (Wood 1976). In the Northern Plains from the eleventh century AD many late prehistoric (AD 1000–1700) villages developed fortification systems that indicated some level of conflict (but see also Oosterbeek this volume who argues the contrary for Chalcolithic Spain), but archaeologists have found little actual evidence of it until the discovery of the massacre at the Crow Creek site (39BF11) along the Missouri River in central South Dakota (Figure 1). Erosion and looting uncovered a pile of human bones buried in one end of the fortification ditch surrounding the village. From examination of the remains of at least 486 individuals all indicators pointed toward a violent death.

This chapter summarises what we know and suspect about the Crow Creek massacre, from how it was carried out to its probable causes. The massacre demonstrates a continuous pattern of intense warfare on the prehistoric Northern Plains, and it has lessons for contemporary people in that the cause of the violence likely stems from conflict over limited resources. The paper will also consider Plains Indian warfare in a contemporary context of image building and stereotyping, as well as the archaeologist's role in the process.

CULTURAL CHANGE ON THE NORTHERN PLAINS, AD 1150

The Crow Creek site is a National Historic Landmark site along the Missouri River, on the present day Crow Creek Sioux Indian Reservation. The site is a massive, heavily fortified village covering some 7.3 ha. Two prehistoric components reflect the cultural changes within the

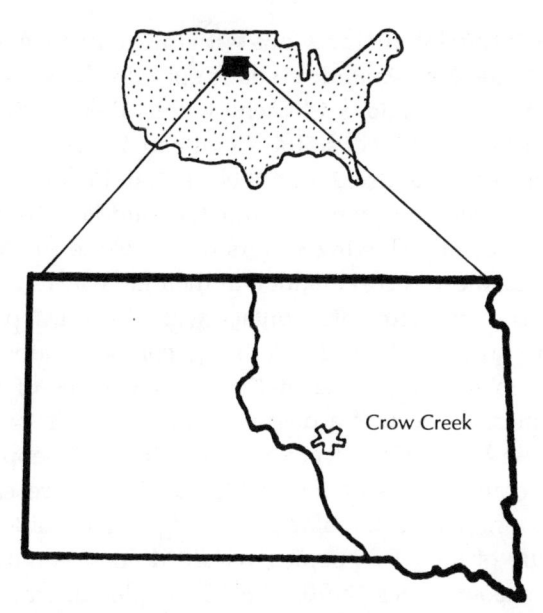

Figure 1. Location of the Crow Creek site, central South Dakota, USA.

Middle Missouri region of the Northern Plains beginning in the twelfth century AD.

The earliest component on the site is from the Initial Middle Missouri tradition (IMM). IMM cultures are ancestral to the Siouan-speaking groups of the region such as the Mandan Indians of the Historic period. IMM culture originated from an admixture of local resident Woodland tradition cultures with influences from major urban Mississippian tradition complexes such as Cahokia to the south and east. Living in villages of rectangular, earth-embanked lodges, these horticulturalists grew maize, beans and squash on the bottom lands near major streams, rivers and glacial lakes. Some of these villages were protected by dry moat fortification systems, as was Crow Creek. With villages located on the uplands above the river floodplain, they sometimes used the steep banks along the rivers as natural fortification.

At the same time, to the south in the Central Plains region, other villagers of the so-called Central Plains tradition (CPT) lived in square earth lodges loosely organised into hamlets and practised maize-based horticulture. They apparently had no involvement with warfare. No evidence of conflict and no fortification systems have been found. These peoples originated from more southerly Mississippian cultures and were Caddoan speakers, ultimately ancestral to the historic Arikara, Pawnee and Wichita tribes.

Both groups thrived in their regions with the moisture and moderate temperatures of the Neo-Atlantic climatic episode allowing the groups to expand horticulture and settlement within their regions. By AD 1150, however, the climatic shifts accompanying the onset of the Pacific climatic episode dried out the Central Plains. Low rainfall caused the CPT peoples to move into the Middle Missouri region where the permanently flowing waters of the Missouri River and its major tributaries allowed continuation of their life ways.

Migration brought them into contact with the IMM peoples. The culture contact apparently did not bring conflict. Rather, the CPT groups began to take on some of the characteristics of the Middle Missouri peoples. There was a degree of hybridisation of the groups emerging as the Initial Coalescent tradition (IC). IC peoples took on some of the ceramic traits of the IMM, but the square earth lodges eventually became larger, circular earth lodges. The shift was mostly with the culture of the CPT peoples; the IMM peoples moved upriver and re-established villages there. The IC peoples often located their villages on the same locations the IMM peoples had occupied. So it was at the Crow Creek site. The site occupies a point of land formed on the uplands by the confluence of two streams, Crow Creek and Wolf Creek. The IMM settlement had been closer to the point, while the IC peoples built their lodges slightly up slope, just inside the outer fortification ditch. The unplanned village structure reflected the loosely organised settlement pattern of their CPT predecessors. Although the climate was unstable, the IC population expanded rapidly, living in a new environmental niche where water supplies were more available for crops. We know that during the IC, at least fifteen villages were established along a 130 km stretch of the river (although we do not know that all were occupied contemporaneously). Several of the IC settlements had fortification systems, but not all of them. The fortified villages tended to be at the ends of the IC range along the river. Crow Creek is the southernmost village at the downstream end of IC range.

THE CROW CREEK SITE

Although large, fortified villages are not uncommon along the Missouri River, Crow Creek is among the largest of any of the prehistoric cultures from the region (Figure 2). The site has been known since late in the last century, and limited excavations were conducted there by the Nebraska State Historical Society and the National Park Service in 1954–55 (Kivett and Jensen 1976). Work was part of the

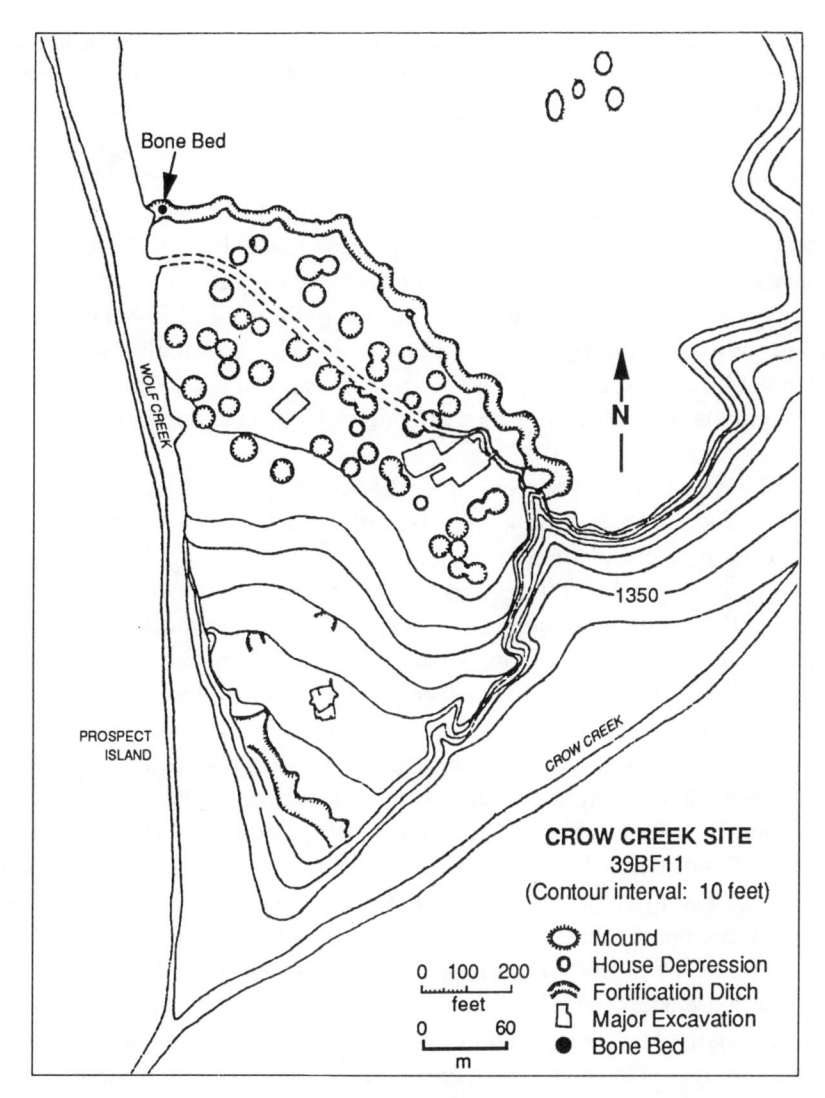

Figure 2. Plan of the Crow Creek site, showing the massacre location at the end of the fortification ditch (after Kivett and Jensen 1976).

River Basin Surveys projects to gather data from archaeological sites threatened by the reservoir created by the construction of the Fort Randall Dam.

Excavations completely exposed six structures, and fifteen smaller test excavations examined parts of other houses, middens, and the three fortification ditches at the site. Work yielded evidence for both the IMM, defined as the Crow Creek component dated to the twelfth century, and the IC, fourteenth century Wolf Creek component, the one involved in the massacre. The Wolf Creek component excavations exhibited nearly square structures reminiscent of the CPT, the houses built in basins up to .6 m deep. All structures contained storage pits and central hearths, with extended, south-facing entryways. Artefacts found were typical of Plains Village cultures. Small, triangular, notched and unnotched projectile points, stone blades, bone awls, shaft smoothers, scrapers and other tanning implements suggest the importance of hunting to the subsistence pattern, but bison bone and other faunal remains provide direct evidence. Horticultural implements abound, including bison scapula hoes, knives and digging implements. Remnants are found from maize and squash, wild plants and shellfish.

Wolf Creek ceramics were likewise abundant with nearly 30,000 pottery sherds, including 4,500 diagnostic rims. Eighty-three per cent of the latter were of three types, Talking Crow, Campbell Creek and Grey Cloud, which firmly places the component within the IC. The IC fortification system at the Crow Creek village is the most spectacular feature of the site. The main structure is an outer ditch, variable in depth and width, but nearly 380 m long, protecting the north-eastern margin of the site. The ditch incorporates ten bastions in its length. The natural topography provided protection for the rest of the site. The ditch supplanted an inner and earlier fortification built by the IC peoples. The 1954–55 excavations indicate that the inner ditch was nearly filled with debris diagnostic of the IC. This ditch also had bastions, and evidence of a palisade line was uncovered. The outer has almost no debris, and evidence of a palisade line is minimal. The remains of twelve lodges lie between the two ditches, suggesting that village expansion required a new fortification. Today, the outer ditch acts as channel for precipitation runoff, causing erosion at both ends of the ditch. It was in the western end of the ditch that erosion uncovered the massacre remains.

Discovery and Excavation of the Massacre

Members of the South Dakota Archaeological Society toured the Crow Creek site in late May of 1978. A member of the tour roamed away from the group toward the end of the fortification ditch, where he discovered human skeletal remains eroding from the ditch. Burials are known from village sites, but some archaeological society members suggested that the remains could be those of a small group of raiders killed during an attack. They little realised how close to the truth they really were! Archaeologists notified the Crow Creek Sioux Tribal Council and the U.S. Army Corps of Engineers, the latter having responsibility for the site. During the time spent deciding on how to proceed, a looter came to the site, saw the exposed remains, and dug a hole approximately a meter into the wall, strewing the remains down the eroded bank. These remains were collected, and a preliminary assessment indicated a minimum number of 45 individuals, including men, women and children. The bones also had cut marks indicating scalping and gnawing marks indicated that the remains had been scavenged before burial. Everything indicated villagers who had been killed in warfare, mutilated, then buried. Although archaeologists had seen evidence of prehistoric warfare on the Northern Plains before, nothing of this level had been uncovered. At this point, little of the actual intensity of the conflict was even suspected.

The University of South Dakota Archaeology Laboratory began excavations under contract with the Corps of Engineers. Because the site was a National Historic Landmark, under the jurisdiction of the U.S. Army Corps of Engineers and on the Crow Creek Sioux Reservation, the politics of the excavation were complex, placing a number of constraints on the project. The bank had been destabilised by the erosion and the looter so the excavation unit had to be larger than originally anticipated to both protect the excavators and to allow a stable bank face. Because it was a National Historic Landmark, we had to minimise "damage" from our own excavation, eventually limiting our ability to take out all the remains. The Crow Creek Sioux had their own concerns (Zimmerman and Alex 1981), including not wanting the remains to leave the state for analysis and demanding reburial of the remains and time limits for study. Budget was also a concern for the Corps of Engineers who funded the project. With these limitations, excavations lasted four months.

The bulk of the remains were located approximately 2.5 m below the current surface of the fortification ditch, with some material placed over the top of the bones when burial occurred and the remainder filling in since that time. By the time the excavations were concluded, an area 6 m by 3 m (maximum) was uncovered, the latter dimension variable to follow the actual ditch edges. Depths ranged from 1.5 m to 3 m. All material was dry screened and much of the material from the bone bed was "floated". More detail on the excavation procedures can be found in Zimmerman et al. (1981).

There were two bone beds. Bone bed A was a thin scattering of

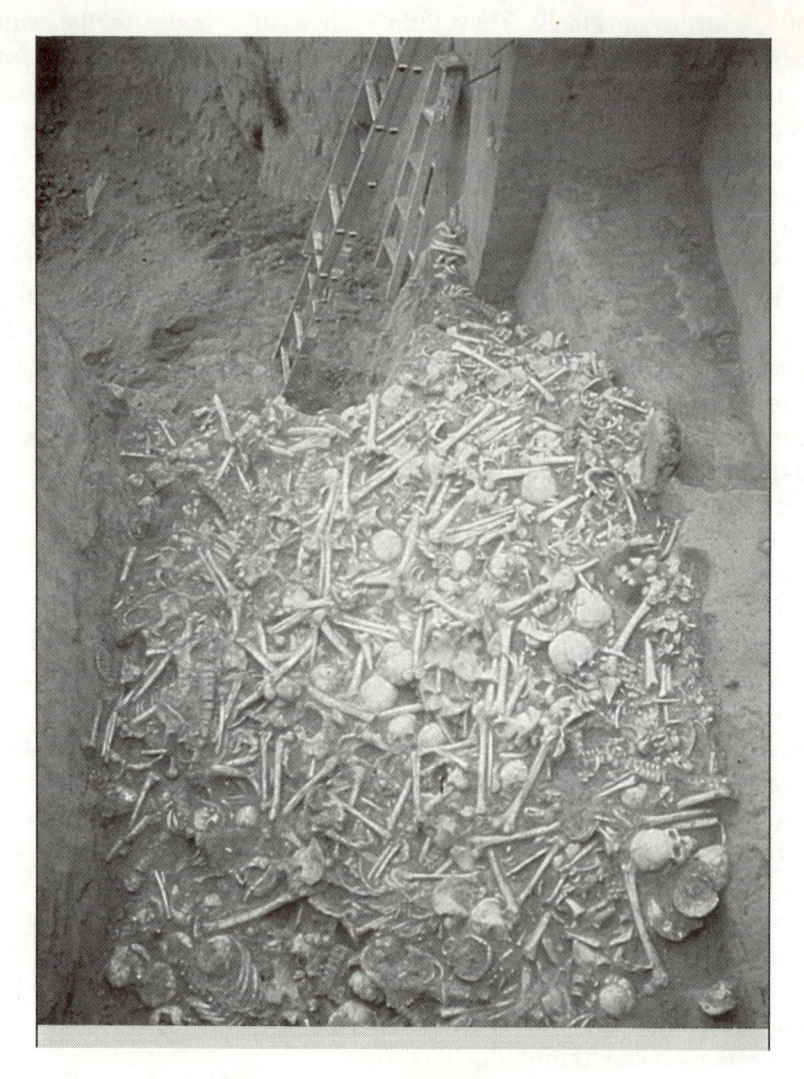

Figure 3. Conical pile of bones from bone bed B.

human remains above bone bed B, the main concentration. Bed B was cone-shaped, about 1.5m thick at its apex, thinning out (Figure 3). The partially dismembered and decayed remains had been carried to the outer edge of the ditch and dumped in the same spot, with a gradual "fan" shape developing. The bone beds were then covered with a 30 cm thick layer of clay brought up from its closest source, the floodplain below. That the clay was brought in to cover and protect the remains, at no small cost in labour, suggests that the burial might have been done by massacre survivors and relatives. A number of bison scapula hoes were found in bone bed A that may have been used for the interment. Mixed with the remains in small quantities were animal bones, pottery, stone tools and other village debris. Ceramics are exclusively those from the IC, linking the massacre firmly to the IC. Carbonised wood taken from bone bed B had a radiocarbon date of AD 1340±55 (WIS-1704) which corrects to AD 1325±55.

Osteology

Archaeological excavation and analysis of cultural materials thus places the remains firmly within the IC. Analysis of the human remains provides substantially greater information about the massacre and gives clues about how and why the massacre happened. Data gathering from the human remains took nearly 6 months, until just before the remains were turned over to the Corps of Engineers and the Crow Creek Sioux for eventual reburial. Analysis and interpretation of the data gathered have continued since that time, resulting in two doctoral dissertations (Bumsted 1984; Willey 1990), a master's thesis (Symes 1983) and numerous papers. Reburial precluded gathering additional information, but the variety and quantity of data gathered ranged from demographic to paleopathological. Some of these findings most pertinent to the conduct of the massacre are summarised here. Very few of the remains were articulated due to dismemberment, scavenging, decay and other taphonomic processes. Not only did this lead to problems for excavation, record keeping and logistics, but simple association of individual skeletal elements to others was often impossible. Even determining the number of individuals represented in the pile was difficult. In the end, counts of the right temporal indicated that at least 486 individuals were present in bone bed B (Willey 1990, 35).

Demography

The 486 individuals do not represent the entire village population. Estimates of village size vary, based on the choice of formulae used. A formula developed by Roberts (1977) for another IC village uses ethnohistoric population figures for the Arikara and other upper Missouri River villagers. His formula suggests that for people of unknown cultural affiliation, 14.88 people per lodge is realistic, but for the Arikara, the direct descendants of the IC, 16.62 people is probable. Kivett and Jensen (1976) estimate that at least fifty lodges were occupied during the IC at Crow Creek. This yields between 744–831 inhabitants of the site. Excavation limits caused some remains, perhaps 50 individuals, to be left in the fortification ditch. This leaves nearly three hundred not accounted for. Some may have been away from the village at the time of the massacre; others may have been killed, but their remains deposited at a different location in the ditch, a situation for which no testing was allowed. Some may have been taken captive as seems to be indicated by the age distribution of the victims. Crow Creek is unique in that the human remains are not from a cemetery sample where bodies are deposited over a period of years. Rather, it is a nearly complete village population killed during a very short time. Demographic reconstruction was difficult due to the problem of disarticulated skeletons and problems associated with ageing and sexing skeletons, but the reconstruction done by Willey (1990, 52) is revealing, demonstrating certain aspects of warfare patterns of the time.

All age groups from infants to elderly, and both sexes, are represented in the massacre. No group was protected from the onslaught. At the same time, in the age ranges from 15–19, 20–24, and 25–29, the number of females is under-represented by about half. This indicates that females of child-bearing age may have been taken captive, a pattern relatively common in small-scale society warfare. In the age ranges from 40 and older, the pattern is nearly the reverse, with older females represented in the population at about twice the number as older males. This could demonstrate a continuous pattern of warfare in which males are more susceptible to early death in combat. This pattern is supported by evidence from mutilations of the victims.

Trauma and Mutilation

Most of the Crow Creek massacre victims exhibit some evidence of paramortem mutilation. Nearly 90% of the skulls show indication of scalping, with no age group or sex immune from it. Willey (1990, 109) has observed that more of the scalp of adults was taken, but that only the top-lock of the scalp of children was removed. He offers that this might have occurred because the hair on the sides of children's heads was undesirable; the scalp was more easily ripped from their heads than it could be from adolescents and adults; the hair style of children and adults differed; or that they had proportionately smaller temporals than parietals when compared to adults. Typically, scalping at Crow Creek had two elements. The primary cut was a circling cut, the deepest, most frequent cuts slicing transversely across the frontal

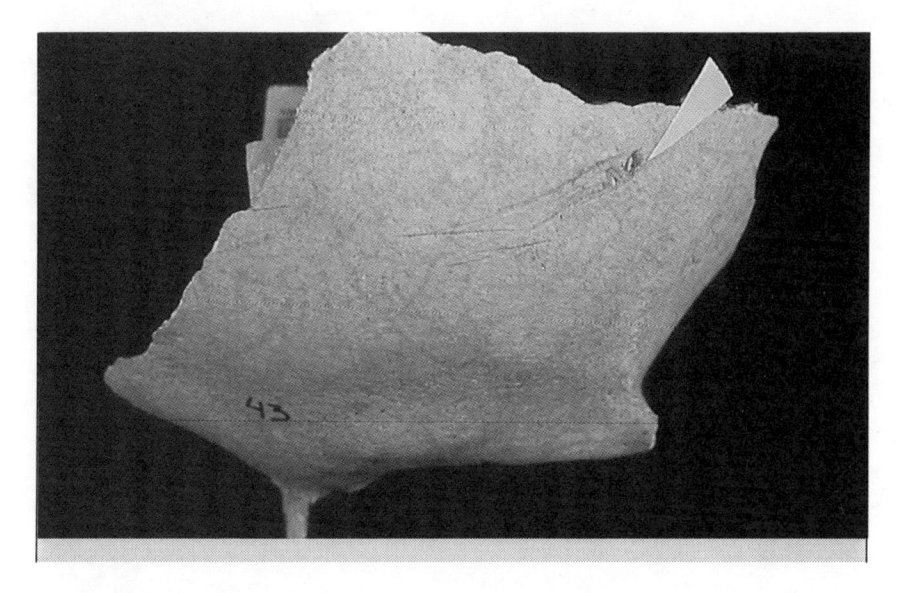

Figure 4. Skull frontal showing cut marks and fragment of scalping knife remaining in the bone.

(Figure 4). Usually there are several groups of short cuts, but sometimes there was a long, single cut. As the circling moved toward the back of the skull, the cuts became fewer and more shallow. Secondary cuts are often scattered over the vault, their most likely purpose to loosen and "skin" the scalp within the primary cuts. Numerous variations on these major themes occur, some perhaps associated with decapitation. Others occur with depressed fractures. When a fracture was present, the primary cuts attempt to avoid gashes or holes in the scalp caused by the fracture, which indicates that scalping frequently occurred after a blow to the head. There is other evidence for scalping. Two skulls show osseous remodelling like that identified as occurring when an individual escapes death but is scalped. Neither scalp shows cut marks due to the remodelling. The importance of these survivors of scalping is that it suggests that a pattern of intermittent warfare for at least three to six months before the individuals were killed in the massacre. Only five (four stone and one bone) projectile points were found with the remains. If bows and arrows were used, the arrows and their points may have been recovered by the attackers, or as the bodies lay out, decay may have caused points to drop out, not to be buried with the skeletal remains. If there was hand-to-hand struggle, other weapons were probably more effective. For many, death came

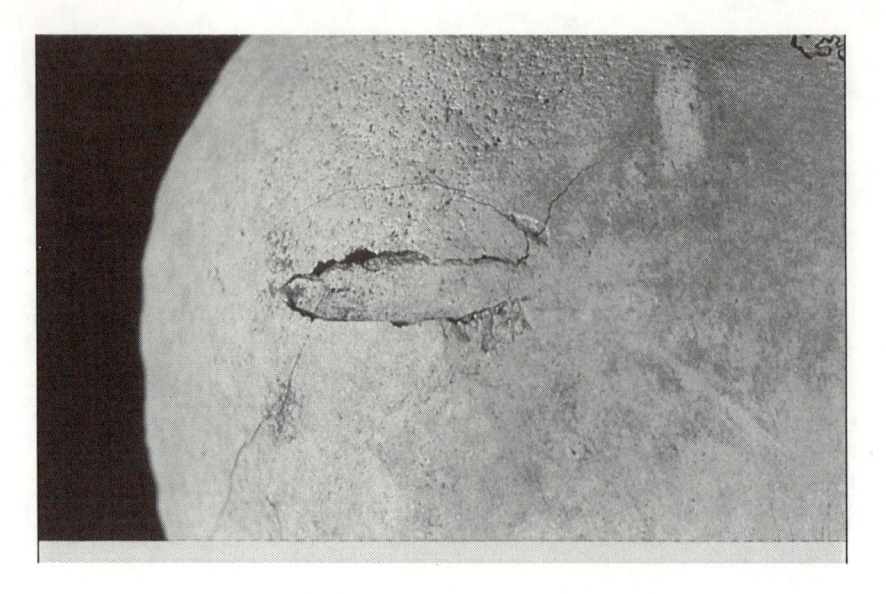

Figure 5. A depressed skull fracture, caused by an axe.

from blows to the head. About 40% of the skulls show depressed fractures, most with only one but some with as many as five. The blows are most common on the top and top-sides of the cranial vault. In some cases, the shape of the fracture may indicate the shape of the instrument hitting the skull. Some were hit with a round instrument striking the skull obliquely while others were ellipsoid, probably from an axe-like weapon (Figure 5). Although scalping and skull fractures are the most common evidences of trauma and mutilation, other mutilations are in evidence. Four nasal apertures were cut, with cut marks lateral and parallel to the long axis of the nose, likely from slashing of faces or removing noses. Evulsion or removal of teeth was fairly common, appearing on about 23% of the victims. Cuts on the ascending ramus of the mandible may have been made during decapitations, but other cuts indicate the tongue may have been removed, and Willey (1990, 119) suggests it may mirror a bison butchering technique whereby the tongue is removed from the bottom of the mandible rather than through the mouth. Decapitation was relatively common, with cut marks evident on the cervical vertebrae and occipitals.

Another very common mutilation form was evident on the postcranial remains, although absolute frequencies were never ascertained. No systematic survey was made. Cuts were present on all three elements of the arm. Efforts may have been made to remove some arms at the shoulder and elbow. Hands were commonly removed, although how much was due to dismemberment and how much due to other taphonomic processes is uncertain. Similarly, cuts marks were evident near hip joints and feet. These assessments are complicated by shattered and splintered ends of bones. How much of this occurred in mutilation and how much occurred later remains a question. Also, there is evidence of gnawing of the ends of bones by canids before the remains were interred. There are accounts from Arikara oral tradition, however, that hands and feet were removed in order to keep the spirits of the dead from exacting vengeance.

Causes and Culprits

With 500 hundred victims and extensive mutilations, the obvious questions relate to how the massacre was carried out, who did it and why. There are no easy answers. The method of the massacre may be the easiest to address.

The 1954–55 excavations give clues. Investigators (Kivett and Jensen 1976, 9) trenched across the outer fortification ditch and found it relatively clean of village refuse. They found no remains of a stockade line or post moulds for it, but along the inner, earlier IC ditch found evidence of an extensive stockade. As well, six of the post holes of the inner ditch contained human skull fragments. This suggests that the inner ditch holes may have been open at the time of the massacre, the posts having been pulled, perhaps to place them along the newer, outer ditch. The outer ditch may well have been under construction at the time of the massacre to protect an expanding village and to replace an old ditch that had lost its effectiveness because filled with village debris. Thus, if the village were under some scrutiny by enemy neighbours, the attackers might have known the best time to breach the fortifications.

When the village was attacked, or soon after the battle, the houses were burned (Figure 6). The 1954–55 excavations found that all the IC lodges they tested or excavated had been set afire. They also found human skeletal remains inside the burned habitations, a cache pit in one house containing a skull and pelvis, another a femur and several phalanges, and a third, a semi-flexed, partially articulated skeleton with skull, right hand and arm, and feet missing. Exactly when the village was attacked is problematic at best, but late autumn or early winter seem the most feasible, based largely on the idea that death happened at a time that decomposition of the remains did not happen quickly as it might have during a spring or summer massacre. Alter-

[87]

Figure 6. The burning of a reconstructed earth lodge (courtesy of the North Dakota State Historical Society).

nate freezing/thawing of autumn/early winter would have allowed slow decay and some disarticulation of skeletons. The burial might then have taken place in spring when the bodies were free of snow and the clay along the floodplain could have been brought up to cover the bone pile.

WHO MASSACRED THE CROW CREEK VILLAGERS?

Among the most intriguing of the questions is "who did it?" Suggested answers have ranged from the incredible (a marauding band of Vikings) to the feasible. Many, and probably most, assumed at first that the conflict was somehow generated from the contact between people of the Initial Middle Missouri culture and those of the Initial Coalescent. Yet nagging questions persisted. Among them were: why did such intense conflict not occur at the start of the incursion of Central Plains tradition peoples in the Middle Missouri? Why was a village at the southernmost end of the group of fortified IC villages attacked? How was such an attack carried out without the other IC villages upstream (the nearest was less than two kilometres away) knowing about the attack and coming to the aid of Crow Creek? Indeed, how could a fortified village of 500 or more people be so thoroughly destroyed?

Others offered the possibility that bands of "proto"-Sioux or Cheyenne carried out the attack. With these suggestions came many of the same questions but with the added dimension of how an outside group could travel with a force of warriors sizeable enough to take Crow Creek while not alerting the neighbouring IC villagers about the attack. True, groups of warriors were known during the Historic period to travel several hundred miles to carry out a raid, but rarely such a devastating attack. Certainly the serious hypotheses offered are feasible. Most, though, demand the complexity of explanation that defy a more scientifically elegant reasoning which suggests that the most simple structure accounting for the greatest variability is the most feasible answer. Therefore, one must look within the cultural system of the IC itself for answers. From available Crow Creek data, data from another IC site, and ethnographic analogy Zimmerman and Bradley (1986) have hypothesised that the massacre was a product of internecine warfare in which another IC village (or villages) carried out the massacre. Their hypothesis is based on evidences of malnutrition in the massacre victims.

In the preliminary evaluation of the skeletal materials, numerous transverse lines in radiographs of long bones were found. Examination also revealed evidence suggesting iron deficiency anaemia in 28 skulls, 18 with orbital cribra, 4 with orbital cribra associated with other skull lesions and 6 with porotic hyperostosis. Both localised and generalised periostial reactions were very prevalent in the Crow Creek bones. Subsequent investigations have uncovered additional supporting evidence indicating repetitious and prolonged malnutrition in many Crow Creek skeletons. The evidence allows much greater insight into the health status of these people and the environmental conditions which surrounded them at the time of their deaths. Information presently available indicates that there had probably been an extended period of unstable weather, especially drought, in the upper Missouri River valley region during the last seasons of occupation of the Crow Creek village. Accompanying the drought were decreased food supplies for both humans and animals and perhaps many of the usual social and psychological responses to famine (Dirks 1980). Detailed examination of the bone morphology and radiographs indicates probable dietary insufficiency in protein and essential minerals and vitamins. The total picture which has emerged from the study of the Crow Creek materials is one of long-standing chronic iron deficiency anaemia, famine, profound malnutrition, and scurvy (Zimmerman and Gregg 1986). These conditions do not appear to have been short-term or temporary. Active and organising subperiostial hematomas along with the other bony alterations provide convincing evidence that nutritional deprivation had been present for some time prior to the deaths of these people and probably was rampant at the time of their demise.

The combined weight of the evidence led Zimmerman and Bradley (1986) to suggest that inter-village warfare resulting from the scarcity of food supplies was the most likely cause for the Crow Creek massacre. Reduction of food supplies was precipitated by an unstable climate which was followed by a shortage of animal and vegetable protein and good sources for other essential nutrients. An exacerbating factor enhancing the food shortage was the apparent high population level of the Missouri River valley during the fourteenth century AD.

Zimmerman and Bradley used a computer simulation to test the hypothesis. In their model, pioneer IC settlements were placed at known locations along the river, and village populations were allowed to grow at variable rates in each simulation run. Land was allocated based on village population, with the simulation aborting if arable land needs were exceeded. They found that population came close to exceeding total arable land along the Missouri River, but that a more crucial variable was the amount of land between villages. This threshold could be quickly exceeded even with modest population growth rates. Thus, disputes may well have been over garden spaces, a cause of warfare and raiding known from many horticultural societies. The only feasible objection to this hypothesis thus far raised has been that it seems unlikely that villagers might be killed and mutilated by their own relatives. In answer, one can only offer that most of the homicides, and many of them brutal, in our own culture are done by close relatives. In addition, the ethnographic record is replete with similar examples from other horticultural societies, most notably the Yanomamo and the Grand Valley Dani (Stewart and Zimmerman 1989).

Internecine warfare, for perhaps no other reason than to satisfy the demands of our own cultural sensibilities, demands causes, or at least contributory factors, of an extreme nature. The data seem to allow a feasible case to be constructed with the causes of the massacre related to chronic malnutrition emanating from population growth, land use patterns, climatic instability, and consequent competition for arable land.

The hypothesis holds lessons for contemporary peoples living in the same river valley. The climate today is still largely unsuitable for the practice of agriculture. Population levels today, approximately 10,000 people, are similar to those projected in the same zone for the IC,

Figure 7. The Crow Creek reburial ceremony.

although today people are aggregated into only two cities and scattered ranches and homesteads. There is a great deal of competition for access to the waters of the Missouri River for irrigation and drinking water. Occupation of the zone certainly seems unstable at best, and the battlefields of prehistory have now become the courts of law.

Warfare Reality, Contemporary Politics and Indian Stereotypes

All archaeological constructions of the past are influenced by contemporary ideology and "politics". From the beginning of the Crow Creek excavations, the archaeologists were faced with the government bureaucracies and Indian concerns. Time to study the remains was limited by the agreement to rebury, and that reburial did occur in 1981 at the Crow Creek site, with a variety of traditional Lakota, Arikara, and Christian ceremonies (Figure 7). Indian concerns about the excavation ranged from outrage at our supposed mistreatment of the bones to worries about the spiritual and actual danger of dealing with the remains (see Zimmerman and Alex 1981 for a discussion). But more than this, the archaeologists largely failed to understand the power of their analyses and interpretations about the massacre. At the discovery of the massacre, the Crow Creek Sioux tribal chairman claimed, as was part of the local folklore about the site, that the Crow Creek site was the location of the last big battle between the Sioux and the Arikara. The tribes were bitter enemies during the late nineteenth century, but there were no historical records of such a battle, making such claims improbable. When the information about the scalping and other mutilations came out, the chairman claimed the Sioux would not have done such things to other Indians and that it must be evidence of a white military massacre of Indians. In another setting, at the 1989 World Archaeological Congress Inter-Congress on Archaeological Ethics and the Treatment of the Dead, a Lakota man vehemently denied that the Sioux and the Arikara ever were enemies, just that they had a few "disagreements". Later, an Arikara man at the meeting privately expressed that "we were enemies".

Beyond the mutilations, the interpretation of causes left Indians uneasy. A public television video, "Wanagi Is Gone", broadcast over several regional public television networks, posed the hypothesis about internecine conflict resulting from competition for scarce resources. Many Indian people expressed anger about this, saying that Indian people were better managers of the ecology than this, and would certainly not go to conflict over land. Archaeological explanations thus challenged Indian perceptions of self and Indian culture.

Indian views about the prehistoric past can become creations of the present, and also may be reflections of the contemporary situations of American Indians as seen by the dominant society. Although archaeologists have known for decades that scalping was practised in North America, Indian people rejected this notion, claiming that they did not scalp until the coming of the white man. That they would reject the practice is understandable when one considers that scalping was used as part of the stereotype of American Indian savagery. Thus Axtell and Sturtevant (1980) demonstrate that Indian rejection of scalping and assigning it to the white man was part of the effort to throw off savage stereotypes during the consciousness raising period of the late 1960s. The harmful effect of the warlike image of Indians is pervasive, even at the seemingly inconsequential level. Consider the impact, for example, when misbehaving, non-Indian children are told by their parents to "stop acting like a bunch of wild Indians." Following Gill (1982), non-Indians are caught up in a complex ambivalence towards Indians. On the one hand, Indians are everything non-Indians are not and everything non-Indians despise; on the other hand, they are everything non-Indians admire. Whites are sophisticated while Indians are crude, naive, and savage. At the same time, Indians are close to the earth, more in tune with the sacred and part of the ecological system, something many whites desire to be. Indians were despised as cunning, ruthless, and bloodthirsty, yet at the same time admired as noble warriors with consummate skill, daring, strategy and tenacity. The images of the dominant society can even come to dominate Indian images of self. They certainly can be and are used against contemporary Indian people in the political arena. That Indian people reject these images is not at all surprising; other cultures do likewise. During the Vietnam War when reports came out about mutilations and massacres like that at My Lai, the general public rejected the evidence out of hand as Viet Cong publicity, until the evidence became incontrovertible.

Thus, where is the reality when it comes to warfare like that at Crow Creek? That people died at Crow Creek and that their bodies were mutilated cannot be seriously questioned. Yet, does the archaeological reconstruction not appeal to people's more macabre interests? It certainly does if the worldwide publicity about the Crow Creek excavations is any indicator. What are the responsibilities of the archaeologist to all this, especially considering that our reconstructions can harm Indians through dominant society stereotyping?

At the very least, we must put our interpretations into cross-cultural context, especially a context that includes the dominant society and its own warfare "histories". In this way, stereotypes may not so easily be formed, or at least their impacts can be blunted. It may be important to discuss our constructions of events like that at Crow Creek with the descendants of the particular groups involved. Doing so may allow them to devise their own strategies to deal with the information. At the same time, there are no panaceas to the dilemmas caused by archaeological reporting of events like the Crow Creek massacre. Archaeologists must be responsible to the data by reporting it accurately, but they must be aware of the theoretical contexts in which the data are excavated and interpreted. They must also be aware of the contemporary social context of doing so and recognise their own responsibilities to that context.

ACKNOWLEDGEMENTS

Thomas Emerson acted as Field Director on the Crow Creek excavations. P. Willey was Chief Osteologist. John Gregg served as paleopathologist. Their work is integral to this paper. The project was funded by the U.S. Army Corps of Engineers, Omaha District under Contract DACW45-78-C-0018. Other support came from the Eastman Kodak Company.

REFERENCES

Axtell, J. and Sturtevant, W. 1980. The unkindest cut, or who invented scalping? *The William and Mary Quarterly* 37, 451.

Bumsted, M. 1984. *Human Variations in Adult Bone Collagen and the Relation to Diet in an Isochronous C4 (Maize) Archaeological Population.* Los Alamos, Los Alamos National Laboratory.

Dietrick, L. 1980 The Occurrence and Interpretation of Trauma at the Larson Site, 39WW2, Walworth County, South Dakota. Unpublished M.A. Thesis, University of Tennessee, Knoxville.

Dirks, R. 1980. Social responses during severe food shortages and famine. *Current Anthropology* 21 (1), 21–44.

Gill, S. 1982 *Beyond the Primitive: The Religions of Nonliterate Peoples.* Englewood Cliffs, N.J., Prentice-Hall.

Kivett, M. and Jensen, R. 1976 *Archaeological Investigations at the Crow Creek Site (39BF11).* (Nebraska State Historical Society Publications in Anthropology 7).

Mishkin, B. 1940. *Rank and Warfare Among the Plains Indians.* (Monographs of the American Ethnological Society 3).

Roberts, R. 1977. Population estimates. In C. S. Smith, *The Talking Crow Site*, 166–76. (University of Kansas Publications in Anthropology 9).

Secoy, F. 1953. *Changing Military Patterns on the Great Plains.* (Monographs of the American Ethnological Society 21).

Smith, C. S. 1977. *The Talking Crow Site.* (University of Kansas Publications in Anthropology 9).

Smith, M. 1938. The war complex of the Plains Indians. *Proceedings of the American Philosophical Society* 78, 425–64.

Stewart, J. and L. Zimmerman 1989. To dehumanize and slaughter: a natural history model of massacres. *The Great Plains Sociologist* 2 (1), 1–16.

Symes, S. 1983. Harris Lines as Indicators of Stress: An Analysis of Tibiae from the Crow Creek Massacre Victims. Unpublished MA Thesis, University of Tennessee.

Willey, P. 1990. *Prehistoric Warfare on the Great Plains: Skeletal Analysis of the Crow Creek Massacre Victims.* New York, Garland.

Wood, W. 1976. Fay Tolton and the Initial Middle Missouri variant. *Missouri Archaeological Society Research Series* 13, 1–58.

Zimmerman, L. and Alex, R. 1981. Digging ancient burials: the Crow Creek experience. *Early Man* 3 (3), 3–10.

Zimmerman, L., and Bradley, L. 1986. Simulation of competition for scarce resources: the Crow Creek massacre in ancient North America. *Proceedings of the 2nd European Simulation Congress*, 763–68.

Zimmerman, L. and Gregg, J. 1986. Malnutrition in 14th century South Dakota: osteopathological manifestations. *North American Archaeologist* 7 (3), 191–214.

Zimmerman, L., Emerson, T., Willey, P., Swegle, M., J. Gregg, J., Gregg, P., White, E., Smith, C., Haberman, T. and Bumsted, M. 1981. *The Crow Creek (39BF11) Massacre: A Preliminary Report*, Contract DACW45-78-C-0018. Omaha, Corps of Engineers Omaha District.

Mightier than the Pen? (an Edgewise Look at Irish Bronze Age Swords)

S. D. Bridgford

A *sword may simultaneously* be, or have the potential to be, a beautiful object, an efficient killing tool, a symbol of power and wealth, an implied or actual threat, a sacrifice, a gift, a reward, a pledge of loyalty and/or an embodiment of the idea of conflict. Many such complex functions and embedded meanings are lost when an object is removed from the society within which it functioned but clues still remain within the object and its context.

Adopted around the start of the first millennium BC, swords were the new weapons of the Irish Late Bronze Age. There are over six hundred examples of Irish bronze swords extant and, in an attempt to shed some light on the society which produced and used these swords, I recently examined some 20% of the National Museum of Ireland's collection in Dublin and all of the Ulster Museum's collection in Belfast. I also examined the Irish bronze swords at the Pitt Rivers Museum in Oxford, which is, as far as I am aware, the only collection to have had all artefacts sampled for metal composition, hardness and metallographic analyses (Allen, Britton and Coghlan 1970). My sample totalled 153 swords, 9 of which were deemed forgeries.

The provenance of Irish bronze swords, especially those found before World War I, is often suspect. Antiquities dealers operated from a number of centres leading to the perpetuation of some "good stories" and of "provenances" based on place of purchase. Inadequate recording of detail and the passage of time have led to some swords being ascribed only to the county of origin, while many have no provenance whatsoever.

Despite the thriving trade in antiquities, there can be little doubt that a large number of finds, especially of fragmentary swords, went unrecognised. Thus one would expect the collections to show a decided bias towards more complete examples. Many swords have been found in the course of peat cutting and river drainage and it is likely that the recorded proportion of swords from such wet contexts would exceed that in areas where such activities are less prevalent.

Well-dated contexts are virtually unknown and the dating of the swords has mainly been performed by typological analysis extrapolated from the few well-associated hoards and by comparisons with artefacts from Britain and continental Europe. The very few settlement and burial sites of the Late Bronze Age excavated have not, so far, yielded much by way of swords though some have produced sword moulds. Sadly, such sites are usually dated by means of the moulds rather than vice versa.

A number of bronze swords have been "modified" to serve other purposes. One, presumably broken, sword (Figure 1, no. 19) became (seemingly in prehistoric times) a short "knife" while retaining the original hilt. Some were, it would seem, used in anger quite recently. Eogan (1965) notes one sword, now in the Royal Ontario Museum, Toronto, purporting to have been "captured" at New Ross, Co. Wexford, during the abortive 1798 rebellion. Presumably similar use was made of one of the swords I examined (Figure 1, no. 138) which retained the remnants of leather binding threaded around the broken tang.

Although swords were clearly mended in prehistory many have been "mended" in modern times. This may obscure the cause of the break, has frequently been achieved by "adjusting" the broken pieces to "aid" the fit and has even joined two completely different swords together (an example was examined in the Pitt Rivers collection). The most unhelpful treatment for my purposes was the "cleaning" of the swords, which in many cases was drastic. Many clues as to the casting, original finish, subsequent treatment and deposition context have been erased.

DESIGN OF THE SWORDS

The major published work on the swords is undoubtedly Eogan's (1965) *Catalogue of Irish Bronze Swords* published almost thirty years

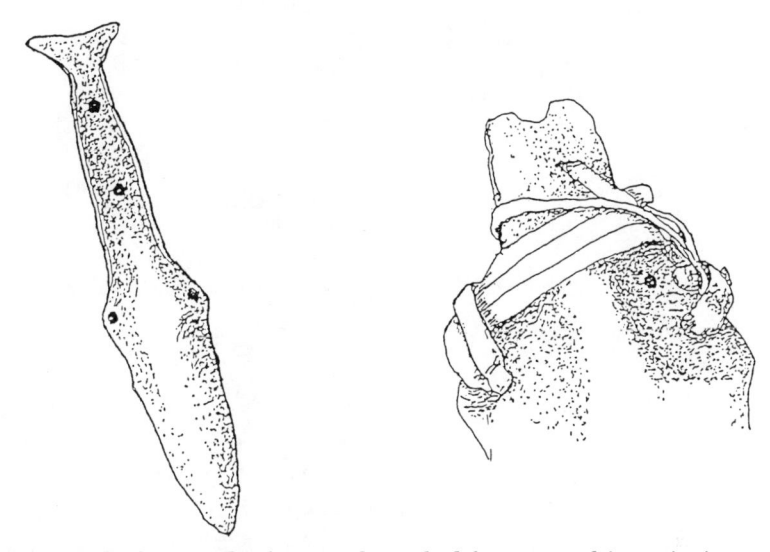

Figure 1. Broken swords: the example on the left was reused in antiquity as a dagger (no. 19, Ulster Museum 1911: 170), the one on the right was presumably "used" until recently, for its break had been "repaired" with leather (no. 138, National Museum of Ireland 1970: 218)..

ago. The typological classification was devised by Eogan to fit the Irish bronze swords into their European context and I have used it for the purposes of my study. The main characteristics of the six sword classes are shown in Figure 2.

Eogan's Class 1 swords (the Ballintober type) are undoubtedly early – some occur late in the Middle Bronze Age contexts. The number of Class 1 swords is small and the similarities so great that it is deduced that they were only produced for a limited period. Their design had a major weakness in the attachment of the hilt to the roughly rectangular tang with its four rivet holes.

Class 2 and 3 swords both present the same broad solution to the tang/hilt attachment problem in the shape of a flanged tang with integral terminal to which hilt plates could be attached using rivets through the butt and tang. Examples of these classes are not numerous and both were superseded fairly rapidly.

The most common Irish bronze sword is the Class 4, known in Britain as the Ewart Park type. Class 4 swords vary greatly in detail of design but typically have straight butt wings and a graceful leaf shaped blade, of pointed oval cross section. The extent of the variations within this class would permit further subdivision but few obvious or useful delineations exist. The variation itself and the numbers

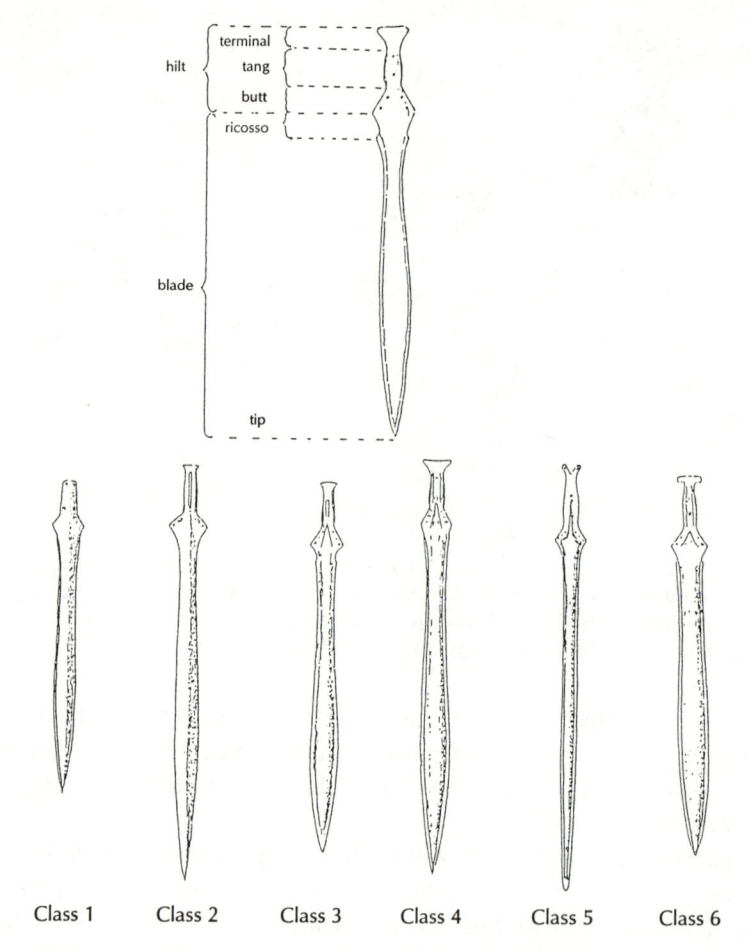

Figure 2. Features of a Bronze Age sword and types of Irish Bronze Age swords (after Eogan 1965).

surviving point to a wide spread of manufacturing and a fairly long period of use for this most successful design, which, despite a lack of examples dated after 600 BC, may have been used well into the European Iron Age (Eogan 1965) and seems equally likely to have been developed towards the start of the millennium.

Class 5 swords form a significant group which probably appeared in the second half of the seventh century BC (Eogan 1965). They are visually very different from the other classes and are clearly similar to the later Hallstatt C Gundlingen type swords. From a functional design viewpoint the thin flangeless tang appears a retrograde step, although the impressive length of the slimmer, almost parallel-sided, blades

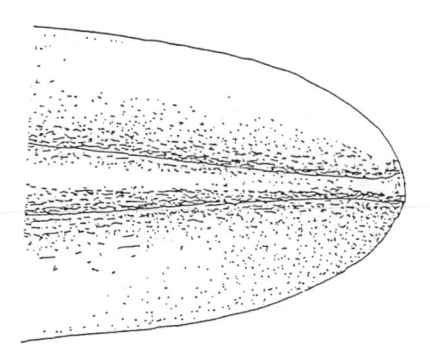

Figure 3. No. 61, Ulster Museum, display sword.

may have been an advantage. The aesthetic design of these swords, and the rather higher quality finish, is undoubtedly more elegant and impressive than that of Class 4 and Class 6 swords with which they evidently co-existed. Class 6 swords are thought to be late given their incorporation, into a basic Class 4 type, of aspects of Class 5 design, including the flangeless tang. Their T-shaped terminal is also present in the Carp's Tongue swords of south-eastern England. They do appear, as Eogan suggests is possible, to be hybrids between Class 4 and Class 5 but bear a strong resemblance to some of the less attractive Class 4 types.

Those few vestiges of hilt plates remaining are of organic material, generally bone, which would have provided a smooth and comfortable surface to grip. The different lengths of the rivets remaining in some swords show that the hilt plates thickened from the terminal to the butt. The majority of the swords have some form of ricasso and the majority of these are an integral, visually obvious part of the sword design. The variety of blade tips is enormous even within each typological class. The very pointed tips do seem to be more common among the "early" types (Classes 1, 2 and 3). Some of the "blunter" tip types, if designed as such (some were broken and reground), would have been totally unsuitable for any "thrusting" sword. The semicircular flat tip surrounding the midrib, exhibited by the example in Figure 3, which is common on Class 5 (and appears on Class 6) swords seems designed solely for aesthetic purposes.

Manufacture of the Swords

Copper was mined in Ireland during the Bronze Age and tin supplies, from Cornwall or Brittany, were fairly close to hand. Northover (1982)

Table 1. Metal composition of Irish Bronze Age swords.

Museum number	sword Class	Cu	Sn	Pb
L37:1934	1	90.3	9.4	<0.1
105:1951	1	88.1	11.3	<0.1
Eogan 7	1	90.4	8.9	<0.1
L34:1934	2	87.8	11.8	<0.1
3890(6.6)	2	85.7	10.0	4.3
188:1913	4	88.1	8.8	2.7
466:1937	4	87.3	9.2	3.4
PR119.298	4		8.0	5.1
PR119.308	4		10.2	7.5
PR119.308	4	78.2	9.9	11.3
PR119.306	4		13.1	3.8
PR119.306	4	84.4	14.5	4.6
PR119.299	4		5.7	0.8
PR119.299	4	83.4	11.7	4.6
PR119.302	4		7.4	9.1
PR119.302	4		17.9	7.7
PR119.267	4		7.3	4.2
PR119.267	4	82.1	11.2	5.6
L24:1936	5	87.0	11.7	0.5
104:1951	5	84.7	14.0	1.2
QUB	5	89.1	10.1	0.5
475:1937a	5	87.4	12.0	0.5
4022(5.4)	6	90.0	7.5	2.2
42:1936	6	91.7	5.7	1.9
42:1936	6	92.1	4.7	2.6

Analyses carried out by the Research Laboratory for Archaeology and the History of Art, Oxford. Chemical analyses (those not listing Cu content) were by I. M. Allen of the Pitt Rivers Museum (Eogan 1965, 182–83; Allen et al. 1970).

has identified several "pools" of metal, with different trace element patterns, which appear to have been used, traded and recycled in quite large geographic units. Long-term participation in the wider trade in metals, alloys and scrap and the arrival of leaded alloys in Ireland is indicated by comparisons with the analyses of the metal composition of some 19 bronze swords, whose results are tabulated above. The Class 1 swords analysed have little or no lead content but proportions of lead were much higher in most examples of the other classes, except for Class 5 swords.

The optimal tin content in bronze intended to be work hardened is around 10% (at high tin levels brittleness is a problem) and this was the median value for the swords analysed. Since lead is insoluble in copper and has a very low melting point, it tends to accumulate in the central midrib of a sword (Northover – personal communication). Thus the addition of lead could improve mould filling without softening the edges. The hardnesses measured (Allen, Britton and Coghlan 1970) indicate that work hardening seldom came near the maximum for the alloy used.

Fragments of bivalve clay sword moulds have been found in several sites. These include site B at Lough Eskragh (Co. Tyrone), Rathgall (Co. Wicklow), Whitepark Bay (Co. Antrim), Dalkey Island (Co. Dublin), Old Connaught (Co. Dublin), and Bohovny (Co. Fermanagh). Eogan (1965) postulates that impressions of either side of a sword or wooden model were made in separate double layered strips of fine and coarse clay. His view is supported by the presence, in the outer layers of several Irish mould fragments, of cavities left by wooden sticks used for support before baking. This process would certainly have facilitated re-use of the mould, cited by Hodges (1954), as a possible explanation of the "slack" outline of typical Irish Late Bronze Age artefacts. Fine clay bivalve sword moulds wrapped completely in a layer of coarse clay, such as those found at Dainton (Devon), could only have been used once (Needham 1980).

Clay moulds must be taken over 400°C to expel all water otherwise they tend to explode on contact with the hot metal. Moulds must be hot during pouring or the flow will falter at any narrow point. Evidently "cores" were not used to form complete rivet holes – they would certainly hamper the flow of metal. The limited capacity of crucibles used and the fairly low temperatures attained by the molten metal, which curtailed pouring, could cause incomplete castings. Such faults may have been rectified by casting on a tang – filling a hilt mould which held an incomplete or broken end of a sword and allowed enough metal to run over the roughened end to form a bond. A number, not properly fused, subsequently became detached.

Three swords from Ballycroghan, Co. Down (Jope 1953) indicate the sequence of finishing, which may well have varied. All have substantial porosity, would not have been functionally viable and were discarded. It is therefore surprising that so much work was carried out. One was as cast but the second, broken at the terminal, had the casting flash removed, the handle beaten and shaped, the ricasso and the blade edge formed, although the blade was not beaten and the rivet holes had not been perforated. The third was fully finished except that the edges were never sharpened.

A number of rivet holes (mostly on Class 1 swords) were incomplete because they overlapped the edge. Rivet marks were often left unper-

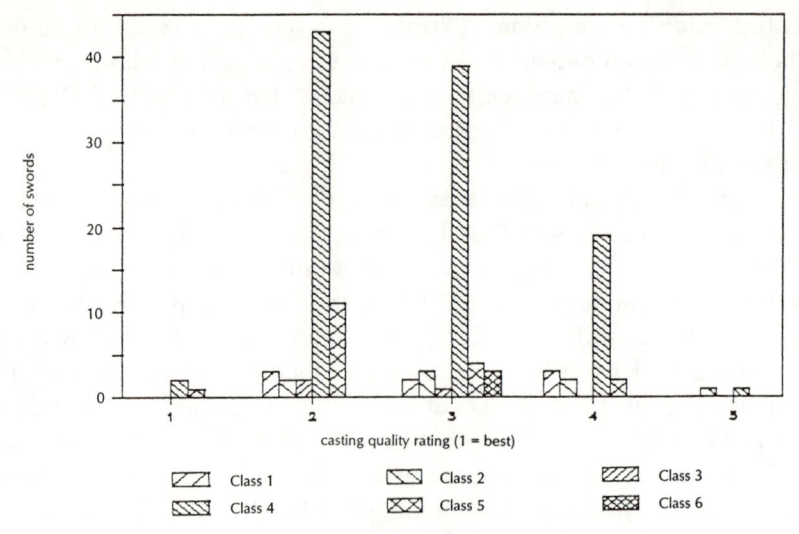

Figure 4. Casting quality rating by Class.

forated and the fact that holes were difficult to bore may have contributed to this unwillingness to weaken the hilt by producing more than were essential. The tang was either roughened or, later, ridged to provide friction with the hilt plate material. Some swords have a definite "step" in the metal where the hilt plates would have ended, showing that the surface of the blade was worked after their attachment.

Two aspects of sword manufacture which I examined were casting quality and edge sharpness. The results were limited by the lack of metallographic, compositional and hardness tests, all of which require samples. The swords were examined using a low power microscope and ranked from 1 (high quality/very sharp) to 5 (excess porosity/blunt) according to the quality of their casting (mainly assessed by the amount of porosity visible) and of their original sharpness. Figures 4 and 5 summarise the distributions of casting quality and sharpness ratings, divided by typological class, for those swords which could be assessed.

Very few swords were of highest or lowest casting quality. About 80% had at most very moderate porosity – the amount concerned would not embarrass a modern metal worker. A higher than average proportion of Class 5 swords were good quality castings, although the Chi-squared test showed significance only at the 6% level. I am inclined to believe that the difference is real, since it is supported by the general impression (and the sharpness ranking results) that Class 5 swords were relatively well made. Only three swords showed little or

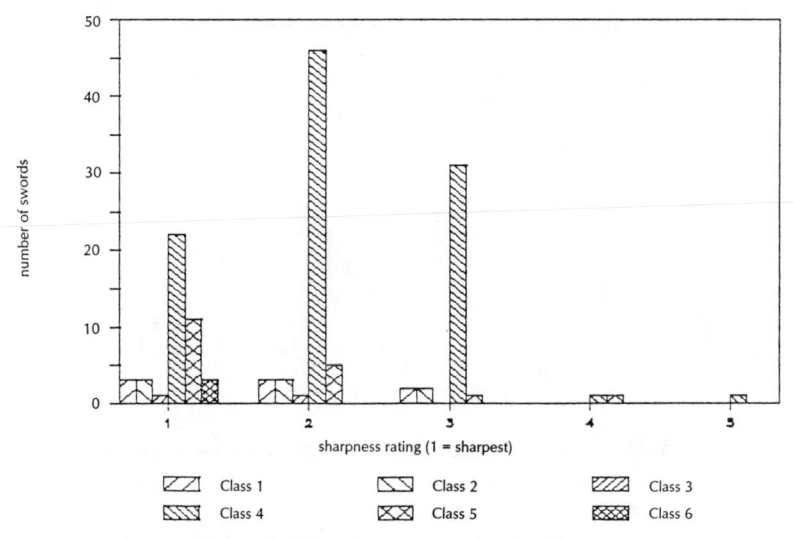

Figure 5. Edge sharpness rating by Class.

no sign of sharpening and a high proportion (significant at the 5% level) of Class 5 swords were rated in the sharpest category compared with both the overall distribution and the dominant Class 4 swords.

USE OF THE SWORDS

There are two main actions involved in sword attack – the thrust and the cut. Swords intended for thrusting will tend to have rather narrow parallel-sided blades with a long thin point and sharp edges which thicken relatively quickly towards a fairly thick centre. Ewart Oakeshott (1960) states that the centre of gravity would be fairly well forward of the hilt, unlike the fencing foils with which I am familiar, to provide forward momentum when thrusting. Cutting swords feature a thin cross section with thin, very gradually thickening sharp edges. Swords intended solely for cutting and slashing do not require a sharp point. A distinct widening of the blade close to the centre of gravity provides maximum force at the point of impact, according to Ewart Oakeshott (1960). However an impact point somewhat below the centre of gravity would travel with greater velocity when the sword was swung which could increase the damage caused while limiting the effort. The mean distances from the centre of gravity to the widest part of the blade, shown below, favour this interpretation since it is least for the swords (Classes 1 and 5) with most "thrust" characteristics.

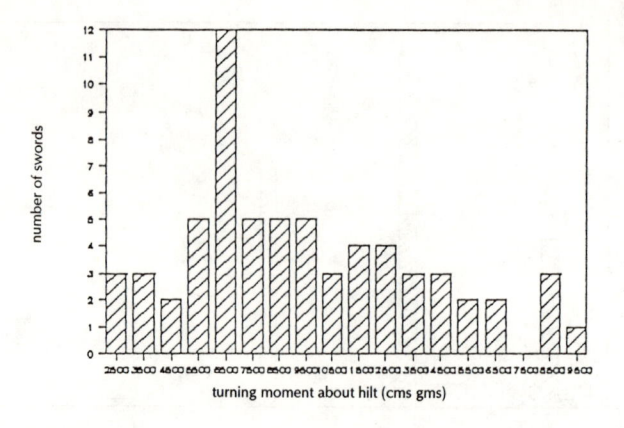

Subjective description of balance by turning moment intervals.

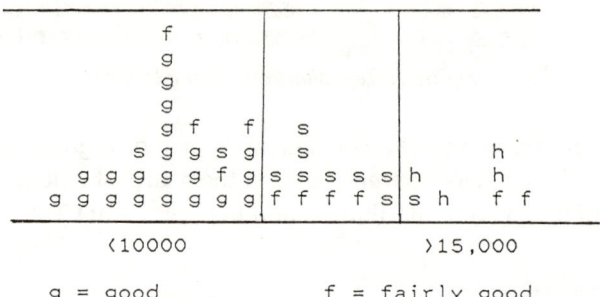

```
                    f
                    g
                    g
                    g
                    g   f     f       s
              s   g g s g     s                      h
          g g g g g f g   s s s s s   h              h
          g g g g g g g g f f f f s   s  h       f   f
          ─────────────────────────────────────────────
                <10000                        >15,000

          g = good                f = fairly good
          s = slightly heavy      h = heavy
```

Numbers of swords per class in each balance category.

Class	Good	Medium	Heavy	Total
1	6			6
2			1	1
3	1	1		2
4	32	14	4	50
5	5	2	3	10
6	1			1
Total	45	17	8	70

Good   = <10,000 cm gm
Medium = 10,000-15,000 cm gm
Heavy = >15,000 cm gm

Figure 6. The balance of swords.

I assessed the balance of effectively complete swords by finding the centre of gravity and calculating the turning moment (weight x distance from centre of gravity) about the hilt, giving an objective, if approximate (no adjustments were made to allow, say, for the absence of hilt plates) measure.

The graph in Figure 6 shows the distribution of the turning moments thus calculated. Below it is the distribution of my subjective assessments of the swords' balance. Clearly the mode of the turning moment fell into the category I described as good (the distributions were surprisingly consistent). The table shows how the categories of balance divide by typological class. The only class with a substantial proportion of blade heavy swords (30%) was Class 5. Such swords, while probably quite effective, would be tiring to use. None of the swords seems intended for thrusting only, unlike the long slim rapiers of the Middle Bronze Age which they seem to have supplanted. Class 1 swords retain a number of "thrust" characteristics and tearing of the sides of the rivet holes would be caused by using the weapons in cutting mode to which the form of hilt attachment was unsuited (Ewart Oakeshott 1960). The lozenge-shaped cross-section in the Class 2 swords, also a "thrust" characteristic, is probably a sign of conservatism in manufacture. The redesigned hilts of subsequent classes, their pointed oval cross-section, more definitely leaf-shaped blades and the wide range of less acutely pointed tips, show that these were better suited to "cutting". Class 4 swords, with their usually less exaggerated leaf-shaped blade, seem excellent combination weapons. Class 5, with their often narrow, oval cross-sectioned blades and thin tangs seem, in some respects, more suited to thrusting than cutting.

The grasp used to wield these Bronze Age swords is described by Ewart Oakeshott (1960) – "the grip is held by three fingers, the forefinger goes forward and below the shoulder while the thumb grips it fast on the other side." This explains the prevalence of the ricasso, which prevented damage to the forefinger. Only 12 of the 65 swords assessed had no sign of a ricasso indent and 5 of these were adequately blunt in the relevant area. The presence in my sample of a number of swords which had "ricasso" blunting added after casting and especially the six "handed" swords, blunted on one edge only, clearly shows that this blunting served a necessary purpose.

This grasp also explains why the distance between the terminal and butt on most swords, at around 75mm for Classes 2, 3, 4 and 6, is smaller than the minimum of approximately 85mm required for a medium-sized male hand to grasp using all four fingers. Class 5 tangs were, however, around 85 mm long. Almost none of the genuine swords I examined had an awkward grip when wielded in the above manner, which felt very "natural".

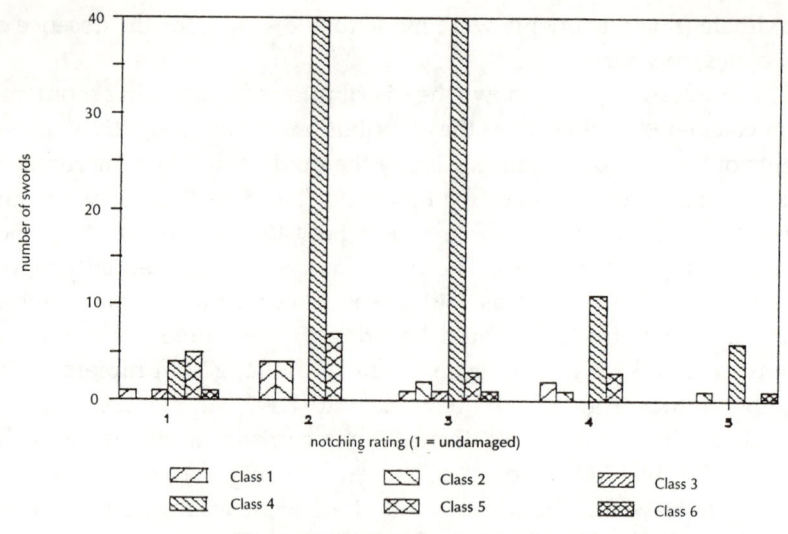

Figure 7. Notching rating by class.

Many swords exhibited damage apparently due to use. Torn rivet holes, so typical of the Class 1 swords, continued to appear in the butt wings of other classes. Sideways pressure caused by "cutting" action clearly remained a problem, although tang rivets would have prevented total failures. The majority of broken hilts were fractured at a tang rivet hole or at the top pair of butt wing rivet holes. Tangs were a weak point, being narrow, perforated by rivet holes and often rather thin. Blade tips seem to have been particularly vulnerable and the demise of the elongated point may have been intended to prevent such damage. Blades also tended to break at their narrow part above the swelling of the "leaf", despite thickening of the midrib there.

The swords were ranked from 1 (undamaged) to 5 (very severely damaged) on the basis of my assessment of the amount and severity of the notches along the edges (excluding the effects of corrosion and other damage, including modern notches). Figure 7 summarises the distribution of notching rating, divided by typological class. Over 90% of the swords examined had been damaged to some extent by edge notching, which is assumed to be the result of a direct impact on the edge most likely to have occurred as a result of combat use. A Chi-squared test, showed a difference, significant at the 5% level, between the notching of Class 5 and Class 4 swords. Although the sample of Class 5 swords is small, it seems reasonable to infer that they generally suffered less damage from edge impact than Class 4 swords. What the tabulated results fail to show is that a few swords had their edges

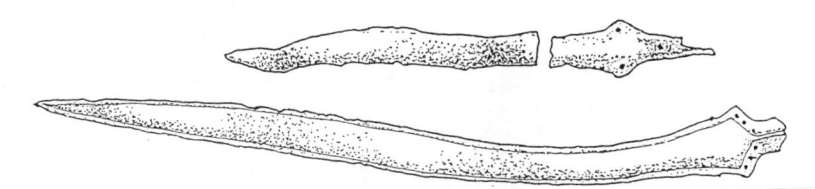

Figure 8. Top: sword no. 128, National Museum of Ireland 1965: 67; bottom: sword no. 113, National Museum of Ireland W80.

"hacked" along the length of the blade in a manner suggesting deliberate destruction. A number showed signs of having been subjected to intense heat as well as trauma damage. Examples include those shown in Figure 8 (nos 128 and 113). Any attribution of such severe distortion to casting errors seems unreasonable – the baked clay mould could not "bend" during casting. Fractures in the metal are consistent with hot bending, as is the twisting of the broken tang. Such swords may have been deliberately destroyed but the size of the pieces means that they were most unlikely to have suffered the heat damage in a crucible used for melting down scrap.

Some clues to uses of the swords other than as practical weapons may lie in their appearance. The presence of applied decoration is so rare as to arouse suspicion as to authenticity. This contrasts sharply with the magnificent gold jewellery, "ritual" objects, and even a number of "weapons", such as spearheads (I examined some examples at the Pitt Rivers Museum) produced in such profusion during the Late Bronze Age in Ireland. The aesthetic qualities of the swords lie therefore in their form and finish. My own general impression is that the surface finish of most Class 5 swords is "better" than that of most Class 4 swords, though this could be an unintentional result of different manufacturing techniques. Class 5 swords may also have been visually "special" due to their "foreign" design attributes.

Another well-attested attribute of swords used symbolically (especially of power) is relatively large size. Indeed this may even be taken, as in some Mycenaean swords, beyond the point where the sword could usefully be wielded, although matters do not seem to have been taken this far in Ireland. As may be seen in Figures 9 and 10 the weights and lengths of the swords produced very wide (possibly bimodal) distributions. All complete Class 5 swords and no Class 4 swords were over 600 mm long. Neither the heaviest sword I examined (a very wide-bladed, fairly long Class 6 example) nor the longest (a fairly parallel-sided, heavy Class 2 weapon, some 762 mm long) was particularly unwieldy. Both were found in rivers.

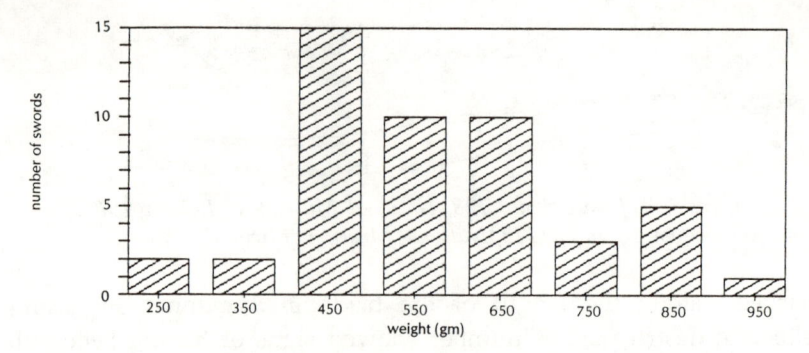

Figure 9. Weights of complete swords.

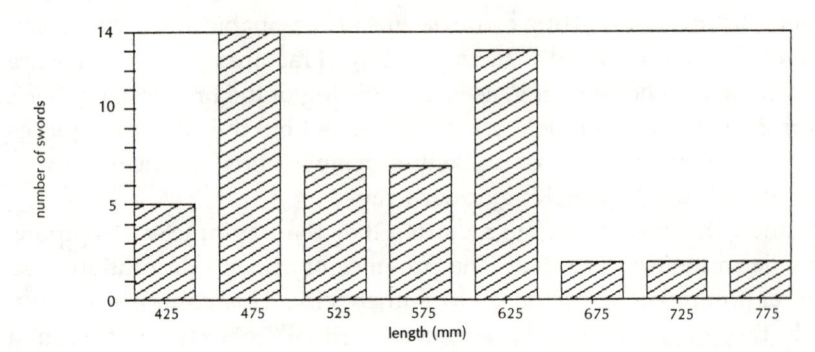

Figure 10. Lengths of complete swords.

DEPOSITION OF THE SWORDS

The mode and context of deposition of objects can provide insight into the economic, social and ideological structures of society. This is especially true of a period such as the Late Bronze Age in Ireland, which has few remains of the settlements and/or burials which provide so much information about other periods. Sadly, poor provenancing meant that I was reduced to considering only the broad categories of "wet" and "other" contexts. The "other" category includes swords with limited or no provenance and is thus almost certain to include examples found in "wet" contexts.

The reasons for examining the differences between swords deposited in wet and dry contexts is the long prevalence in Europe of an association between wet places and religious practices, including the deposition of objects. Such depositions are widely accepted as "gifts to the gods" given the peculiarity and/or richness of many of the objects de-

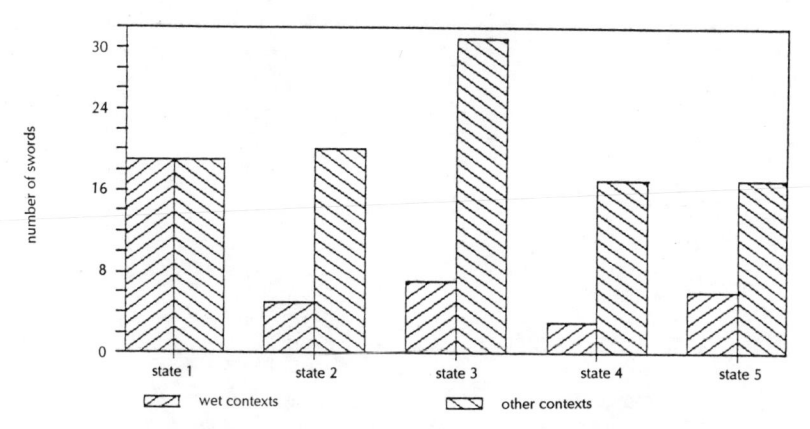

Figure 11. State of completeness and context type.

posited, their accumulation over very long periods and the implication that they were not deposited with any intention of retrieval. The actual number of known Irish Bronze Age swords found in hoards is fairly low (less than 40) (Eogan 1965). This excludes the rumoured 200 from the "Golden Bog of Cullen", of which only four were ever published – there is considerable doubt as to Cullen's status as a hoard. The majority of the swords from hoards were deposited in bogs.

It has already been noted that a number of the swords examined were subjected to intense heat and/or quite deliberately destroyed. None is shown as having been found in a river, although one came from Lough Gur (no. 133) and one from Littleton Bog (no. 128). In some cases the deliberate damage would be in keeping with a motive such as the ritual destruction of the blades, perhaps on death or after capture. In others it could be consistent with the sword being with or near a body being cremated. The presence, at one of the very few known Late Bronze Age burial sites (within Rathgall hillfort, Co. Wicklow), of a portion of the blade of a leaf-shaped sword supports the theory that weapons could have been cremated along with bodies.

Figure 11 shows the relationship between the context and the state of completeness of the sword. Complete swords and those with very minor damage were rated 1. Those with more substantial damage to the terminal, hilt and/or blade tip were rated 2. If most or all of the hilt or blade was missing, the sword was rated 3, while sword fragments were rated 4. A separate category, 5, was used for swords with more than one piece present. Chi-squared tests also showed a significant relationship between context and state of completeness with greater than expected numbers of swords from the "wet" contexts being

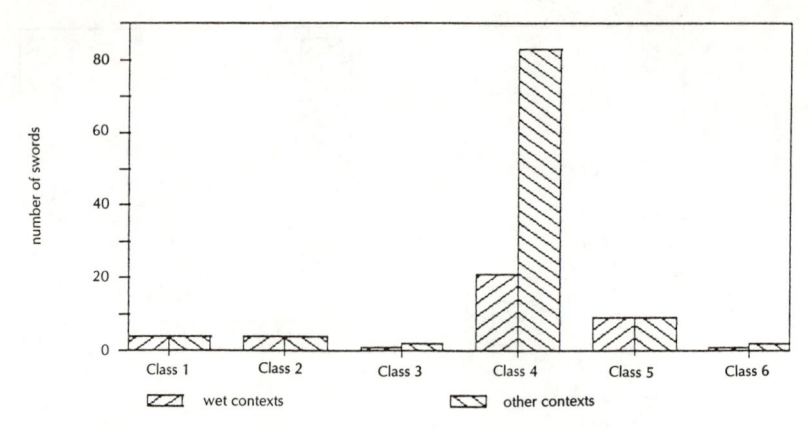

Figure 12. Class and context type.

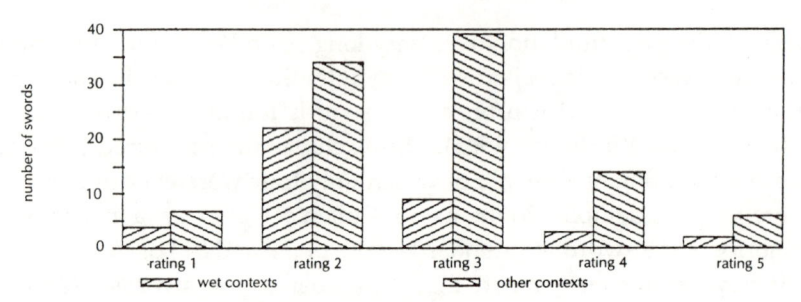

Figure 13. Edge notching and context type.

complete or almost complete. This was especially marked in the case of swords found in rivers. Figure 12 shows the relationship between the context and the state of completeness of the sword.

Figure 13 shows the relationship between amount of edge notching and the context. There was a statistically significant relationship between the two with a higher than expected proportion of swords from "wet" contexts (almost two thirds) being undamaged or almost undamaged. Over 70% of the swords found in rivers had little notching.

Figure 14 shows the casting quality and edge sharpness of the swords according to deposition context. The tendency to a deficiency of the "medium" grades (3) of casting quality and edge sharpening in those swords found in "wet" contexts was tested but the difference was significant only at the 10% level.

Figure 15 shows the rating of various ergonomic features of the swords according to type of context. Although no differences can be accepted as significant, it may be observed that the proportion of swords with a ricasso formed after casting (a clear sign of practical

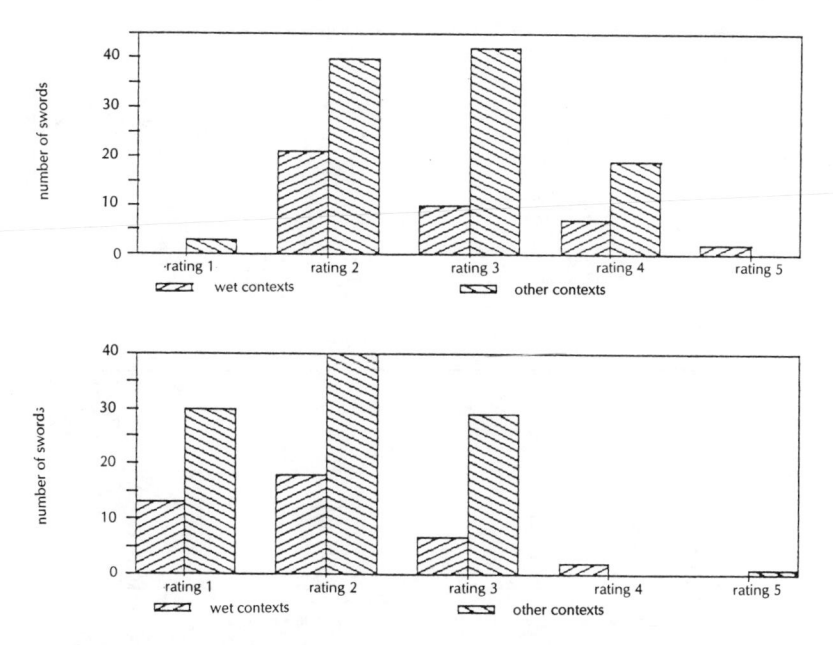

Figure 14. Casting quality and context type (above) and edge sharpness and context type (below).

use) found in "wet" contexts is rather low and that the proportion with no ricasso at all, which would have made practical use difficult, is rather high.

The differences observed between the populations of swords discovered in "wet" contexts and those from "other" contexts point to there being at least a tendency for the swords to have a different history prior to deposition. The quality of manufacture of the swords seems to have had some effect, in that the swords of medium quality may show a greater tendency not to be found in "wet" contexts. The handling characteristics may also have had some slight effect but only in that those which would have been most difficult to use show a tendency to form a higher proportion of swords found in "wet" contexts.

If, as the above may indicate, actual use was important, one would expect the amount of breakage and edge damage to show some correlation with context, and this is indeed the case. There was a significantly high proportion of "wet" context swords which were complete, or nearly so, and/or had little or no edge notching. The relatively low proportions of Class 4 and 6 swords coming from "wet" contexts was also statistically significant. While this may be chronological it could also be, at least partly, due to their seemingly utilitarian design.

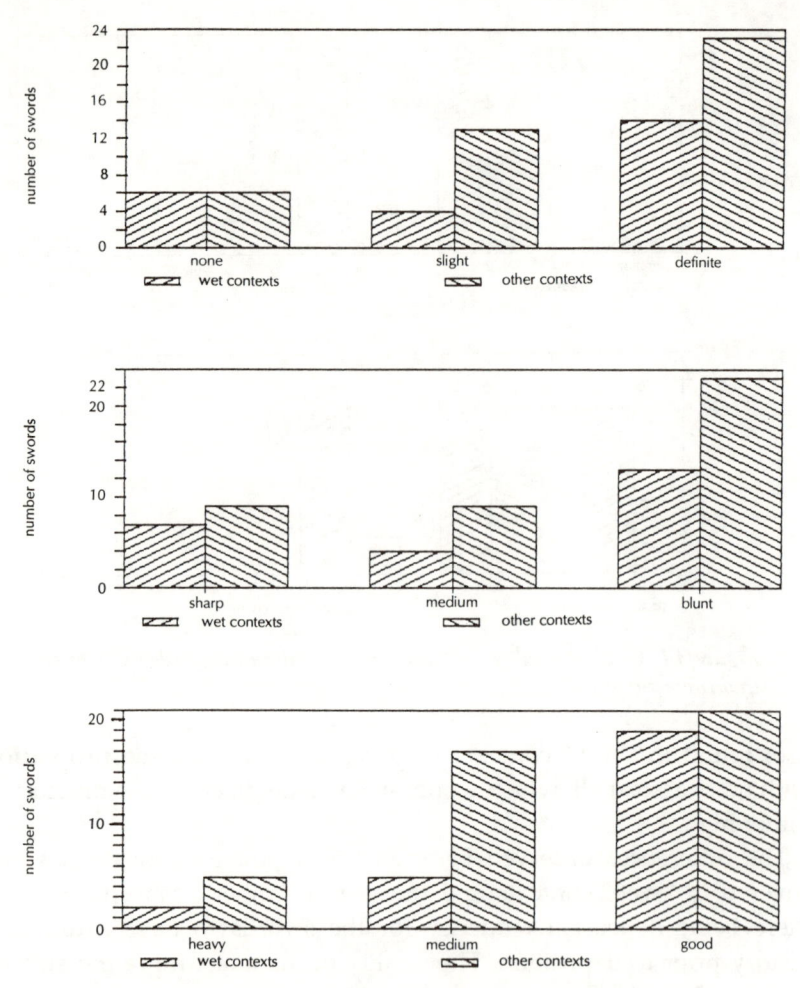

Figure 15. Ricasso presence and context type (top); ricasso blunting and context type (middle); sword balance and context type (bottom).

Overall it would seem that swords deposited in "wet" places were less likely to have been used than those found elsewhere and were more likely to appear "different" (e.g. Class 5 swords). They seem to have tended to be of above average quality but also to have had little attention paid to possible faults in design, manufacture or finishing liable to affect usefulness in combat but not appearance.

The effect was more noticeable if "river" deposition only was used as the dividing line. This, combined with the virtually complete lack of hoards deposited in rivers (one only, found in 1895, "in the bed of a small river"), the tendency of hoards to be found in bogs and the relatively few swords deposited in hoards, leads me to infer that certain swords were specially deposited in rivers and that the nature of this deposition differed from that on dry land and, probably, from depositions in other "wet" places.

Conclusions

It is clear that almost all the swords were of a suitable design and adequately manufactured to be useful as weapons and, from the damage exhibited, that a large proportion were physically used, most probably in combat.

Provided the chronological sequence of the sword classes proposed by Eogan is accepted, it can be inferred that the number of swords deposited increased with time and that sword design changed from that better suited for thrusting to incorporate adaptations for cutting.

The exception to this "progression" seems to be the "intrusive", la Tène influenced but locally produced, Class 5 sword, which shows a reversion to some characteristics more in keeping with thrusting action. Plausible explanations include use in a different type of combat and/or an aim at visual impact, including, possibly, deliberate exaggeration of foreign attributes.

I postulate that the type of combat itself changed over time. "Thrusting" swords are efficient for killing in single combat but are of much less use in the hands of relatively unskilled combatants against wooden or hardened leather shields such as that found in a bog at Cloonlara, Co. Mayo. Thin bronze shields, such as that from a bog near Lough Gur, Co. Sligo, were probably intended for display and/or ritual purposes only. Most unskilled foot soldiers and almost all cavalry tend to use a sword primarily as a cutting and slashing weapon (Turney High 1949). Indeed, the use of a slashing sword and a fairly small round shield certainly continued in the Highlands of Scotland well into the time of firearms. The paucity of artefactual evidence for the use of horses for riding and chariotry in the Irish Late Bronze Age makes me favour expansion of sword combat among the populace rather than the arrival of cavalry based warfare to explain the increase in numbers combined with the adoption of the "cut and thrust" swords. The combination of a spear, for initial encounter, a sword for closer contact, a dagger, as a weapon of last resort, and, possibly, a round shield for defence, may well have been the standard equipment of the time.

Such an explanation also implies a change in the organisation of combat. It seems probable that individual combat with swords gave way to groups using swords. The inference that there was an increase in inter-group hostility during the Late Bronze Age may also be supported by the initial construction, during the Bronze Age, of ditches and other, possibly defensive, earthworks at some "Iron Age" raths and hillforts (e.g. Haughey's Fort, Co. Armagh, and Rathgall, Co. Wicklow). It has been suggested, based largely on flooding of lakeside sites and rapid peat bog development, that a climatic deterioration led to lower agricultural production in Ireland during the Late Bronze Age and that this may have led to conflict. It is far from clear that, in what seems to have been a rather pastorally based, but mixed, economy, any such climatic change would have had a dramatic effect. On the contrary, the artefactual evidence supports the view that there was considerable wealth in Ireland at the time. The stunning, but sadly depleted, collections of gold objects mark Ireland as an area exploiting its mineral and agricultural resources to the full. If an explanation need be sought for any perceived increase in organised conflict, it is likely to lie within the social organisation and its adaptation to this wealth.

Analysis of deposition context brings out a different aspect of Irish Late Bronze Age society and the role of the sword within it. While the proportion of swords found in rivers may have been exaggerated, especially in the Bann and Shannon, only one of the many bronze hoards purports to have come from a river. I am inclined therefore to see the high proportion of swords deposited in rivers (around 20%) both as indicative of a real phenomenon and, as argued above, as representing a special relationship between swords and river deposition.

The fact that the swords so deposited do tend to have a history of less damage, less actual combat use and, probably, "different" appearance, leads me to infer that they functioned in a symbolic manner when so deposited, and probably tended so to do before deposition. It certainly negates the proposition that such swords were "lost" in battle at fording points, or were deposited by the victors after battles. More mundane explanations, such as erosion from riverside settlement deposits or loss in transit by riverboat (supported by the presence of some other, less spectacular, items in rivers), does raise questions as to why only riverside settlements and/or river cargoes should contain so many swords (and why their swords differed from those elsewhere).

There is no evidence in favour of river deposition of swords in place of grave good deposition, such as the human bones which caused Bradley (1990) to propose this for some Thames sword deposits. In the absence of such evidence, I am inclined to search for swords performing such a function among the burnt and/or deliberately destroyed blades. I am thus forced to the view that the swords deposited in rivers were most probably "gifts to the gods" and that the symbolism was quite likely to be concerned with the conduct of "warfare". I would further speculate that swords were the only weapons used in such a manner at that time.

The evidence of the swords shows that society during the Late Bronze Age in Ireland exhibited ingenuity, technical competence, considerable capacity to accumulate wealth, substantial overseas contact, increasingly organised "military" activity and a special position for such activity in the ritual of the time.

ACKNOWLEDGEMENTS

I would like to express my gratitude to Richard Warner and Sinead McCartan of the Ulster Museum, Raghnall O'Floinn and Mary Cahill of the National Museum of Ireland, Ray Inskeep, Julia Cousins and John Simmons of the Pitt Rivers Museum, Paul Craddock of the British Museum, Peter Northover of Oxford University and Barbara Ottaway of Sheffield University for their invaluable assistance to me in undertaking this study.

REFERENCES

Allen, I. M., Britton, D. and Coghlan, H. H. 1970. *Metallurgical Reports on British and Irish Bronze Age Implements and Weapons in the Pitt Rivers Museum.* Oxford, Pitt Rivers Museum (Pitt Rivers Museum Occasional Papers on Technology 10).

Bradley, R. 1990. *The Passage of Arms.* Cambridge, Cambridge University Press.

Eogan, G. 1965. *Catalogue of Irish Bronze Swords.* Dublin, Stationery Office.

Ewart Oakeshott, R. 1960. *The Archaeology of Weapons.* London, Lutterworth.

Hodges, H. W. M. 1954. Studies in the Late Bronze Age in Ireland. 1. Stone and clay moulds and wooden models for bronze implements. *Ulster Journal of Archaeology* 17, 62–80.

Jope, E. M. 1953. Three Late Bronze Age swords from Ballycroghan, near Bangor, Co. Down. *Ulster Journal of Archaeology* 16, 37–40.

Needham, S. P. 1980. An assemblage of Late Bronze Age metalworking debris from Dainton, Devon. *Proceedings of the Prehistoric Society* 46, 177–215.

Northover, J. P. 1982. The exploration of the long distance movement of bronze in Bronze and Early Iron Age Europe. *Bulletin of the London Institute of Archaeology* 19, 45–72.

Turney-High, H. 1949. *Primitive War.* Columbia, University of South Carolina.

War in the Chalcolithic? The Meaning of Western Mediterranean Chalcolithic Hillforts

Luiz Oosterbeek

Archaeologists, *perhaps because* of their preference for major processes, tend to miss the action of change by stressing those cultural traits that maintain inequality over time, after the change has been established.

– Hastorf 1993: 16

WHAT? WHO? WHY? LOOKING FOR THE QUESTIONS

The study of Mediterranean Chalcolithic hillforts has attracted the attention of archaeologists since the pioneering work of the Siret brothers at Los Millares, in the last century (Siret 1890; 1892). Fortifications, collective burials and metallurgy lie at the heart of the models of interpretation of cultural change in the area, in the fourth to the second millennia BC (Renfrew 1967). Mediterranean hillforts are characterised by stone walls reinforced with added features such as bastions, towers and barbicans.

Directly related to these features is the discussion over war and violence. Most authors agree that warfare is associated with an increased hierarchy that dominated the social process in the Chalcolithic. There are a number of pieces of evidence in favour of this assumption. The architecture of the stone hillforts themselves is accompanied by rock-art depictions of archery combat (as in the Abrigo IX de La Casulla, Castellón-Camps 1992), the increasing number of weapons (e.g. arrows, daggers, maces), the presence of skeletons pierced by arrows, the evidence for wealth accumulation (revealed through storage vessels and pits, as well as through artefactual differentiation among burials and settlements), and other "defensive" structures (ditches, palisades). And yet, the main issue in question is not the description of these features, but their understanding. To answer the question "who built these structures and what does this evidence mean?", archaeologists have searched for parallels in the eastern Mediterranean (Renfrew 1967; Best and de Vries 1982; Daniel and Evans 1975), revealed the local traditions and ideological renewal (Jorge 1983; 1990; Blagg and Jones et al. 1984), stressed the morphological similarities throughout the western Mediterranean (Camps 1992; Almagro Gorbea 1973b), suggested population growth and wealth accumulation and control as primary factors (Chapman 1990; Harrison 1985), and indicated the importance of trade in those societies (Lillios 1991; Harrison and Gilman 1977; Gilman and Thornes 1985), as well as craft specialisation (namely metallurgical – Chapman 1990; Sherratt 1981).

An alternative question, which may help to broaden the views over these issues, is not "what happened", but "why did what happened happen?" Here, diffusionist models tend to seem stronger, since they provide an explanation (defence of the colonies) rather than an often confused statement of war or warfare whose parameters are not clearly defined. Diffusionists and evolutionists share, though, the same common reduction of the structures in question to a defensive purpose.

In opposition to these approaches, I believe that an interpretation of Mediterranean fortifications, and the understanding of violence in the Chalcolithic, must be built upon the concept of endogenous social contradiction. I will briefly examine some aspects of the typology of the sites, their context and alternative meanings and I expect to demonstrate that only a dialectical model can account for the variability (and yet unity) of the discussed phenomena.

Us and the Other

By Chalcolithic Mediterranean hillforts, the archaeological literature understands a set of stone-built structures found throughout the western Mediterranean, bearing formal similarities with their counterparts in the eastern Mediterranean (Chalandriani, Troy – Blance 1961; Renfrew 1979a). Without intending to be exhaustive, I will briefly examine a number of areas and the structures within them, stressing their variability concerning shape, size, construction and location. It is also useful to understand their relationships with other, non-fortified sites.

These structures have been recognised in Iberia, southern France, the Balearic islands, Sardinia and Sicily. Most of these are either coastal or easy access to the sea. Yet others are to be found further inland. Their chronology varies over a great range, some being occupied from pre-Chalcolithic periods (although with no fortification), while others were first used at various times throughout the Bronze Age. Their shapes and sizes also vary a lot.

In Sicily (e.g. Petraro di Melilli, a sub-rectangular walled 800 square metres enclosure, with bastions) and Sardinia (e.g. S'Urecci, Monte Claro) the sites are located in high well-defended hills, close to the sea. The chronology of these sites extends into the Bronze Age.

Similar locations with a Chalcolithic chronology are present in the Balearic islands (Ets Antigors and So'n Ferrandell-So'n Oleza in Maillorca, or Torralba d'En Salord in Menorca). These sites may attain very large sizes (Ets Antigors, with over 10.000 square metres), and the structures may include towers (Ets Antigors) or bastions (So'n Ferrandell). J. Lewthwaite (1985) points out that their setting, in calcareous areas, contrasts with the later Bronze Age Navetas, when they tended to occupy fertile landscapes.

In southern France, several of these features have been noted (Camps 1992), consistently located on hilltops and not far from the sea. They may be very small (as Campmau, with 600 square metres), or fairly large (e.g. Lébous, with 8000 square metres – Arnal 1973). Their shapes vary from sub-rectangular (La Tailladette) to sub-oval (Boussargues – Colomer and Coularou et al. 1980), and may include only bastions (Lébous, Camp de Laure) or also towers (as at Campmau).

It is Iberia, though, that has attracted the greatest attention for archaeologists, largely due to the site of Los Millares, and all the importance it acquired (together with Vila Nova de São Pedro or Zambujal) in the "colonialist" theories. Different regions may be recognised in Iberia. First, the region of Almeria, dominated by Los Millares, includes several hillforts (Campos, Trez Cabezos, Loma de la Galera) with impressive stone structures. Los Millares itself is actually a complex of settlement and necropolis, protected by a line of eleven fortified enclosures, the whole complex occupying over 50,000 square metres (Almagro Gorbea 1973a; Clara Barrionuevo et al. 1909; Guai-Jener 1975; Walker 1986). To the west, in the Granada region, a number of off-shore settlements seem to have evolved under the impulse of the Millares influence (Aguayo 1977; Molina and Aguayo et al. n.d.), showing less impressive structures, but often occupying wider areas and with later survival into the Bronze Age, such as Cerro de la Virgen, Cerro de las Canteras, Cerro de los Castellones or El Malagón (Mendozel and Molina et al. 1975; Arribas and Molina 1977b).

Moving further west, to Portugal, coastal fortified sites are known from the Algarve, such as Santa Justa (Gonçalves 1980; 1981a; 1981b; 1982a; 1982b), the coast south of the Tagus, with Sesimbra (Marques 1967), Chibanes, Rotura (Silva 1970) and Monte da Tumba (Silva and Soares 1987), or north of the Tagus, with sites such as Vila Nova de S. Pedro (Savory 1959), Zambujal (Sangmeister and Schubart 1981), Leceia (Cardoso 1979; 1981; 1984), Outeiro da Assenta, Outeiro de S. Mamede (Gonçalves 1991), Lexim (Arnaud 1977), Baútas (Arnaud and Gamito 1972), Columbeira (Schubart and Ferreira 1969) or Olelas (Serrão and Vicente 1958). Most of these sites are about 1500 square metres or less in size (e.g. Penedo, Pedra do Ouro), but again their shapes (from rectangular at Pedra do Ouro, to circular at Vila Nova de S. Pedro) and elements (bastions with or without towers) vary considerably (Barbosa 1956; Spindler 1969). These are hilltop sites, but are located in a variety of settings and include differing artefactual assemblages. Many of them have an early pre-fortified occupation, suggesting that they would have been selected as naturally defended places, and only later fortified (Cardoso and Soares et al. 1984), passing through a succession of building phases, that may either be understood as an architectural evolution (from large enclosed spaces to massive structures) or as strategic variations (Gonçalves and Cardoso et al. 1984).

In the Iberian inland, these structures are also present, often much less impressive, with a late Chalcolithic to Bronze Age chronology, as well as later survival. They are usually close to main Iberian rivers that are thought to have been important prehistoric routes, such as the Tagus (Cerro del Castrejón, Los Castillejos, Sierra de la Pepa, Charneca do Fratel – Arribas and Molina 1977a; Jorge 1990), the Guadiana (Escoural, Castelos de S. Brás – Parreira 1983), the Douro (Castelo Velho de Freixo de Numão – Jorge 1990) or the Zêzere (Maxial – Oosterbeek 1992b).

This evidence must be understood in a wider context, where non-fortified sites played an important part (Arnaud 1971; 1982; Ferreira and Castro 1967). Some authors suggested the existence of an important trade or exchange links between the Portuguese coastal areas, rich in flint, and the inland regions with no flint but rich in hard rocks for producing polished implements. This would explain the importance of "coastal artefacts" from the Portuguese Estremadura in inland sites such as the open settlement of Carriceiras in the Beira Alta (Martinez 1992). A similar acceptance of intensive long-distance contacts has been supported by V. Gonçalves (Gonçalves, Cardoso et al. 1984), when considering that the formal typological similarities between Iberian, Sardinian or Aegean fortifications was the result of the circulation of ideas and technologies, and not the product of eastern colonisation. Also, the consistency of either coastal or riverine location of these sites suggests the importance of sea links in the period, contrasting with what will be observed in later periods (van Schoor 1991). By contrast, S. Jorge (1990) rejects the hypothesis of significant exchange, and suggests that the period was, above all, one of ideological renewal, although not clarifying what he means by this. This importance of the sea to these sites contrasts with other economic data. Zambujal, being one of the best studied sites, is a good example. Although rich in flint and copper implements, as well as revealing a dominance of agricultural activities for subsistence (Sangmeister and Schubart 1981), it stands seven to twenty kilometres from the nearest flint source, over thirty minutes walk from quartzite, basalt or sandstone sources, and it has poor soils. Yet, by the same time, other areas were also occupied, such as Matacães or Fórnea, apparently specialised in cereal production, copper metallurgy or even defensive activities (Fórnea ?), enabling one to understand Zambujal as a central site of a larger network. A similar explanation has been put forward by V. Gonçalves concerning Vila Nova de S. Pedro (thirty minutes from the Atlantic ocean). This is a reasonable assumption if one considers the input of human labour needed to build these enclosures, which has no correspondence to the area they occupy (even considering the external zones enclosed by minor walls). An important issue is to assess the significance of the signs of violence and warfare in this period. M. V. Gomes (in Gonçalves and Cardoso et al. 1984), in a reasoning that approaches S. Jorge's opinion, considers that there are signs of a symbolic break in the Chalcolithic, expressed for instance in the demolition of Neolithic menhirs in the Alentejo or in the Chalcolithic settlement of Escoural, which was built on a previous sanctuary. One may argue, though, that while these features are not indisputable, and there are clear signs of continuity both in the bulk of the artefactual assemblages (including the burial architecture) and the settlement patterns in many regions. There are greater differences between Los Millares, Ets Antigors or Zambujal, then there are similarities, except from the point of view of the building techniques, a recurrent use of bastions and, above all, the common material expression of an enormous input of human labour (which itself has important social implications). The hillforts may be found associated with megalithic burials or false corbelled chambers; they may be found associated with neighbouring hillforts or undefended open settlements; they may include signs of metallurgic activity or not; they do not stand apart in term of the artefactual assemblages of the region where they have been built.

Thus, one finds that, as in many other transcontinental features (e.g. the megaliths, or the Beakers), it is not easy to attribute the fortified enclosures to a single complex (Chalcolithic? Bronze Age?), one single symbolic meaning (continuity? break?), a single function (central place? peripheral site?) or a clear origin (eastern? local?). It is also likely, one must conclude, that they had no single purpose. This is not to say that the mentioned similarities are of no importance. The fortified enclosures are built with a similar technological knowledge and they share a dichotomy between the inside (us, be it our ethnicity, our wealth, our status or something else) and the open space (the other).

Meaning vs. Meanings

The social evolutionists of the nineteenth century sought to portray primitive society in quite obvious and plain steps. Bands, tribes and states were founded as superstructures of the human evolutionary path, created by different people at different rates, but tending to the same increasing complexity of behaviour. In this picture, the growing differentiation of society, from savagery to barbarism and to civilisation was marked by an increasing loss of egalitarianism, the same way children are supposed to lose innocence while growing into adults. Actually, children are not so innocent and prehistoric people were no inhabitants of paradise.

Study of prehistory has suffered from this bias, and still partially does. When discussing the origin of war and violence in human societies one should first of all avoid all previous assumptions of this kind and clearly define what one intends to clarify. War and violence are not directly reflected by material culture, because they deal with political, social and generally ideological links among men. These may have left traces in the archaeological record, but at best only few. One's inquiry into the hillforts starts with questions derived from the above assumptions. Was there social differentiation? of what nature and range? How was it reflected in material culture? Do the hillforts have a meaning, or different meanings, and depending on what?

Following Service and Sahlins, A. P. Phillips (1973, 50) explains that while in bands "all the functions of the culture (economy, religion, political organisation) are practised within the family group and the status is only related to age and sex." Tribes live in a state of permanent warfare, due to the competition for land and based on the ideas of property and territoriality. In the same sense, Colin Renfrew (1973, 342) sustains Service's and Sahlins' concept of chiefdoms, including in it the transition "between the relatively egalitarian tribal society which we may imagine from some early Neolithic cultures of Europe – Starecevo perhaps, or Danubian I – and the civilisations of Crete, Mycenae, Classical Greece or Rome." Renfrew (1973, 342) defines a chiefdom as a "ranked society, hierarchically arranged, sometimes in the form of a conical clan where the eldest descendent in the male line from the clan founder ranks highest, and the cadet branches are ranked in seniority after the main line."

Either we follow the romantic picture of the nineteenth century or we accept, as Phillips does, that status is present in those societies, though related to age and sex. And even if only related to age and sex, the most significant aspect of status is that it had a social function. Even in very small groups it is possible to find at least one particular person (maybe the father, the mother, the oldest, the strongest, the best hunter or prophet) who acts not exactly as a "big-man" (Binford 1988, 215) but as the leader of the group, accomplishing both the task of making the group fit for everyday life and, often acting as a living reference for the consolidation of the group. In societies where human life had reached a level of rather complex and diverse activities, apart from this leader (possibly a syncretic version of chief, prophet and sorcerer), the specialisation of some individuals particularly fit at specific tasks, such as hunting or preparing flint tools, will enlarge the number of those who, even without economic compensation, will tend to gain status in the group. This has nothing to do with Service's often-quoted "redistribution" model (Eslick 1988).

In the Neolithic one sees two traditions running side-by-side until they meet. On the one hand, the social need of a group of rulers to co-ordinate the increasingly more diverse activities and greater number of people; on the other, the pre-existence of individuals with a particular status that tended to transform that group into a caste (later as a class). These are the roots of differentiation, and of the notions of power and privilege. The former is the more immediate cause of differentiation, while the latter is the tradition that enables a slow and unconscious transition to a new social organisation. Chiefdoms should be seen as expressions of this trend, and the archaeological record of these periods can be read as the material expression of permanent conflict within the society, between the existing individual status and the pressure to develop and consolidate a clear caste in power. This conflict, not necessarily immediately violent, is of much greater significance than an eventual state of warfare.

I do not agree that "a system will remain stable until acted upon by forces external to its organisation as a system" (Binford 1988, 221) or that "there must exist some pressures for change in the Darwinian sense" (Binford 1988, 231) as an alternative to an endogenous process. I see the whole process as being mainly genetic in Piaget's (1968) terms and the particular systems as fragile equilibria tending to be upset by any external, but most often by internal, pressures.

The questions addressed at the beginning of this section, can be better answered by looking at a few specific examples. Considering the problem of social differentiation, it has already been argued that even the collective burials from late in the Neolithic are not to be read as necessarily the expression of egalitarianism (Renfrew 1973). In the Late Neolithic and Early Chalcolithic in the Nabão Valley (central Portugal), archaeologist have recognised a marked variability of artefactual assemblages between contemporary burials (Oosterbeek and Cruz 1991). Settlements have been located which are associated with regional groups of burials, but again they vary from small groups of huts to enclosed fortifications (Oosterbeek 1992a; Oosterbeek and Cruz 1992). In the Algarve (southern Portugal) a Chalcolithic assemblage of Tholoi at Alcalar showed a similar pattern of differentiation (Arnaud and Gamito 1978).

Despite this variability, the introduction of Bell Beaker pottery is associated in most of Iberia with major changes in all regional sequences: burials tend to become individual and carefully arranged; artefacts proclaim long-distance links increase (copper and other rare raw materials, but also ostrich egg-shells or amber); the use of cattle for traction seems to start or significantly increase, high arable soils, very hard to work, being planted for the first time; most fortified enclosures begin to decay, especially the coastal ones, in a trend that increased in the Bronze Age (Case 1987; Eogan 1979; Ferreira 1966; Guilaine 1984; Leisner 1946). These processes indicate a social and political shift. The old individual status of Palaeolithic tradition was gradually redefined, first through the increasing number of leaders in larger communities (still not implying particular individual benefits). Differences between collective burials could go along with more or less important ranked clans, according to lineages. The Bell Beaker and the later individual burials may express the consolidation of a ruling caste, with personal, permanent and hereditary benefits and differences of wealth. It is significant that collective burials go together with the first big hillforts (McKay 1988).

The problem of the function and meaning of the hillforts starts with their name. If they were hill"forts" against whom were they built? There are no general signs of war or even warfare, though we may suppose that warfare, based on intergroup rivalry, could exist. The diversity of activities and specialised crafts developed through the Neolithic, together with population growth and economic intensification, imposed the need for central co-ordination. This does not necessarily imply a social hierarchy. Consolidated political power implies a recognition of a ruling caste. The hillforts may be seen as large public works that suited the double purpose of material expressions of the territories' central places (which itself was a shift that complement the previous marking of the space with burial monuments) and of monuments to an emerging leading power. These hillforts would not then be of immediate practical purpose (even if they could be useful during periods of war, or to meet other needs of protection) but of an ideological one, to consolidate the ruling caste, the unity of their territory and the emerging state (Clare and Gowie et al. 1985; Nocete 1989).

The use of major public works, with a more-or-less practical utility, is a practice recognised in critical periods of political consolidation. The megaliths had the same purpose in the previous phase (Jorge 1979; 1989; Kinnes 1975; Oliveira 1986) and pyramids, temples, statues and irrigation works played the same role in the origin of the Asian mode of production of the so-called hydraulic civilisations (Anderson 1976). Throughout history one can find examples of this trend, increasingly complex as it corresponds to more and more hierarchical and developed societies, up to the present day (Fortes and Evans-Pritchard 1940). One significant aspect is that in the Bell Beaker phase and in the Bronze Age in Portugal settlements no longer had this input of human effort in building, although the state of warfare would have tended to grow after the economic basis of society received a major impetus as a result of the use of animals for agricultural work and other implements associated with the "secondary products revolution" (including the growing production and trade of metal tools). Here one sees clear evidence that the ruling caste/class was firmly consolidated as a particular rank with a defined social status, and that society no longer needed to invest in those prestigious buildings at the same scale.

By this, one does not exclude alternative views (Neustupný 1977). Although considering the endogenous social contradiction of regional and local segmentary societies as the prime factor for the building of the fortified enclosures, other elements may be considered. The typological and technological similarities do indicate Mediterranean contacts (Camps 1976; Childe 1969), and there is local evidence of violence probably associated to warfare. But there is no reason to look for a specific prototype area (the Aegean or other), just as there are no signs of permanent warfare, other then present-day preconceptions about a meaning attributable to these structures. In this sense, the actual understanding of these enclosures must be found at two levels: a general one, which is social; the other cultural, contingent, depending on the regional understanding of local traditions and economic systems. We shall deal with the former in the concluding section. [4]

THE END AND THE BEGINNING

As Guidoni (1978, 23) emphasises, "cooperation and conflicts develop within the territory . . . but here, too, the struggle between different groups for possession, control, and exploitation of the natural resources . . . has as back-ground and basis a very precise architecture of the terrain and its landmarks." Built structures are a minor part of the architecture of the landscape, which is, in other words, the human/social/ethnic perception of it, mediated by several cultural products (and not only material culture). Stone-built structures, though, are of major relevance, since they may dominate the view of the landscape, and from that they become an active element in the building of the group's perception of it (Frémont 1980; Roncayolo 1986). Discussions on the symbolic meaning of primitive and prehistoric architecture are a recurrent theme in anthropological and archaeological debates (Guidoni 1978; Hodder 1990). I think that in order to understand the hillforts of the Chalcolithic, one must consider this element of interpretation.

The previous sections argued for an interpretation based on the concept of endogenous social contradiction (as opposed to external conflict, but with a long-term prevailing influence), and a multiplicity of approaches. One understands the hillforts as defining a landscape of oppositions, of contradictions: land/sea; the inside/the outside (both of the acropolis and of the wider walled and worked areas, thus materialising a more complex hierarchy); centre/periphery (within the group, and in some cases, within a region); production/consumption (and also extraction/transformation, with particular emphasis in metallurgy and pottery); collective/elite (be this military, political, social); the inheritance of the past through the dead (as with megaliths) as opposed to through the (a few?) living.

Therefore, it is only by understanding the context of each structure, the economic activities, the artefacts and associated symbols, the burials, the technology, that one may start understanding these monuments. The complexity of Los Millares contrasts with Zambujal or Lébous, and not only in the size of the architecture. On the other hand, the different phases of construction do represent more than material transformations, they stand for a "progressive endogenous reformulation of the space" in the words of Paul-Lévy (Paul-Lévy and Segaud 1983). The fact that both these and their roots (bastion-type constructions, locations dominating the landscape) cross-cut different regional cultural sequences, does stand for some kind of link.

Violence and warfare have been accepted as that link, after a preconception that the evolution of the Chalcolithic societies, and their increasing complexity, derives from competition. The control of critical resources has been posited as a prime basis for the emergence of inequality, and for inter-societal competition. It is interesting, though, that apart from south-eastern Spain, where water control seems to have been a crucial aspect, archaeologists have experienced much greater difficulties in assessing the "critical" resources in other areas. The control of exchange routes (for flint, amber or whatever) and the protection of production surplus have also been indicated as alternative "critical" aspects. It is difficult to imagine rivalry for control of stock in an apparently rich environment such as the Tagus valley. Unless one considers, again, that this rivalry is not primarily between groups, but within them. Anthropologists suggested, a long time ago, that population increase generates increasing endogenous conflict and tension (Lévi-Strauss 1980), and from it emerging elites tend to consolidate their status not only through armed repression, but by ideological means, as religious activities, prestige goods, or unproductive public works. I believe that this is what the hillforts are all about. In this sense, they are the accomplishment and the end of an era – the Neolithic – that enabled an enormous accumulation of wealth and experienced a gradual social ranking, expressed in material terms by collective burials. But they also announced the beginning of something new, individual status (expressed in individual burials, for instance), towards a class-divided society and the emergence of the state. They are, in essence, a political tool for social transformation, and therefore appear in the archaeological sequences at different moments, according to the strength of the new emerging social order (which in fact occupied the whole third and part of the second millennium). In this sense, the abandonment of the hillforts, does not necessarily represent a regression, since it may simply correspond to the consolidation of the ruling elite, no longer needing such public works. But the fact that they cease to be used after some time, while symbols of violence are reinforced (arms depictions in art and associated with burials), acts as a counter-proof against the primarily defensive character of the constructions.

REFERENCES

Acosta Martínez, P. 1983. Estado actual de la Prehistoria Andaluza. *Habis* 14, 197-205.

Aguayo de Hoyos, P. 1977. Construcciones defensivas de la edad del cobre peninsular. El cerro de los catellones (Laborcillas, Granada). *Cuadernos de Prehistoria de la Univcersidad de Granada* 2, 87-104.

Alexander, J. 1977. The "frontier" concept in prehistory: the end of the moving frontier. In J. Alexander (ed.), *Hunters, Gatherers and First Farmers beyond Europe*, 7-29. Leicester, Leicester University Press.

Almagro Gorbea, M. J. 1973a. *El Poblado y la Necropolis de el Barranquete (Almeria)*. Acta Arqueologiaca Hispanica 6.

Almagro-Gorbea, M. J. 1973b. *Los idolos del Bronce Hispanico*. Madrid, Bib. Praehistorica Hispanica.

Anderson, P. 1976. *Lineages of Absolutist State*. London, New Left Books.

Arnal, J. 1973. Le Lebous à Saint-Mathieu-de-Treviers. Ensemble du Chalcolithique au Gallo-Romain. *Gallia Préhistoire* 16, 131-200.

Arnaud, J. M. 1971. Os povoados "Neo-eneolíticos" de Famão e Aboboreira (Ciladas, Vila Viçosa) Notícia Preliminar. *Actas do II Congresso Nacional de Arqueologia*, 199-221. Lisboa, Instituto de Alta Cultura.

Arnaud, J. M., Oliveira, V. S., and Jorge, V. O. 1971. O povoado fortificado neo- e eneolítico do Penedo de Lexim (Mafra). campanha preliminar de escavações – 1970. *O Arqueologo Portugues* 5 (3ª série), 97-131.

Arnaud, J. M. and Gamito, T. J. 1972. O povoado fortificado neo- e eneolítico da Serra das baútas (Carenque, Belas). *O Arqueologo Portugues*, 119-61.

Arnaud, J. M. 1977. Escavações no penedo do Lexim. *O Arqueólogo Português* 7-9 (3ª série), 398-406.

Arnaud, J. M. and Gamito, T. J. 1978. Povoado Calcolítico de Alcacar. Notícia da sua idetificação. *Anais do Município de Faro* 8, 275-83.

Arnaud, J. M. 1982. O povoado calcolítico de Ferreira do Alentejo no contexto da bacia do Sado e do Sudoeste peninsular. *Arqueologia* 6, 48-64.

Arribas, A. and Molina, F. 1977. *El Poblado de Los Castillejos en Las Peñas de los Gitanos (Montefrio, Granada). Resultados de las campañas de 1971 y 1974*. Univ. de Granada.

Arribas, A. and Molina, F. 1979. El Poblado eneolítico de "El Malagon", de Cullar-Baza (Granada). *XIV Congreso Nacional de Arqueologia (Vitoria 1975)*, 67-101. Min. Educación.

Barbosa, E. 1956. O Castro da Pedra do Ouro (Alenquer). *O Arqueologo Portugues* 3, 75–85.

Barbosa, E. 1956. O Castro de Ota (Alenquer). *O Arqueologo Portugues*. 3, 117–24.

Beguiristain Gurpide, M. A. 1978. Los Yacimientos de habitición durante en Neolítico y edad del bronce en el alto valle del Ebro. *Trabajos de Arqueologia Navarra* 3.3, 59–156.

Best, J. G. P. and de Vries, N. M. W. 1982. *Interaction and Acculturation in the Mediterranean*, vol. 2. Amsterdam, Gruner.

Binford, L. R. 1988. *In Pursuit of the Past: Decoding the Archaeological Record*. London, Thames and Hudson.

Blagg, T. F. C., Jones, R. F. and Keay, S. J. 1984. *Papers in Iberian Archaeology*, vol. 1. Oxford, British Archaeological Reports (International Series 368).

Blance, B. M. 1961. Early Bronze Age colonists in Iberia. *Antiquity* 35.

Bosch-Gimpera, P. 1945. *El poblamiento y la formación de los pueblos de España*. Mexico.

Burnham, B. C. and Kingsbury, J. 1979. *Space, Hierarchy and Society. Interdisciplinary sudies in social area analysis*. Oxford, British Archaeological Reports (International Series 59).

Camps, G. 1976. Navigations et relations interméditerranéennes préhistoriques. *Chronologie et Synchronosme dans la Préhistoire Circum-Méditerrannéenne*, 77–89. Nice, Union Internationale des Sciences Préhistoriques et Protohistoriques.

Camps, G. 1992. Guerre ou paix? Origines des conflits intraspécifiques humains. *Préhistoire et Anthropologie Méditerranéennes* 1, 9–15.

Cara Barrionuevo, L. et al. 1989. Fronteras Culturales y Estrategias Territoriales Durante el III Milenio A. C. en el Valle Medio y Bajo del Andarax (Almería). *Arqueologia Espacial* 13, 63–76.

Cardoso, J. L. 1979. O Povoado Pré-Histórico de Leceia (Lisboa, Portugal). Nota Prévia sobre a Colecção de Ólvaro de Brée. *Boletim da Sociedade Geologica de Portugal* 21, 265–69.

Cardoso, J. L. 1981. O povoado pré-histórico de Leceia. *Revista de Guimarães* 91, 206–33.

Cardoso, J. L. 1989. *Leceia Resultados das Escavações Realizadas 1983–1988*. Oeiras, Câmara Municipal de Oeiras.

Cardoso, J., Soares, J. and Silva, C. T. 1984. O Povoado Calcolítico de Leceia (Oeiras). 1ª e 2ª campanha de escavações (1982–83). *Clio/Arqueologia* 1, 41–68.

Case, H. J. 1987. The Oxford International Western Mediterranean Bell Beaker Conference 1986. In W. H. Waldren and R. C. Kennard (eds), *Bell Beakers of the Western Mediterranean*, 3–13. Oxford, British Archaeological Reports.

Castro Martínez P. V. and G. M. P. 1989. El Concepto de Frontera: Implicaciones Teóricas de la Noción de Territorio Político. *Arqueologia Espacial* 13, 7–18.

Champion, T., Gamble, C., Shennan, S. and Whittle, A. 1991. *Prehistoric Europe*. London, Academic Press.

Chapman, J. 1988. From "space" to "place": a model of dispersed settlement and Neolithic society. In C. P. T. Burgess, C. Mordent and M. Maddison (eds), *Enclosures and Defenses in the Neolithic of Western Europe*, 56–70. Oxford: British Archaeological Reports.

Chapman, R. 1990. *Emerging Complexity: the Later Prehistory of South-East Spain, Iberia and the West Mediterranean*. Cambrdge, University Press.

Childe, V. G. 1969. *A Aurora da Civilização Europeia*. Lisboa, Portugália ed.

Clarke, D. V., Gowie, T. G. and Foxon, A. 1985. *Symbols of Power*. Edinburgh. Edinburgh, National Museum of Antiquaries of Scotland.

Colomer, A., Coularou, J. et al. 1980. l'enceinte en pierres seches de Boussargues (Argelliers, Herault): premiers resultats. In J. Guilaine (ed.), *Le groupe de Véraza et la fin des temps néolithiques dans le Sud de la France et en Catalogne*, 79-88. Paris, CNRS.

González Cordero, A., Castillo Castillo, J. and Hernández López, M. 1991. La sequencia estratigrafica en los yacimientos calcolíticos del área de Plasenzuela (Cáceres). *Extremadura Arqueológica* 2, 11-26.

Crubézi, E. and Raymond, C. 1988. Le passage de la sépulture individuelle à la sépulture de groupe du IIIe. au XIIe. siècle dans le sud-ouest de la France. In *Actes des 3èmes Journées Anthropologiques*, 195-208. Paris, CNRS (Notes et Monographes Techniques 24).

Cruz, A. R. 1991. Estudo Preliminar do Ossário da Gruta dos Ossos (Tomar). *Revista de Ciências Históricas* 6, 91-121. (Porto, Universidade Portucalense Infante D. Henrique.)

Daniel, G. and Evans, J. D. 1975. The western Mediterranean. In H. I. E. S. Edwards et al. (eds), *The Cambridge Ancient History. History of the Middle East and the Aegean Region*, 480-562. Cambridge, Cambridge University Press.

Eogan, G. 1979. Objects with Iberian affinities from Knowth, Ireland. *Revista de Gvimarães*, 69, 670-77. (Guimarães, Sociedade Martins Sarmento.)

Eslick, C. 1988. Hacilar to Karatas: social organization in south-western Anatolia. *Mediterranean Archaeology* 1, 5-22.

Evans, J. 1973. Priests and people – a note on evidence for social distinctions in prehistoric Malta. In J. M. Motes (ed.), *Estudios dedicados al Profesor Dr. Luis Pericot*, 56-70. Barcelona, Universidad de Barcelona.

Ferreira, O. V. 1966. *La Culture du Vase Campaniforme au Portugal*. Memórias. Lisboa, Serviços Geológicos de Portugal.

Ferreira, O. V. and Castro, L. A. 1967. O povoado neo-eneolítico das Salenas (Ponte de Lousa). *Revista de Guimarães* 77, 39-45.

Ferreira, O. V. 1975. Acerca dos Monumentos de Planta Quadrada ou Rectangular encontrados em Portugal. *Boletim Cultural da Junta Distrital de Lisboa* 81, 49-55.

Fortes, M. and Evans-Pritchard, E. E. 1981. *Sistemas Políticos Africanos*. Lisboa, Fundação Calouste Gulbenkian.

Frémont, A. 1980. *A Região, Espaço Vivido*. Coimbra, Livraria Almedina.

Gallay, G., and Spindler, K. 1972. Varatojo and Lapa do Suão. Zum Neolithicum Westen der iberischen Halbinsel. *Madrider Mitteilungen* 13, 35-58.

Gilman, A. and J. B. Thornes. *Land-use and Prehistory in South-east Spain*. London, George Allen & Unwin.

Gonçalves, V. S. 1978. Para um Programa de Estudo do Neolítico em Portugal. *ZEPHYRVS* 28-29, 148-62.

Gonçalves, J. L. M. and Serrão, E. C. 1979. O Povoado Calcolítico do Alto do Dafundo. *Actas da 1ª Mesa-Redonda sobre O Neolítico e o Calcolítico em Portugal*. Coimbra, Grupo de Estudos Arqueológicos do Porto.

Gonçalves, V. 1980. Cerro do Castelo de Santa Justa (Alcoutim). Escavações de 1979. *Clio* 2, 133-39.

Gonçalves, V. 1981a. Cerro do Castelo de Santa Justa (Alcoutim). Campanha 3 (81). *Clio* 3, 171-76.

Gonçalves, V. 1981b. Cerro do Castelo de Santa Justa (Alcoutim). Campanha 2 (80). *Clio* 3, 165-70.

Gonçalves, V. 1982a. Cerro do Castelo de Santa Justa (Alcoutim): Campanha 4 (82). *Clio* 4, 155-63.

Gonçalves, V. 1982b. O Povoado Calcolítico do Cabeço do Pé da Erra (Coruche). *Clio* 4, 7-18.

Gonçalves, J. L. M. 1991. Cerâmica Calcolítica da Estremadura. *Actas das IV Jornadas Arqueológicas*. Lisboa, Associação dos Arqueólogos Portugueses.

Gonçalves, V., Cardoso, J. et al. 1984. Povoados Calcolíticos Fortificados no Centro/Sul de Portugal: génese e dinâmica evolutiva. *Clio Arqueologia* 1, 141-54.

Grant, E. 1986. *Central Places, Archaeology and History*. Sheffield, University of Sheffield.

Guidoni, E., 1978. *Primitive Architecture*. New York, Harry N. Abrams Inc.

Guilaine, J. 1976. *Premiers Bergers et Paysans de l'Occident Méditerranéen*. Paris, Mouton.

Guilaine, J. (ed.) 1984. *L'Age du Cuivre Européen – civilizations à vases campaniformes*. Paris, CNRS.

Gusi Jener, F. 1975. La Aldea Eneolítica de Terrera Ventura (Tabernas, Almería). *XIII Congreso Nacional de Arqueologia (Huelva 1973)*, 111-19. Huelva, Min. Educación.

Haas, J. 1981. Class conflict and the state in the New World. In G. D. Jones (ed.), *The Transition to Statehood in the New World*, 17-29. Cambridge, Cambridge University Press.

Halstead, P. 1981. From determinism to uncertainty: social storage and the rise of the Minoan Palace. In A. Sheridan and G. Bailey (eds), *Economic Archaeology*, 32-45. Oxford, British Archaeological Reports.

Harrison, R. J. 1985. The Policultivo Ganadero or the secondary products revolution in Spanish Agriculture, 5000-1000 BC. *Proceedings of the Prehistoric Society* 51, 118-37.

Harrison, R. and Gilman, A. 1977. Trade in the second and third millenia B.C. between the Maghreb and Iberia. In V. Marcotics (ed.), *Ancient Europe and the Mediterranean*, 90-104. Warminster, Aris & Phillips Ltd.

Hastorf, C. A. 1993. *Agriculture and the Onset of Political Inequality before the Inka*. Cambridge, University Press.

Hodder, I. 1990. *The Domestication of Europe*. Oxford, Basil Blackwell.

Jorge, S. O. 1979. O Megalitismo no Contexto Neolítico Peninsular. *Revista de Guimarães* 88, 19.

Jorge, S. O. 1983. Habitats de la préhistoire récente du Nord du Portugal (III et début du II millénaire avant J.-C.). Resultats et problèmes des fouilles des dernières années. *Bulletin de la Société Préhistorique Française* 80, 183-86.

Jorge V. O. 1989. Arqueologia Social dos Sepulcros Megalíticos Atlânticos: Conhecimentos e Perspectivas Actuais. *Trabajos de Arqueologia* 2ª (série 6), 365-443.

Jorge, S. O. 1990. Desenvolvimento da Hierarquização Social e da metalurgia. In J. Alarcão (ed.), *Portugal das Origens à Romanização*, 163-212. Lisboa, ed. Presença.

Kinnes, I. 1975. Monumental function in British Neolithic burial practices. *World Archaeology* 7, 16-29.

Leisner, G. 1946. A Cultura Eneolítica do Sul de Espanha e suas Relações com Portugal. *Arqueologia e História* 1 (8ª série), 11-28.

Lévi-Strauss, C. 1980. *As Sociedades Primitivas*. Grandes Temas. Rio de Janeiro, Biblioteca Salvat.

Lewthwaite, J. 1983. The Neolithic of Corsica. In C. Scarre (ed.), *Ancient France – Neolithic societies and their landscapes 6000–2000 B.C.*, 146–83. Edinburgh, Edinburgh University Press.

Lewthwaite, J. 1985. Social factors and economic change in Balearic prehistory, 3000–1000 B.C. In G. Barker and C. Gamble (eds), *Beyond Domestication in Prehistoric Europe. Investigations in subsistence archaeology and social complexity*, 47–68. London, Academic Press.

Lillios, K. 1991. Competition to Fission: the Copper to Bronze Age Transition in the Lowlands of West-Central Portugal (3000–1000 BC). Unpublished PhD dissertation, Yale University.

Marques, M. G. 1967. Castro Eneolítico de Sesimbra. Notícia do seu Achado. *Boletim do Centro de Estudos do Museu Arqueológico de Sesimbra* 1, 10–16.

Martinez, J. C. S., 1992. O Sítio de habitat das Carriceiras (Carregal do Sal). Notícia Preliminar. *O Megalitismo no Centro de Portugal*, 68–76. Mangualde, Centro de Estudos Pré-Históricos da beira Alta.

Mckay, M. 1988. *The Origins of Hereditary Social Stratification. A study focusing on early prehistoric Europe and modern ethnographic accounts*. Oxford, British Archaeological Reports.

Mendozel, A., Molina, F. et al. 1975. El Poblado del "Cerro de los Castellones" (Laborcilhas, Granada). *XIII Congreso Nacional de Arqueologia (Huelva 1973)*, 315–32.

Molina, F., Aguayo, P. Fresneda, E. and Contreras, F. n.d. Nuevas Investigaciones en yacimientos de la Edad del Bronce en Granada. *Homenaje a Luis Siret (1934–1984)*, 55–65. Madrid, Consejeria de Cultura de la Junta de Andalucia – Direccón Genaral de Bellas Artes.

Neustupný, J. 1977. The time of the hillforts. In V. Marcotics (ed.), *Ancient Europe and the Mediterranean*, 128–41. Warminster, Aris & Phillips Ltd.

Nocete, F. 1989. *El espacio de la coerción. La transición al estado en las campiñas del Alto Guadalquivir (España)*. Oxford, British Archaeological Reports.

Oliveira, D. L. 1986. Monuments and social complexity: a new line of enquiry? *Oxford Journal of Archaeology* 5, 103–07.

Oosterbeek, L. and Cruz A. R. 1991. A Arqueologia da Morte: considerações a propósito da interpretação dos contextos sepulcrais na região de Tomar. *Boletim Cultural*, 99–117. Tomar, Câmara Municipal de Tomar.

Oosterbeek, L. and Cruz, A. R. 1992. O rio Nabão há 4000 anos. O Povoado da Fonte Quente e o mais antigo povoamento no vale do Nabão. *Boletim Cultural da C.M.T.* 17, 27–42.

Oosterbeek, L. 1992a. Habitat et territoires dans la Préhistoire récente dans le Haut-Ribatejo (Portugal). *Mediterrâneo* 1, 79–93.

Oosterbeek, L. 1992b. O Megalitismo no Ribatejo Norte. *O Megalitismo no Centro de Portugal*, 112–21. Mangualde, Centro de Estudos Pré-Históricos da beira Alta.

Pader, E.-J. 1982. *Symbolism, Social Relations and the Interpretation of Mortuary Remains*. Oxford, British Archaeological Reports.

Parreira, R. 1983. O Cerro dos Castelos de S. Brás (Serpa). Relatório preliminar dos trabalhos arqueológicos de 1979 e 1980. *O Arqueologo Portugues* 1 (4ª série), 149–68.

Paul-Lévy, F. and Segaud, M. 1983. *Anthropologie de l'espace*. Paris, Centre de Création Industrielle/Centre Georges Pompidou.

Phillips, A. P. 1973. The evolutionary model of human society and its application to certain early farming populations of western Europe. In C. Renfrew (ed.), *The Explanation of Culture Change: Models in Prehistory*, 529-37. London, Duckworth.

Piaget, J. 1968. *Le Structuralisme*. Paris, P.U.F.

Piggott, S. 1965. *A Europa antiga. Do Início da agricultura à Antiguidade Clássica*. Lisboa, Fundação Calouste Gulbenkian.

Renfrew, C. 1967. Colonialism and Megalithismus. *Antiquity* 41, 276-88.

Renfrew, C. (ed.) 1973. *The Explanation of Culture Change. Models in Prehistory*. London, Duckworth.

Renfrew, C. 1979. *Before Civilization*. Harmonsworth, Pelican Books.

Renfrew, C. and Shennan, S. (eds) 1982. *Ranking, Resource and Exchange: aspects of the archaeology of early European society*. Cambridge, Cambridge University Press.

Rowlands, M. 1987. Centre and periphery: a review of a concept. In M. L. M. Rowlands and K. Kristiansen (eds), *Centre and Periphery in the Ancient World*, 15-55. Cambridge, Cambridge University Press.

Sangmeister, E. and Schubart, H. 1981. *Zambujal-Die Grabungen 1964 bis 1973*. Madrid, Madrider Beiträge 1.

Savory, H. N. 1959. A section through the innermost rampart at the chalcolithic castro of Vila Nova de S. Pedro, Santarém. *Actas das 1 Jornadas Arqueológicas*. Lisboa, Associação dos Arqueólogos Portugueses.

Schubart, H., Ferreira, O. V. et al. 1969. A fortificação eneolítico da Columbeira - Bombarral. *O Arqueologo Portugues* 3 (3ª série), 17-36.

Serrão, E. C. and Vicente, E. P. 1958. O Castro Eneolítico de Olelas. Primeiras escavações. *Comunicações dos Serviços Geológicos de Portugal* 39, 87-125.

Service, E. R. 1962. *Primitive Social Organization*. New York, Random House.

Sherratt, A. G. 1981. Plough and pastoralism: aspects of the secondary products revolution. In I. Hodder, (ed.), *Patterns of the Past: Studies in Honour of David Clark*, 261-306. Cambridge, University Press.

Silva, C. T. 1970. O Povoado Pré-Histórico da Rotura (Setúbal). Vestígios de Estratigrafia. *Arquivo de Beja* 25/27, 31-44.

Silva, C. T., and Soares, J. 1987. O povoado fortificado calcolítico do Monte da Tumba I - Escavações arqueológicas de 1982-1986 (resultados preliminares). *Setúbal arqueológica* 8, 29-79.

Soares, J., Barbieri, N. and Silva, C. T. 1973. Povoado Calcolítico do Moinho da Fonte do Sol (Quinta do Anjo - Palmela). *Arqueologia e História* 4 (9ª série), 235-68.

Spindler, K. 1969. Die kupferzeitliche Siedlung von Penedo/Portugal. *Madrider Mitteilungen* 10, 45-117.

Siret, L.1890. *Las primeras edades del metal en el SE de España*. Barcelona.

Siret, L. 1892. La fin de l'époque néolithique en Espagne. *L'Anthropologie* 4, 77-119.

Walker, M. J. 1986. Society and habitat in Neolithic and Early Bronze Age S.E. Spain. In A. Fleming (ed.), *The Neolithic of Europe*, 37-50. Southampton, The World Archaeology Congress.

The Dread of Something after Death: Violation and Desecration on the Isle of Man in the tenth century

Sarah Tarlow

About *five years ago*, some of the gravestones in a Jewish cemetery in north London were smashed by neo-nazis, and others daubed with swastikas and anti-Semitic slogans. This vandalism was widely reported in the national papers, and was the first time I remember hearing about the modern desecration of graves in Britain. I, like most of those who heard about the incident, felt shocked and upset by the violence of the action and the hatred which lay behind it. Although physical damage was done only to inanimate things, the threat implied by such wanton desecration was deeply disturbing. Violent action such as desecration is a trespass which implies not only antipathy towards the individual or group against which it is directed, but also for all their most profoundly held beliefs and principles, everything that they stand for. In many societies, graves and memorials are particularly imbued with emotional symbolic meaning, and violation of the grave is an offence against those for whom its meaning is of great personal value. As a locus of violent expression, the grave is especially powerful because of the force of the emotions and the strength of custom which guides their treatment. Antagonism between groups can be articulated through violence upon non-sentient things, in this case human remains, to which end I want to consider in some detail one pagan burial in the Isle of Man.

Fear of grave violation is widespread anthropologically (see e.g.

many of the papers in Humphreys and King 1981; Bloch and Parry 1982), and it has been suggested that early Christians believed that the violation of the grave jeopardised one's chance of resurrection (Ariès 1981, 32).

The boat burial at Chapel Hill, Balladoole on the southern coast of the Isle of Man is an example, or so Wilson (Bersu and Wilson 1966, xiv) claims, of how the pagan Norse of the Isle of Man "respected the Christian Celtic graveyards". The burial, dated by the grave goods to the later part of the ninth century or the early part of the tenth (Bersu and Wilson 1966, 87), was discovered by accident during Gerhard Bersu's 1945 excavations on a hill in the southern part of the island. Bersu unfortunately died before the report was complete and only a small preliminary report had appeared before 1966 when David Wilson finished, edited and published the full report.

In his overview of the Viking graves of the British Isles, Haakon Shetelig (1945, 36) commented on the particularly "intimate relations between the Celtic and the Norse elements of the population" in the Isle of Man. This observation is inspired both by the sculptured crosses of the late Norse period (these are crosses which are Celtic in form, with Norse style carved decoration) and by the frequent appearance in the Isle of Man of Norse interments in Christian graveyards. These graves Shetelig (1945, 36), Wainwright (1962, 160) and others (Crawford 1987, 163) have seen as representing a transitional stage when paganism and Christianity were both practised. Shetelig equated both the amalgamation of different styles in a single artefact and the proximal occurrence of the archaeological remains of different groups with cultural assimilation.

I contest that the co-occurrence of the two types of burial are actually part of a very different relationship. The cemetery was in fact the locus of the expression and creation of antagonistic relations between groups/individuals. Funerary ritual is an arena in which relationships between people are produced and perpetuated (Thomas n.d.). Interpretation of the meaning of mortuary practices demands more sophisticated analysis than Shetelig's simple equation of the degree of physical proximity with the degree of social or cultural "mixing". According to his understanding, the process of cultural assimilation will correlate directly with the degree of blending of artistic styles or spatial closeness. Therefore, since the process of assimilation is considered to be gradual, so the appearance of pagan graves in Christian cemeteries is anticipated as "a transitional stage" for the Norse (Wainwright 1962, 160) between being fully pagan and fully Christian.

Under a layer of black earth a large number of clench-nails indicated the presence of a boat. Remains of one adult male, and possibly a female as well, were in the boat. The burial was particularly "rich", accompanied by a shield, a considerable amount of elaborate horse tack, some of which was of Carolingian metalwork, knives, a cauldron, a ring-headed pin and various other bits and pieces. The boat itself was probably about 11 metres long by about 3 metres broad at the widest part (Bersu and Wilson 1966, 4). Above the boat a mound had been built, but was seriously eroded by the time of the excavation. Bersu estimated its original size as about twelve by five metres and two metres tall. The mound was capped with stones and covered in a layer of pale, burnt animal bone. Just outside the mound, to the north-west, was a large post hole, sixty centimetres square at base and nearly a metre deep. Stripping of the surrounding area failed to reveal any other Norse remains.

The boat sits at the highest point of Chapel Hill, and appears to be an isolated feature of its kind. However, it was not a burial in virgin soil. Immediately beneath the boat are a number of lintel graves, dug into the occupation layer of an earlier (Iron Age) settlement and dating, therefore, from some time between the abandonment of that settlement and the Norse burial. In fact it can be more closely dated to the period immediately preceding the Norse burial from the condition of the human remains when the boat burial was made. These earlier burials comprised at least sixteen individuals in long shale cists, aligned west-east, lying in two rows (Figure 1). Only one of them is undisturbed. The other graves all have at least some capping stones missing; several are substantially disturbed or have been almost completely destroyed. Isolated human bones and pieces of shale were found in the mound, which were presumably thrown up when the hollow in which the boat was to sit was scooped out. In several cases the bones had been removed from the cists and either replaced in a partial and jumbled fashion or laid on the ground surface adjacent to or beneath the boat. The small bones of the hands and feet were still articulated when they were removed from their graves and placed on the ground, which indicates that the tendons had not yet decayed (Bersu and Wilson 1966, 9). We can thus infer that little time had passed since the earlier burials before the Norse burial took place. After the boat burial there were no subsequent Christian burials in the same location, and the boat burial was emphatically punctuated by the positioning of a mound over virtually the whole of the cemetery area. A large post hole at the edge of the mound, to the south-western end

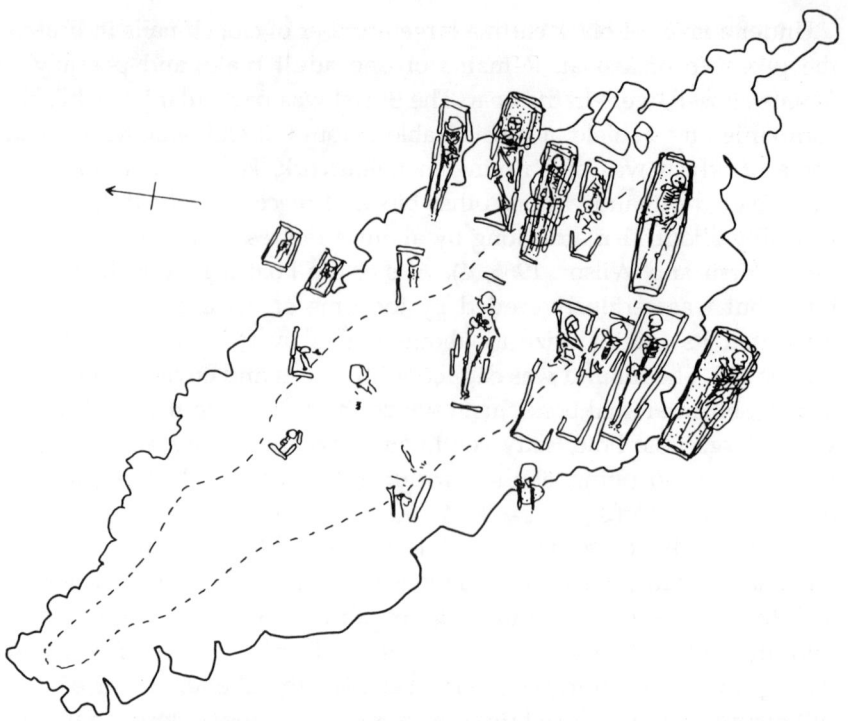

Figure 1. The Christian burials at Chapel Hill, Balladoole, Isle of Man. The solid line represents the edge of the overlying cairn; the dotted line shows the position of the boat burial (after Bersu 1966).

of the boat, suggests that a substantial marker proclaimed the Norse appropriation of the site (the hole is 0.6 m square at the deepest part, and extends almost a metre into the earlier layers).

In his original report Bersu interpreted the siting of the burial and the treatment of the previous interments as a deliberate "slighting" of the island's Christian community. "It is clear," he wrote (Bersu 1966, 12), "that the Vikings had little respect for the earlier burials." However, Bersu's interpretation received little support from others involved with the site. He (1966, 13) recorded in his report the dissent of Basil and Eleanor Megaw who saw the juxtaposition of the burial with the earlier burial ground as purely co-incidental. They maintained that the position chosen for the Norse grave was only motivated by a desire for a prominent position. Wilson agreed with the Megaws for the "subjective" reasons that such behaviour is "out of character for the Vikings, as we know them in literature, and does not agree with the later harmony between the two populations, evidenced by the Manx crosses" (Bersu 1966, 13n). He also says that such an event appears to be unique in British Norse archaeology.

The Megaws' argument, denying any particular significance to the placing of the Norse burial within the earlier cemetery, is hard to support with reference to either the geographical or temporal co-incidence of the Christian and Norse burial events. The main burial was directly over the centre of the Christian cemetery. It is hard to believe that the people who carried out the second burial were unaware that their chosen spot had been used for burials already, especially since burials had taken place there so recently that the tendons joining the small bones of the hands and feet were still undecayed. The linear alignments of the Christian burials also suggest that the graves were, if not marked somehow, at least well known in local tradition, so that new burials could be placed appropriately according to the existing system. But even supposing that somehow the earlier burials were not known to those who carried out the boat burial, it is inconceivable that they could have remained unnoticed. The decision to proceed with the burial even after the other graves had been encountered was a deliberate act involving the remains of the dead. The articulated remains of the Christian dead were removed from shale cists and spread out on the ground surface. If such behaviour seems unlike the Vikings as Wilson characterises them, than surely it is by specific examination of this act, rather than disputing the validity of the evidence, that our understanding of social and political relationships at this time might be enhanced.

Although such behaviour is without known parallels in Britain, analogous practices are recorded archaeologically from Norway. Brogger (1953) discussed the phenomenon of "mound-breaking" at Gokstad and Oseberg. The latter is a late ninth century boat burial in Norway, where the upper layers of the mound over the boat had been disturbed shortly after the burial took place. Almost all of one of the two female skeletons was removed. Some of her bones were scattered around the top part of the mound, most were removed completely and her bed was chopped into pieces. Brogger (1953, 100) pointed out that this is excessively vandalistic behaviour for mere plundering. One might add that the intrusive activity seemed more concerned with destruction than theft, since many rich grave-goods remained untouched, while the attention given to the skeleton and the chopping up of the bed make little sense in terms of material gain. Rather, as Brogger says, "the object was to 'annihilate' the deceased and *render the grave uninhabitable*" (ibid., his italics). From the saga literature one Norse concept which comes across very strongly is that the dead person "lives" in their mound (e.g. Hord's encounter with Soti in *Harðar saga og Hólmverja*).[1] The grave is the dwelling place of the dead and the location of interaction between the dead and the living. According to this Norse understanding of the grave as a place where the dead dwelt, the disordering of the Christian graves at Balladoole appears a distinctly deliberate act. The disturbance of graves was not merely incidental to the preparation of the new burial, but constituted part of its meaning. By disarticulation and removal of the human remains, the Christian ancestors were "evicted" from the burial ground, which was then reoccupied by the Norse dead. Action occurring at the place of burial was necessarily a meaningful communication between the living and the dead, and by extension between the living and the living.

The picture which emerges is not one of cultural integration between Norse and "native" elements, but one of violent antipathy. If, as Wilson claims, the disturbance of earlier burials is an unusual act for the Vikings, then the particular character of violent desecration was surely apparent to those who carried it out, as well as to the Christian community of Balladoole. The violence here evidenced suggests the forceful expression of difference. The Norse are not integrating their burial practices into existing structures, by continuing to use the same locale, but committing violence upon those existing structures, and replacing them with their own, aggressively Norse, practices. In order to develop this point, it is necessary to consider Norse boat burials in the late ninth century.

It is first of all remarkable how few elaborate pagan burials there are. There are two known Norse boat burials on Man, and a handful of other sites which probably represent pagan burials (Wilson 1966, xiii, 91–92; Cubbon 1962, 11). One might ask where are the grave fields of common pagan graves? Where are the less elaborate boat burials, involving small rowing boats and more modest equipment, as are known from Scandinavia? Our idea of the number of Vikings far exceeds the number implied by known graves. The boat burials demand and attract so much attention because of their rich and spectacular nature. It is to this unusual richness we could profitably look in order to understand the British boat burial phenomenon. The assumption that pagan boat burials represent the first generation of settlers is based upon a circular argument which dates the coming of the Norse by the dates of the pagan graves. On this basis, suggestions that the Norse might have been present in Man up to a century earlier than the orthodox estimate of the late ninth or early tenth century (as is implied by some of the literary sources) are dismissed (Sawyer 1971, 64;

Megaw 1978, 269; Crawford 1987, 174).

Lamb (1993) suggests that these burials represent not a survival of paganism amongst the first generation of settlers, but a self-conscious and aristocratic revival of Norse paganism in the late ninth century. "We seem . . . to be in a world of quite self-conscious romanticism, closer in spirit to Wagner and William Morris than the Norse scholars possibly would care to allow" (Lamb, pers. comm.). This revival, if such it is, is limited to an elite phenomenon, associated with the cult of Odin, an aristocratic, warrior god, rather than the more commonly worshipped and proletarian Thor. Such an interpretation is suggested by the absence of "Thor's hammers" from the Norse pagan graves on the Isle of Man and elsewhere in Scotland and the islands, and the frequency of large boats, horses and their tack, and battle equipment. For those who followed the cult of Odin, god of the dead, to locate a burial in a place already occupied by "enemy" dead might have had particular significance.

If Lamb is right and the elaborate boat burials are connected with a self-consciously romantic revival, then they are better considered as part of a continuous discourse between a small aristocratic group and the wider Christian population. Such a discourse was concerned both with the establishment of identity and with the legitimation of power relations between groups, by strategies of representation which refer to religious and ethnic associations. These relations were articulated in, amongst other situations, the cemetery. The early Christian burials show a very small degree of differentiation. Although personal identities were recognised in the provision of separate and individual stone cists, there is no indication that the graves were differently marked. The spatial arrangement of the cemetery shows no differentiation on the grounds of gender or status, except that the infant burials are concentrated to the north of the cemetery. The burials are all aligned west-east and are organised in rows parallel to each other. The graves contain no surviving burial goods. They uniformly lack ostentation, and do not appear to be an arena for the articulation of individual status in a competitive manner. Rather, the graves can be said to articulate, in social terms, an ideology of egalitarianism and group cohesion, and perhaps to express Christian ideals of modesty and the rejection of personal material display.

The contrast with the Norse burial, which violently rejects this Christian ideology, is dramatic. The boat burial is highly individualised. It is accompanied by rich and fine goods, including a boat and the equipment of a horse, which were powerful symbols of the aristocratic elite

(Foote and Wilson 1970, 232; Cramp 1982). It is an isolated occurrence, elaborately commemorated, and symbolically "sealed" with a cairn some two metres high and a very substantial marker. Situated, as it is, on the highest point of the hill, the grave would be visible from a considerable part of the surrounding landscape, and would thus intrude upon the daily lived experience of people of the area. It would be a constant reminder of the presence of the Norse, as well as referring to the preparations for the burial and the funeral itself. From the descriptions of contemporary writers (e.g. Ibn Fadlan in 921–922 [Jones 1968, 425–30]), it can be suggested that there was probably considerable pomp at the funeral itself. It is likely that the layer of cremated bone over the mound is evidence of ritual activity at the funeral. The cremation of animals and incorporation of cremated animal remains into the burial (in this case the layer of white animal bone could also have accentuated the visibility of the mound), ostentatiously flaunts a practice quite antithetical to Christian burial.

The Chapel Hill boat burial does not read like the actions of the first generation of Norse settlers, intermarrying with the local population and rapidly converting to Christianity (Cubbon 1962, 12; Crawford 1987, 163). An interpretation which incorporates the assertion of a romantic identity with reference to a heroic past and intentional disregard for Christian society comes closer to explaining the Balladoole burials.

Rather than ethnic harmony, or geographical chance, I believe that this boat burial expresses particular tensions between a small elite group and the rest of the population. These differences were not only acted out in the struggle for symbolic and actual possession of the most prominent position in the landscape, but the graves themselves were the location in which political and ethnic relations were violently expressed.

CONCLUSIONS

Thinking about violence is problematic. Archaeologists, despite their claims to some academic objectivity, have generally avoided taking a position on violence in their discourse, frequently ignoring or underplaying evidence of violent behaviour or aggressive intent in the past. The past with which we are generally presented is sanitised. The passionate, dangerous, physical aspects of human experience are written out of our histories, even though we know through our own daily experience how fundamental are emotional responses and psychological conditions to all aspects of human practice and interaction. Not only does violent behaviour present the archaeologist with an aspect of the human self which is uncomfortable because it demands a moral response, it also comes into the realm of passionate expression, which generally makes the scholar uncomfortable. Emotional responses are held to be incompatible with proper logical thought, and seriously out of place in an academic discipline. Perhaps it is fear of our own credibility which makes us shy away from passionate action such as violence as an area of consideration, choosing instead "logical" dynamics such as exchange or political relations (and neglecting to consider the emotional basis of such practices).

Wilson and others have been unwilling to acknowledge brutality in the past, preferring to discuss the trading relations suggested by the burial goods rather than the context of the burial itself. Atrocity is uncomfortable, but it is only by making a consideration of such things a part of archaeology that archaeologists can help fulfil their responsibility in the modern world. This includes not only warfare but also a consideration of brutality in all its forms: punishment, domestic violence, murder, injury, even sacrifice and cannibalism. It must also include violence towards the non-human: desecration, iconoclasm, sacrilege. All these are imbued with strong emotions, and have profound meaning for the perpetrator as well as the victim.

There is also a danger that in an academic discussion such as archaeology the profound and passionate human experience of the violent and the violated is trivialised or marginalised by the use of language which softens the impact of acts such as that which occurred at Balladoole. Thus I have suggested that "violent expression" was part of a "negotiation" or "discourse". Nevertheless, it is not only possible but necessary to bring the discussion of violent and other passionate expression within the constraints of academic discourse. We cannot discuss Balladoole, and sites analogous to it, without considering aggression. To ignore violence in the past is to de-problematise and effectively naturalise it, which has real consequences in the modern world. To ignore or diminish the human consequences of violence impoverishes our understanding of the past and abdicates our responsibility to the present.

Acknowledgements

I would like to thank Brian Boyd, Bill Sillar, Koji Mizoguchi, Lesley McFadyen and Diura Thoden van Velzen for reading and commenting on an earlier version of this paper. I am also grateful for John Carman's editorial help and advice.

Note

1. Although the saga literature is distant from the Balladoole burial both chronologically and geographically, that the burial mound was metaphorically understood as the dwelling place of the dead is suggested by widespread archaeological evidence of the chamber grave (*Kammergrab*) and analogous house or room shaped graves (e.g. at Birka (Gräslund 1981)) throughout the period and area of pagan Norse influence. Wilson (1966, 69, n.) persuasively argues that the Norse burial at Cronk Moar in the Isle of Man is a *Kammergrab* by analogy with several Scandinavian examples.

References

Ariès, P. 1981. *The Hour of Our Death*. Harmondsworth, Penguin.

Bersu, G. and Wilson, D. 1966. *Three Viking Graves in the Isle of Man*. London, Society for Medieval Archaeology.

Bloch, M. and Parry, J. (eds) 1982. *Death and the Regeneration of Life*. Cambridge, Cambridge University Press.

Brogger, A. 1953. The ship graves. In A. Brogger and H. Shetelig (eds), *The Viking Ships: their ancestry and evolution*, 52–71. Dreyers Forlag.

Cramp, R. 1982. The Viking image. In R. Farrell (ed.), *The Vikings*, 8–19. London, Phillimore and Co.

Crawford, B. 1987. *Scandinavian Scotland*. Leicester, Leicester University Press.

Cubbon, A. 1962. *The Ancient and Historic Monuments of the Isle of Man*. Douglas, Manx Museum and National Trust.

Foote, P. and Wilson, D. 1970. *The Viking Achievement*. London, Sidgwick and Jackson.

Gräslund, A.-S. 1981. *Birka IV: The Burial Customs: a study of the graves on Björkö*. Stockholm, K.Vilterhets Historie och Antikvitets Akadamien.

Humphreys, S. C. and King, H. (eds) 1981. *Mortality and Immortality: the anthropology and archaeology of death*. London, Academic Press.

Jones, G. 1968. *A History of the Vikings*. Oxford, Oxford University Press.

Lamb, R., 1993. Carolingian Orkney and its transformation. In C. Batey, J. Jensch and C. Morris (eds), *The Viking Age in Caithness, Orkney and the N. Atlantic: select papers from the Proceedings of the 11th Viking Congress*, 260–71. Edinburgh, Edinburgh University Press.

Megaw, B. 1978. Norseman and native in the kingdom of the Isles: a reassessment of the Manx evidence. In P. Davey (ed.), *Man and the Environment in the Isle of Man*, 265–314. Oxford, British Archaeological Reports (British Series 54 (ii)).

Sawyer, P. 1971. *The Age of the Vikings*. London, Edward Arnold.

Shetelig, H. 1945. The Viking graves in Great Britain and Ireland. *Acta Archaeologica* 16, 1–55.

Thomas, J. n.d. Death, Power and the Body in Prehistoric Britain. Unpublished paper.

Wainwright, F. 1962. *The Northern Isles*. Edinburgh, Edinburgh University Press.

The Victim or the Crime: Park Focused Conflict in Cambridgeshire and Huntingdonshire 1200–1556

Twigs Way

This *paper examines* park-related violence and disorder between the thirteenth and the seventeenth centuries in the counties of Cambridgeshire and Huntingdonshire and utilises current documentary and archaeological research on the social and economic impact of imparkment in that area. Violence associated with imparkment took both physical and social forms and was committed both by the creator of the park and by those affected by its creation. In this paper greater stress will be laid on the response to imparkment rather than the actual imparkment process, which will be addressed more fully in a forthcoming study (Way 1994).

Imparkment during this period regularly involved the re-positioning of key components in the parish landscape such as the church and the manorial site. Frequently changes were made to the size and/or layout of the village itself and customary routeways were subjected to alteration, defining areas of exclusion and seclusion within the local landscape. Customary rights might be violated, rights of access restricted or denied and labour demands modified.

The changes consequent on imparkment led to dislocation both of established social relations and the landscape in which they were embedded, frequently inciting a violent response as new social patterns were negotiated. "Trespass" and "park break" both feature commonly in medieval and post-medieval records as testimony to this response.

Such transgressive acts included the throwing down of fences and barriers, injuries to keepers and widespread poaching and trespass. Crimes were carried out by groups of various social backgrounds both from within the parish and from surrounding areas. The very alienation between social class groups which had been both articulated and enforced by imparkment was further intensified by the privatisation of the landscape, whilst existing factional feuding and conflict within the gentry classes were fuelled by the status "statement" of the park. Thus the park can be seen as both a reflection of, and a subsequent focus for, social tensions and aggression during the period under consideration.

I suggest that in the past categorisation of park-related violence and crime has been greatly over-simplified. Instead, a complex picture of disturbances and conflicts associated with specific social groups can be presented. In this study I have excluded crimes which took place within the park boundaries but appear not to be directly related to the issue of imparkment; I have also chosen to restrict the study to those actions which are physically focused on the park, although it is recognised social response to imparkment is not invariably located within the park, for example, a manorial centre located outside of the imparked area may be assaulted as a response to imparkment elsewhere within the parish.

Imparkment

The act of imparkment can be seen as embodying two types of "violence". Firstly, the re-organisation of the landscape resulting in the removal of certain social "resources" from the public domain and the dislocation of established social patterns; secondly the restriction or removal of economic resources.[1] These economic resources were often closely linked to customary rights and thus also formed part of the established social order. It can be argued that this act also resulted in less frequent interaction between the manorial landholder and the tenants by the creation of physical exclusion areas and barriers within the landscape. Documentary material relating to the imparkment process is rare (unlike that for the later enclosure episodes), but the available evidence concerning park breaks indicates that the process was extremely unpopular. Both the act of imposition and the resultant social and economic changes were therefore harmful to established social relations. Aggravation of established relations took place not only across social divisions but also within groups; as expansion of areas of private land fuelled factional violence within the nobility, contributing to an unbalancing of power relations.

Landscape change resulting from imparkment has been recovered using archaeological and documentary sources relating to Cambridgeshire and Huntingdonshire and in my research I have used these two types of data to establish the impact of imparkment in these counties. At least sixty parks were created in Huntingdonshire and Cambridgeshire during the period 1200 to 1550 and in each case re-organisation of the central social elements of the parish have been studied in order to assess the degree of alteration and its likely social impact (Way 1994).

Social elements

In the past it has frequently been suggested that early imparkment was not associated with settlement disruption; physical displacement or constraint of village settlement being judged to have occurred mainly after the mid-sixteenth century. However, my research indicates that at least ten settlements in Cambridgeshire and Huntingdonshire underwent some degree of re-organisation as a direct result of imparkment prior to 1550. This reorganisation ranged from complete de-population to relatively minor re-routing of road systems and consequent readjustment of settlement development. Removal of parts of a village to achieve seclusion of the manorial dwelling and/or church appears to have been a relatively common aspect of imparkment since the thirteenth century. Constraint of village development or the imposition of an "interrupted" or "dispersed" pattern of settlement is also common. These latter need not be associated with any population decline, they are, however, likely to have had a harmful impact on existing social structures as there is adjustment to the loss of communality associated with nucleated patterns of settlement.[2] The imposition of change also indicates an important stage in power relations and class conflict.

Within the Cambridgeshire/Huntingdonshire area at least thirteen manorial sites were situated within private parkland by 1550 with a further eleven being sited on the boundary between the park and the main settlement area (Way 1994). The "removal" of the manorial dwelling (frequently used for events such as meetings of manor courts) from within the village community to the exclusive landscape of the parkland is found both accompanying and independent of more general settlement disruption. This physical separation of the manorial centre from the community echoed and further engendered increasing social distancing.

Churches were also increasingly subject to appropriation by the land holding sector of society and consequent removal from the public domain. At least ten churches were situated within or on the boundary of private parkland by the mid-sixteenth century in the area under consideration, a figure that was doubled within the following century. With reference to the appearance and contents of the parish church Williamson and Bellamy (1987, 191) claimed that "it is a communal space which has been used by the rural community for centuries, and it has been shaped by the way this community ordered itself"; I would extend this claim to the spatial positioning of the church within the community and suggest that the appropriation of the church, and by implication the power embodied within it, signals change in the power structure and organisation of the local community.

Economic resource

Imparkment of economically valuable land could have a significant impact on available resources. The most common conflict of interests resulted from the enclosure of woodland and waste areas, curtailing rights of grazing, pannage or wood collection. Stamper (1988) has recently drawn attention to the many economic rights associated with woodland and emphasised its key importance in the peasant economy. Imparkment of areas of arable or pasture land became relatively common by the fifteenth century. Where that arable was part of demesne land other consequences need to be considered, such as reduction in the amount of labour required to work the demesne.

Prior to 1550 there is evidence for imparkment of arable land in fifteen locations in Cambridgeshire and Huntingdonshire. Meadow and pasture land were removed from cultivation in eight cases while a further six documentary references are made to the imparkment of "land" or other land use categories (such as fen). This indicates that approximately half of the parks created during this period removed land other than woodland from the parish economy. Analysis of national documentary records of the type of land imparked from 1232 to 1430, taken from the Calendar of Patent Rolls records of licensed parks, also indicates a figure for intake of land other than woodland of 50% from 1360 onwards – although prior to 1360 there is a stronger emphasis on the imparkment of woodland rather than arable.

Stamper (1988, 129) has argued that "woodland was a vital, much used and financially valuable resource" for this period and in addition to its production of essential raw materials it "often served as grazing land . . . sometimes the only common land on which animals could be put". In several of the Cambridgeshire examples the woodland imparked was the only woodland available in the parish and its enclosure represented the complete removal of this resource from the local economy.

Bushaway (1992) has recently considered the erosion of custom and rite in eighteenth century southern England and his comments on the ideological importance to the poor of customary collective activities might equally well be applied to the area under discussion; thus emphasising the overlap between the social and the economic impact of imparkment. It is possible that certain common rights could be continued following imparkment, however, no references to this have been encountered in the present study. Continuation of common access as a right would both create problems for the control of poaching and also negate one of the central purposes of imparkment – the creation and control of specific areas of exclusion.

Summary

In this section I have briefly demonstrated the impact that imparkment could have on local social and economic resources. In the examples given the numbers of parishes affected are minimum numbers, as in many other cases either the date or extent of the park or the placement of the manorial centre or church are not sufficiently well established to form part of the original data set. In many cases the curtailment of rights or removal of access will have gone almost unrecorded. Reorganisation of the local landscape with its impact on social relations and destabilising of power relations can be seen to have been a common consequence of imparkment. To this extent imparkment can undoubtedly be defined as an action of violence – one which caused harm both at an individual level and on a wider social basis. The fact that this reorganisation was imposed upon a largely unwilling and often aggrieved local populace can be seen by the response that these changes engendered.

RESPONSES TO IMPARKMENT

Types of park-related crime and violence

Park-related disorder and conflict has commonly been fragmented and included within other categories of crime in the past. Some of these, such as poaching, have received considerable attention whilst others, such as the group park break (categorised as assault), have received little. Due to a misunderstanding of the nature of imparkment there has been little differentiation between certain crimes (in particular poaching) when they occur outside or inside a park, even though the themes of privacy and enclosure were emphasised by parks in contrast to those of unenclosed areas. I would argue that this approach to the data has resulted in an underestimation of the importance of parks as a focus for social tensions. Similarly, the variety of ways in which those tensions were expressed has been unappreciated.

In the first part of this paper evidence for landscape reorganisation associated with imparkment was taken from both archaeological and documentary sources, evidence for criminal response to that disturbance is however almost entirely documentary and the data restricted to those cases which were brought to trial. Disorder and violence associated with parks varied both in the severity of that action and the sector of society participating, this results in reference to those actions appearing at various "levels" in the judicial system from manorial courts to Star Chamber. This makes a complete study of park-related violence extremely difficult. In addition to this, not all of the courts with responsibilities for park-related crime are present throughout the period under consideration and changes in the popularity or perceived effectiveness of certain courts also resulted in fluctuations in the number of incidents brought before that court.[3]

King (1982) has argued that any analysis based on only one type of court but dealing with a crime which might be adjudicated at others will be distorted, particularly in terms of frequency. An analysis which aimed to look quantitatively at the incidence of park-focused disorder regionally or nationally would have to tackle an enormous range and wealth of court documents both local and national. Assessment of the relative frequency of each type of crime, i.e. was small-scale poaching more or less frequent than group park breaks, is also hampered by these problems. Differential preservation of the records of these different courts also makes any quantitative analysis extremely difficult (if not impossible). This paper is therefore concerned not with the absolute frequency of park-related crime but instead with the types of disorder represented in Cambridgeshire and Huntingdonshire and their relationship with the initial act of imparkment.

Table 1 is a list of currently known instances of park-related disorder in Cambridgeshire and Huntingdonshire based on a variety of primary and secondary sources as referenced within the table. For this area very few manorial court rolls have been transcribed as yet, although examples can be selected from the work of de Windt (1990) and Coleman (1984 and forthcoming). Quarter sessions records do not survive prior to the mid-seventeenth century (with the exception of the

Isle of Ely which are intermittent from 1607) and assize records, whilst extant, have not yet been calendared for the Norfolk circuit (of which Cambridgeshire is part). Despite this unpromising circumstance the detail provided by the cases listed in Table 1 has enabled a more detailed analysis and categorisation of park-related disorder to take place than has been attempted previously. This has then been combined with further examples on specific types of disorder and conflict from a wider area, as provided by national records for various courts, and a category suggested for each recorded incidence. These categories are as follows: i. poaching[4] by single persons or small groups (under 3) carried out by non-gentry; ii. poaching carried out by gentry and nobility as single persons or small groups; iii. peasant-led group park breaks including diverse actions such as tree felling, fishing, and assault but typified by breaking down of park pale; iv. gentry/nobility-led group park breaks including diverse actions such as tree felling, fishing and assault but typified by breaking down of park pale; v. park breaks, usually by single persons or small groups, to gain or regain resources such as underwood, pannage etc.; vi. park breaks by groups of various sizes to recover animals impounded within the park.

Categories have been partially based on historically contemporary legal definition with the addition of distinctions based on the social class and number of the perpetrators. Although these social distinctions were not explicitly recognised in the law code of the time they are indicated by the appearance of "similar" disorders at different courts dependent on the social status of the accused. These categories are thus defined by the nature, scale and social origin of the disorder. This in turn enables identification of those acts which appear to be a direct response to imparkment, the aim of this paper being not merely to distinguish different types of park-related disorder but to further examine these as responses to the disruption of social relations brought about by the imparkment. Analysis also allows us to distinguish those acts which appear to have as their basis violence against the concepts of private land or the breakdown of social "custom".

In contemporary law, gatherings of more than three people could be prosecuted under a charge of "riotous assembly" and technically there is some overlap here between small groups which appear to have been brought together for poaching expeditions and those prosecuted for "assembly". However, records of the assize courts for the Home Circuit for the latter part of the sixteenth century suggest that, by that period, the accusation of "riotous assembly" was usually only made when activities other than poaching took place within the park, i.e.

Table 1. Park conflicts in Cambridgeshire and Huntingdonshire, 1200–1556.

Parish	park date	crime date	source	details	category
Alconbury	1234	1255	Select Pleas of the Forest (Turner, G. J. 1901, 23)	entrails of deer found in park, possibly poached from forest	i or ii
Kingston	1269	1269	Cal. Pat. Rolls 1266-72, 388	park break, poaching of deer, few details (first mention of this park)	i or ii
Camps, Castle	1263 subsequent enlargement	1283	Cal Pat Rolls 1281-92, 97	park break, poaching of deer, few details	i or ii
Buckden	1214	1286	Hunts Eyre Roll (de Windt 1981, 343)	removal of other resources; two young boys found collecting fallen branches in park	v
Great Staughton (Dillington)	1271	1286	Hunts Eyre Roll (de Windt 1981, 334)	removal of "beasts", possibly poaching but "beasts" unspecified	i/ii/iv
Southoe	1235	1286	Hunts Eyre Roll (de Windt 1981, 333)	recovery/theft of ox from park, single person	vi
Gamlingay	1289	1289	Cal Inq Misc, vol. 1, 1219-1307, no. 1478	poaching of deer, few details (first mention of this park)	i/ii
Doddington	1222	1298	Cal Pat Rolls 1292-1301, 355	park trespass, few details (named culprit, Walter de Spalding)	?
Somersham	1279	1301	Cal Pat Rolls 1292-1301, 626	park break and burning fence, culprits not named but appears to be a group park break	iv/v
Doddington	1222	1302	Cal Pat Rolls 1301-07, 42	park break, no details (named culprit, William de Colne)	v
Ramsey	1280	1305	Court Rolls (de Windt 1981)	poaching (peasantry?), five men, appears to have taken place with connivence of keeper	i
Somersham	1279	1306	Cal Pat Rolls 1301-07, 446	park trespass and burning of fences, few details (named culprit, Phillip L'archer)	iii
Elm (Coldham)	1308	1308	Cal Pat Rolls 1307-13, 89	park break, hunt and carry away game, few details (this is the only mention of the park)	iii
Castle Camps	1263 subsequent enlargement	1313	Cal Pat Rolls 1313-17, 63	group park break, fell trees, fish, etc. (by Edmund de Gegdinge and others)	iii/iv
Great Staughton	1271	1316	Cal Pat Rolls 1313-17, 427	park break, no details, cuplrits unknown	iii/iv
Great Staughton	1271	1316	Cal Pat Rolls 1313-17, 591	group park break, hunting of deer	iv
Kirtling	1086/1319	1319	Cal Pat Rolls 1317-21, 469	group park break, including servants of de Vere	iv
Glatton	1218	1334	Cal Pat Rolls 1330-34, 561	group park break to recover animals impounded, culprits include reeve and parson	vi

[150]

Table 1 (cont.). *Park conflicts in Cambridgeshire and Huntingdonshire, 1200–1556.*

Parish	park date	crime date	source	details	category
Ramsey	1280	1335	Court Rolls, (de Windt 1990)	park break, single person	v
Buckworth	1279	1343	Cal Pat Rolls 1343–45, 168	factional group park break, including assault led by John fitz Richard	iv
Isle of Ely	–	1357	Cal Pat Rolls 1354–58, 500	group park break with fishing and tree felling; probably more than one park and more than one occasion, during vacancy of bishopric	iii/iv
Ramsey	1280	1370	Court Rolls (de Windt 1990)	"opening the close of the lord's park", single person	v/vi
Kirtling	1086/1319	1374	Cal Pat Rolls 1370–74, 493	gentry led group park break concerned with hunting and other game (named culprit, William de Clopton)	iv
Ramsey	1280	1382	Court Rolls (de Windt 1990)	breach of lord's park, single person	v/vi
Somersham	1279	1385	Cal Pat Rolls 1381–85, 600	group park break with trees felled, servants assaulted, etc.	iii/vi
Ramsey	1280	1382	Court Rolls (de Windt 1990)	park breaks by single person (the miller), four times	v/vi
Kirtling	1086/1319	1410	Dr Lewis, pers. comm. PRO CP 40/595 rot. 28	Ralph Parker and others accused of forcible entry and hunting without permissioin in park of Richard Beauchamp	iii
Ramsey	1280	1382	Court Rolls (de Windt 1990)	park break and rescue of cattle impounded there, single person	vi
Ramsey	1280	1382	Court Rolls (de Windt 1990)	park entry to take wood, single person	v
Castle Camps	1263 subsequent enlargement	1526	In Parsons 1914, 3	group park break and assault; gentry-led with 300 persons (!); factional, related to further park breaks in another county; also reference to other park breaks (no details) from 1530 to 1534	iv
Great Staughton Rushoe and Whitley	1536	1554	STAC, Bundle vi, 77	group park break and assault, gentry-led, factional	iv
Castle Camps	1263 subsequent enlargement	1526	STAC, Bundle vii, 16; Parsons 1914	group park break and assault; gentry-led, factional	iv
Little Downham	1221	1310–1374	Court Rolls 1310–74; in Coleman 1984	various, poaching, trespass, etc., no details given (awaiting transcription, Coleman forth.)	various

1. Ramsey court roll references to the "common" park are not included.
2. References to non-park related poaching (such as that within the Gamlingay Court Rolls) are not included.

[151]

assault or destruction. There are exceptions to this, as in the early 1570s when three labourers were accused of "illicit assembly and trespass" for entering the Petworth park and "trampling the grass".[5] These categories of crime and disorder are predominantly peasant-based with the exception only of categories ii and iv. However, due to the better preservation and availability of national court records, discussion in the past has focused almost entirely on gentry led actions (e.g. Hanawalt 1975, Birrell 1982) and extremely little attention given to peasant-led disorder or attempts to regain or recover resources. Poaching at all levels has always been a popular subject particularly in discussions of the definition of "social crime" (Hobsbawn 1972; Emmison 1970).

DISCUSSION AND CASE STUDIES

i. Poaching by single persons or small groups (usually under three) carried out by non-gentry

This type of park-related crime commonly appears in several records including those of manorial and assize courts. Full descriptions given in these accounts allow us to establish a pattern for this activity. The assize records for the Elizabethan period for the Home Circuit (Sussex, Essex, Kent, Surrey, and Hertfordshire) contain many examples of small-scale peasant poaching,[6] involving between one and five people. Larger groups than this (technically over three) could be prosecuted under riotous assembly. The crime almost always took place at night and usually only single deer were taken. Poaching of rabbits from warrens within parks also took place.[7] Prosecutions in the assize courts for this type of crime are overwhelmingly of "yeoman" or "husbandmen" at least by the sixteenth century, although there is evidence for occasional overlap into gentry-led poaching, and this will be examined below.

Physical violence is rarely associated with this type of crime but social antagonism created by the constant flaunting of the strict game laws at both this and later periods has been well documented (Munsche 1981; Thompson 1975). Poaching may be considered as subsistence-related crime, as protest "social" crime (responding to the imposition of imparkment) or just a form of theft. In fact most poaching appears to lie somewhere between these. Emmison (1970) has suggested that, at least during the Elizabethan period (1550–1602), "there is little to suggest that the poorer poachers were driven after disastrous harvests to seek animal protein where it could be found."

Whilst Birrell (1982) supports the division of poaching into peasant-led and gentry on the grounds that peasant poaching had its own characteristic motives and techniques. Transcribed records of peasant led poaching in Cambridgeshire are at present not sufficient to indicate whether this type of action embodied a strong "social" element. On some occasions this type of poaching appears to have little to differentiate it from poaching outside parks, as recorded in the Gamlingay Court Rolls for the manor of Merton (Cambridgeshire) in the fifteenth century (Brown, pers. comm.) and it must be questioned whether the park is incidental to the main crime; the combined elements of game taking and disregard of land ownership being also present outside of the park. The Merton Rolls, for example, record cases of prosecution for "being common poachers and fence breakers" or "breaking the hedges of the lord and tenants" outside of the park area.[8]

ii. Poaching carried out by gentry and nobility as single persons or small groups

Gentry-led poaching and general park-related disorder has been the subject of considerable discussion and analysis in the past due, in part, to the greater availability of records recording this type of crime. However, there is little evidence that poaching (as opposed to park breaking) was committed with any frequency by individuals or very small groups of gentry. The few documented small-scale poaching activities do not appear to have led to physical violence with any frequency. The lack of evidence for this category may be connected with the role of the "familia" in gentry and nobility society during this period, so that activities were rarely undertaken without a considerable retinue. This would suggest that the park-breaking category for gentry-led activities may encompass both the factional elements and a poaching element – the latter of which would, in the lower classes, be undertaken by individuals or smaller groups.

iii. Peasant-led group park breaks, including diverse actions such as tree felling, fishing and assault but typified by breaking down of park pale

This type of crime is usually described by contemporary chroniclers as involving both park breaking and riotous assembly. It was considered a serious enough disorder to merit a commission for oyer and terminer,[9] rather than merely being tried within the manorial court system.

Somersham park (Huntingdonshire) was originally created by the Bishops of Ely in 1279 and appears to have been a focus of conflict and park breaks throughout the fourteenth century. The first group park break recorded here was in 1301 when the "hay" of the park was broken and burnt by a group of "malefactors" and deer and hares carried away. In 1306 an indictment was brought against Philip Larcher for non-appearance following burning of the fences. Given the five-year gap this is most likely to be a separate park break. Significantly, Larcher was only accused of fence burning and trespass, not of removal of any game. A further incident took place in 1385 when servants were assaulted and timber felled and removed in addition to game being taken. The licence to enlarge the park at Somersham in 1390[10] indicates that this involved encroachment on the rest of the parish. The licence of 1390 gave permission for the inclusion of a further 36 acres in addition to the initial 200 acre imparkment, and by 1650 the park included a staggering 621 acres of the parish of 4,000 acres, with much of the rest of the parish being technically "chase".

Neave (1991, 12) interprets the breaking down of the park pale by peasants at Leaconfield, eastern Yorkshire, as stealing of wood rather than an attack on the park itself, although she does consider some poaching incidents (notably at Beverley, eastern Yorkshire) as "deliberate expressions of discontent" over loss of land or common rights.

Many of the cases of gentry-led park breaks were carried out with the predominant and, indeed, active participation of the local tenantry. For example at Wilstrop (Yorkshire) following depopulation for park creation, a force of 200 tenants attacked the park and uprooted the pale and hedge on several occasions. Although the raids were led by some of the local gentry, and therefore on superficial examination would be categorised as "gentry park breaks", the context of the attacks and the numbers of peasants involved suggest a "popular" protest (Beresford 1957 in Stamper 1988, 147). There is no doubt that on many occasions of park break appearing in the Patent Rolls although local gentry appear as figure heads the mass of the break was carried out by a retinue of local peasants and tenants. In these cases, we may be able to detect an overlap between popular protest and factional feuding, the two very different types of social conflict being focused on one physical feature. For the gentry involved, the park represented increasing privilege and status of the opposing faction, and a relatively easy target of attack, whilst for the accompanying peasants it was the physical embodiment of the ideological attack on common rights and resources. The frequent concentration of the assault on the park pale or fence suggests aggression being focused on the symbol of exclusion, the boundary between private and public. It is to be noted that complaints

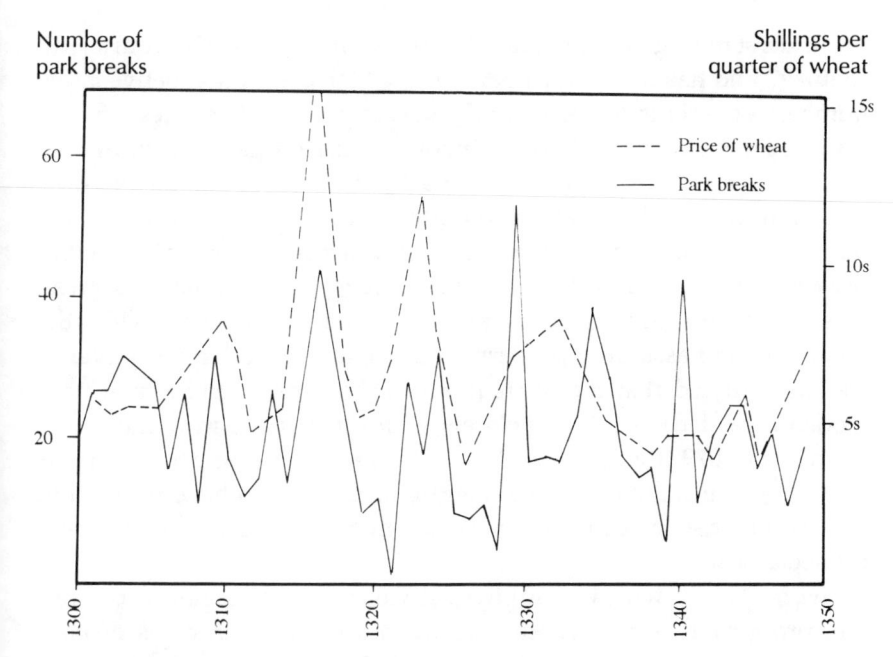

Figure 1. Park breaks recorded within the Calendar for Patent Rolls compared with the price of wheat in the county of Norfolk, 1300–1348.

of "hedge or fence breaking" outside of parks were also often made and these acts were held to be serious attacks on the established social fabric of the landscape.

In many cases it can be difficult to establish whether a park break was gentry- or peasant-led, or indeed how many people were involved in the attack. Many commissions of oyer and terminer refer only to "malefactors" whilst others name the supposed leader of the attack but no more. In many cases it must be assumed that the names were unknown to the (complainant), and such seems to have been the case for example at Great Staughton described below, where Sir Oliver Leader submitted that the "whole names and dwelling places [of the culprits] are ... as yet unknown."[11]

The suggestion that "gentry park breaks" frequently combined with more "popular" revolt could help explain the close link between years of famine and hardship and peaks in commissions for oyer and terminer resulting from park breaks in the early to mid-fourteenth century. Figure 1 compares the number of park breaks resulting in commissions of oyer and terminer for the period 1300–1348 with the price of wheat for the area of Norfolk in those years.[12] Hanawalt (1979) has argued that "it is agricultural production that will provide the key

[155]

to understanding fluctuations in crime for the early fourteenth century" and has produced a particularly high correlation between the number of criminal cases and wheat prices. If entries in the commissions of oyer and terminer solely reflected gentry disorder we may presume these would not fluctuate with years of famine and high prices, however the peak in reported park conflicts in 1315–1316 mirrors a peak in price of wheat as does, to a lesser extent, a secondary peak in the early 1320s. This link would suggest that some park break episodes may be regarded as "subsistence" related, with the accompanying assault to property and persons secondary, however, it should be noted that the fluctuations in the general crime rate (non-foodstuff related) also tallies closely with fluctuations in wheat prices (Hanawalt 1979, fig. 12). Social disorder resulting from these periods of economic instability and hardship thus appears to have resulted in both an increase in crime in general and in park-focused conflict across the social scale.

The frequency with which physical violence and assault to persons and property is encountered is substantially higher in cases of park break than for poaching incidents, both for peasant- and gentry-led cases. With reference to violent crimes amongst local communities King (1982) has drawn a distinction between group attacks and individual assaults based on the records of the court leet. He suggests that group attacks are typified by being planned whereas assault involving only a couple of individuals may suggest spontaneity. In the case of park-related violence this would imply that group park breaks are planned conflict whereas the physical violence occasionally documented for small-scale poaching incidents is the result of an unexpected encounter. Both types of conflict involve violence towards property but only group park breaks involve purposeful physical assault.

iv. Gentry/nobility-led group park breaks, including diverse actions such as tree felling, fishing and assault but typified by breaking down of the park pale

This category is the most commonly violent form of park-focused conflict in terms of injury both to persons and property. As discussed above, ease of access to transcribed national records have resulted in a predominance of studies of this type of crime for this period and the relative frequency of this type of crime is most probably over-emphasised. However, gentry-led park breaks were undoubtedly fairly common and at certain periods appear to have reached an almost epidemic scale nationally with over two hundred documented in some decades

[156]

Number of park breaks

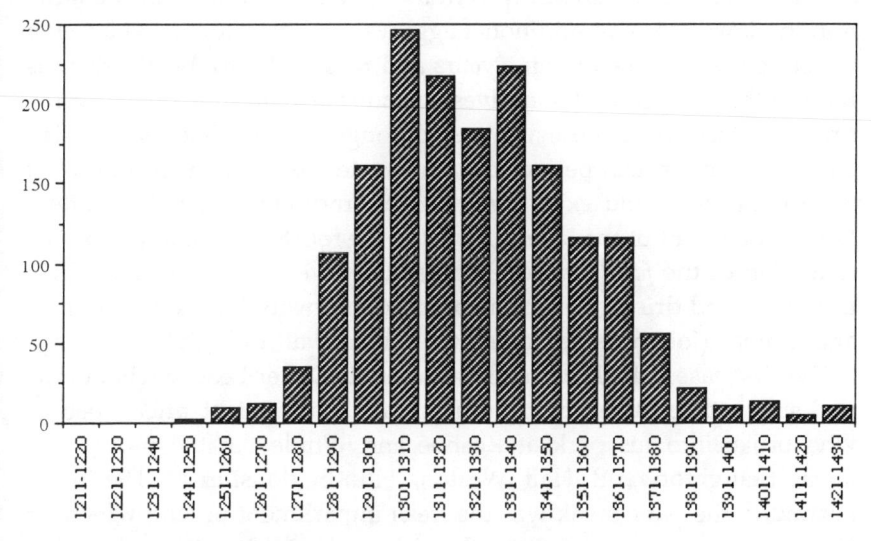

Figure 2. Park breaks recorded within the Calendar for Patent Rolls per decade for the period 1210–1430.

of the fourteenth century (Figure 2). In Cambridgeshire and Huntingdonshire there are seven definite cases of this type of crime known between the thirteenth and mid-seventeenth centuries, and a further six where the gentry status of the group leader is suspected, it is possible that more await recovery as present research on Patent Rolls only extends to the mid-fifteenth century. Much of the violence in this type of disorder was focused on the landscape of the park itself. The park pale, fences, hays, trees and stews were often destroyed along with the deer and other livestock contained within the park. Assault on the parker, or other servants of the household was frequent, particularly in cases where the house of the parker or a manorial dwelling was located within the park.

In addition to the standardised reporting of this type of disorder within the Patent Rolls, several excellent and detailed descriptions of park breaking survive as records of cases that went as far as Star Chamber[13] and these act as examples of the type and degree of violence associated with this crime. These cases, and those recorded in the Patent Rolls, demonstrate a high level of mob violence and tension focused on the private area of the park and sometimes appear, as in the case of Rushoe, Huntingdonshire, to be specifically in response to recent imparkment. The main motive for this type of disorder appear to be factional feuding amongst the gentry (and this may be particularly relevant for the sixteenth century[14]) with discontent at the strict hunting laws being an additional aggravation. Despite the evidence of the close link between famine years and recorded park breaks there is little within the cases themselves to indicate that subsistence was a primary objective in these assaults; although it is possible that subsistence poaching in this period may have extended further up the social scale than we would expect. A contemporary chronicler drew attention to the plight of the lay magnates in the fourteenth century and the reduction of the *familia* who "because they were unsuited to a life of little food and drink . . . became parched and were thus led to murder and rapine" (Johannes de Trokelowe in Hanawalt 1979, 251).

The first case I shall examine is that of Sir Oliver Leader who, in the mid-sixteenth century, brought a private case against fifteen people who broke into his park at Rushoe and Whitley in the parishes of Great Staughton and Hail Weston, Huntingdonshire.[15] The background to the park break was the fresh imparkment of land which Sir Oliver had acquired in 1539–1543. In his testimony Sir Oliver describes the area as being composed of "one hundrethe acres of pasture and one hundrethe acres of woodd with th'appurtenaunces" which he claims "tyme out of mynde hathe been emparked and replenyshed with dere". He goes on to state that about sixteen years previous he had rescoured the ditches and repaired the hedges and "made a great dyche and a quycke set aboute the same parke". Leader described the accused as coming "in most ryotouse and forcyble manner and agenste your peace . . . in warlyke manner arrayed" and identifies the leader as one Robert Sapcote "essquyuyer . . . man of great mysorder". Sapcote held the Hall Fee at Elton parish some sixteen miles north of Rushoe, a holding which had only been recognised as a manor in the late fifteenth century. The rest of the gang was composed of "yeoman", undoubtedly under the control of Sapcote, coming mainly from Elton and Yaxley with many unspecified. There is strong evidence that Robert Sapcote himself held a park in Elton, this is described as being "enlarged" in 1577[16] and is most likely to have been in existence since the late fifteenth century. The gang is described as having with it weapons, including cross bows, long bows, swords, bills, arrows and other "weapons of war" as well as more than seven brase of grey hounds. It is difficult to conceive that this was merely a hunting expedition, even an extremely well-equipped one. It was certainly unlikely to be an expedition which desired any degree of secrecy – thus contrasting with the much smaller, night time, poaching incidents.

The attack on the Rushoe and Whitley park does not appear to have the taking of deer as its primary motive but instead focuses on the park and its keeper; on arrival at the park it is recorded that the "ryotous persons" threw down a length of the hedge around the park and went immediately to the keeper's lodge where they attacked the keeper, his wife, and another of Leaders' servants. Following this they killed deer and drove off several cattle and two geldings. The deer were mostly left to rot in the ditches of the park – an action untypical of smaller poaching incidents. The *Victoria Counties History* entry concerning this riot notes that it was inspired by "adjoining tenants who claimed rights over [the imparked land]"[17] and I would concur with this. However, there also appears to be an element of factional feuding present. Although Oliver Leader was one of the Chancery clerks at the time of the riots he has been classed as "new gentry" whilst the aggressor, Robert Sapcote, was from a family whose manorial holding had only been recognised a couple of generations previously. Both the creation of the park by Leader and the aggressive response to it are typical of this period of intense social competition as outlined by Stone (1967).

The second case concerns the park of Castle Camps, Cambridgeshire. The case went to Star Chamber and both the plaintiff (Countess of Oxford) and defendant (Sir Giles Allington) were of gentry/nobility status. This case was transcribed in the early part of this century (Parsons 1914) and it is this secondary source which has been used here.

Both the plaintiff and defendant held parks; Sir Giles created a park around his hall at Horseheath in 1448[18] and this had been further enlarged in 1550.[19] On both occasions a licence had been obtained for this imparkment. The park of the Countess of Oxford had a much greater antiquity, being first mentioned in 1263[20] and enlarged subsequently.[21] The date of this enlargement is unsure although it was after 1331 and before 1450.[22] Parsons suggested that feuding between the two parties may have been caused by the Countess obtaining the nearby Nosterfield Priory Farm in 1538 for further enlargement of her park, an area which Parsons (1914, 5) believed Sir Giles wanted for his park. However, it should be noted that this area lay some distance from the southern edge of the known maximum Horseheath Park.

This park break followed a similar pattern to that at Rushoe and Whitley; the attack took place at night, approximately a dozen men were involved, all under the control of Sir Giles Allington, although not led by him. The park boundary was forcibly broken and swords, bows and arrows were used both to attack the deer and to assault the keeper and other servants of the Countess. One of the men employed by Sir Giles on this occasion had previously worked for the countess within her park and it is claimed that Sir Giles had "exhorted [him] to leve my ladye of Oxford's service, saying . . . that yf he contyneuyd in hit, he would be slayne" (Parsons 1914, 19).

The third case is of a considerably earlier date but similar in its pattern. In 1343[23] the park at Buckworth, held by John Mauduit of Weremynstre, was broken by a number of people led by one John fitz Richard. Fitz Richard had two years previous witnessed the deed that released the manor at Buckworth to John Mauduit. It was claimed that the Mauduit family had originally entered unlawfully into the manor previously held in the family of John fitz Richard. This case may be a combination of factional feuding by the gentry involved whilst the "gang" were motivated by a more general discontent focused on the park. In addition to hunting and, in this case, carrying away deer, the accused also broke the house and assaulted the servants of John Mauduit carrying away other goods. That the assault resulted in "the loss of their service for a great while" suggests a severe physical assault, though this comment is often recorded in oyer and terminer commissions and may be justificatory for bringing a case. The park at Buckworth was by no means a new creation by the mid-fourteenth century, being mentioned in the Hundred Rolls in 1279[24] and the park break may therefore have been motivated by more recent aggravations of social relations, the aggressive physical response to which was then focused on the park.

These three cases, although displaying similarities in terms of numbers and class of peoples involved, type and focus of aggression, display apparently different combinations of motives. Factional feuding, social discord and anger at loss of resources are all present. Examination of the many hundreds of entries in the Patent Rolls of other park break episodes suggests that at certain periods an element of subsistence poaching may also be present, in particular when gentry-led outlaw bands are involved (such as the Coteral or Folville gangs documented by Bellamy (1964) and Stones (1957)). A further aspect, which there is no space to examine in detail here, is the involvement of members of the lower gentry and religious orders, for whom hunting of any kind was in direct conflict with the strict social hierarchy regulating this activity.

v. Park breaks, usually by single persons or small groups, to gain or regain resources such as underwood or pannage

This type of park-related crime was typically carried out by one or two persons and is exclusively a peasant crime.

It is most usually recorded within manorial court rolls and rarely involved physical violence, except in those cases where the perpetrators were unexpectedly discovered by the parker. It is perhaps one of the most important "social crimes" associated with parks as the imposition of private enclosed land conflicted with common rights and resources. A typical example of this crime is included in the Ramsey View of Frankpledge in 1460 where John Water was amerced for entering the lord's park and "carrying off wood and undergrowth" (de Windt 1990). A further example is found in the Huntingdonshire Eyre Rolls of 1286, where two young boys are recorded as having been collecting the fallen branches in the Buckden park when they were discovered by the parker. It is probable that the large number of pigs which "invaded" the Downham park in the mid-fourteenth century, rather than accidentally straying into the park, were in fact "directed" there by owners intent on regaining pannage and thus provides another example of this type of social conflict (Coleman 1984, 34).

This is a very different crime from the large group park breaks in which timber was cut and taken and entire trees removed. Instead, it suggests the illicit continuation of previously held rights of *haybote* or *housebote* which would have been present prior to imparkment. Thus the conflict is between the newly established social and economic order and customary social practice. Following the Statute of Merton in 1232 it was the duty of the lord of the manor to compensate any loss of common land and rights following enclosure, but it seems that this was not strictly adhered to. In some cases, such as at Burrough Green (Cambridgeshire) where the entirety of the main woodland was imparked, there was little or no alternative source of wood or pannage.

This type of disorder might be classed either as a "social crime" (illicit regaining of common rights) or as straightforward theft. It must be remembered that in some cases a park may have been in existence for several generations prior to the crime being committed. Although a constant source of irritation to the manorial tenants, these cases cannot be seen as direct action with the intention of regaining recently held rights. Where this type of crime is recorded in Cambridgeshire and Huntingdonshire punishments were not usually severe. In the Downham case outlined above the ammercements were 2d a piglet, while the fine for the case of John Water at Ramsey was only 1d. In common with other categories involving small numbers of people, violence appears to rarely be associated with this sort of crime, except when park officials were encountered. Occasional examples of physical assault are found, for example in the 1286 Buckden case, which appeared at the Eyre not as a result of the initial crime but as a result of the boy's death following the beating he received from the park keeper when they were unexpectedly disturbed.

vi. Park breaks by groups of various sizes to "recover" animals or other belongings impounded within the park.

The retrieval of animals impounded within a park involved both trespass and park break and in some cases could verge on the riotous activity which we have seen associated with full park breaking. Words for "park" and "pound" can be easily misread in the original Latin – particularly when heavily abbreviated – resulting in problems with the examination of records of this type of conflict. The terms p̄cum and p̄cam are occasionally noted in "inappropriate" contexts or associations, the frequent references to breaking the "common park" in the translation of the Ramsey, Bury and Hepmangrove court rolls is a case in point.[25] Recovery of animals within the park would usually be tried in the manorial courts. For example, in the Ramsey View of Frankpledge for 1429 it is recorded that John Newman was fined 3d for breaking into the lord's park and taking away cattle detained there. At Southoe a bull/ox was "foraged" from the park in 1286 and this may be another example of this type of crime, although the rather severe punishment (the culprit was hanged) may indicate that the animal in fact belonged to the park holder.[26] In other cases animals that were detained within the park could be driven off as part of a more general park break of the sort discussed in the previous section. In 1334 at Glatton, Huntingdonshire, more than twenty people were involved in the recovery of impounded cattle from the park. These included the bailiff and parson from the adjoining parish of Denton. This action appears to have developed into full-scale "riot" as goods and livestock in excess of the original cattle were taken (a total of twelve horses and sixty-six cattle as well as "goods") and servants were assaulted. The conflict was judged to be sufficiently severe for a request of oyer and terminer.[27]

These last two types of disturbance (v and vi) have common elements, such as the social position of the culprits and the (usual) mildness of punishment. However, they contrast in their concept of the focal area of the disorder. Attempted continuation of common rights appears to indicate a dissatisfaction with the status of the imparked area whereas the recovery of impounded animals disputes the process which has put them there[28] but does not appear to comment directly on the right to impark. In both cases, however, there is conflict resulting from refusal to accept the imposed social and economic order.

Conclusion

In this paper I have examined the "park" as a focus of social tensions and violence. Evidence for the impact of landscape reorganisation has been drawn from both primary documentation and fieldwork whilst primary and secondary documentation records the numerous acts of reactive aggression directed at landowners, park keepers and parks themselves. This violence is evidenced not only in the social and economic conflict created during initial imparkment, but continued through the lifetime of the park as it became the focus for social disturbance and disorder. I have suggested that this social disorder may be categorised according to both the group size and social origin of the perpetrators and, further, by their motives. Whilst I recognise the existence of social tensions which led up to the creation of the park these have been deemed to be beyond the scope of this essay.

In his discussion of crime and social disorder Hobsbawn defined "social crime" as one in which "acts of law breaking have a distinct element of social protest in them or when they are closely linked with the development of social and political unrest" (Hobsbawm 1972, 5–6). It has been argued here that application of this definition would result in the inclusion of several categories of park-related violence and disorder within the category of "social crime". In those cases of group park break where it appears unlikely that the attack was carried out by local peasants we must consider whether, in order to be considered as a form of social crime or conflict, the action has to be carried out by those directly affected. It could be argued that the act of imparkment generally was sufficiently widespread as to initiate response at a more general level as with later enclosure episodes. Figures for Cambridgeshire and Huntingdonshire, for example, indicate that over the 350-year period considered approximately one parish in every four was affected directly by imparkment.

Imparkment can thus be seen to have not only exacerbated economic stress and social conflict at a local level but also resulted in worsening social relations as power struggles occurred both within and between social groups at local and regional level. This in turn led to actual physical violence in the form of assault on persons and destruction of property and game, actions which engendered further social conflict and alienation. At certain periods during the thirteenth to seventeenth centuries this conflict appears to have reached almost epidemic proportions with aggression rooted in a wide range of social and economic ills taking the park as their focus.

Acknowledgements

Thanks are due to Steve Kemp, Dr Lewis, J. Brown, Rosemary Hoppit and John Carman.

Notes

1. Imparkment of areas which led to diminution or termination of certain common rights, including access, was a "crime" in the stricter sense of "an act punishable of law" following the introduction of the Statute of Merton in 1232. However, there is little evidence for any adherence to this statute.
2. Social changes consequent on restructuring of settlement have been discussed by Roberts (1985) and Pred (1985).
3. For example, gentry-led park break cases were frequently brought to Star Chamber in the sixteenth and seventeenth centuries as part of the increasing popularity of litigation as an extension of gentry and nobility feuding at this period.
4. Emmison (1970, 232) notes that the legal term "poaching" does not appear until after 1600, previous to this references are made to "unlawful hunting".
5. Calendar of Home Circuit Assize Records, Sussex Circuit, case 469.
6. A typical set of entries concerning this type of crime, although slightly later than the period under consideration here, would be those in the Essex Assize Indictments for 1569, 1572, 1573, 1575, *passim* (entries 430, 585, 709, 854 respectively).
7. For example, Assize Records Essex, 3275, 3338.
8. MCR 5482 and 5486; Brown pers. comm.
9. Oyer and Terminer was a commission to "hear and determine" cases dealing with treasons, murders, insurrections and offences judged to be of a sufficiently serious or treasonable nature. Commissions were set up for each county and heard cases only for that county.
10. Cal. Pat. Roll 1388–92, 365.
11. STAC Bundle vi, 77.
12. Hanawalt does not give the figures for Cambridgeshire.
13. The Star Chamber was operating from its revival in 1487 until its final abolition in 1640. During this time cases that were allegedly endangering "the kings peace" could be brought before it, its main stated function being to curb disorder (Barnes 1962). All prosecutions were ostensibly made on the king's behalf although they were brought usually by private persons (Barnes 1962, 226) and a typical case would be one of riot, fraud, conspiracy or defamation. Barnes' discussion of the importance of the Star Chamber during the sixteenth century draws attention to the role of the court in the massive increase in private litigation in this period, often as part of a wider context of faction/feuding.
14. See for example, Stone's (1967) discussion of the crisis of the aristocracy from the mid-sixteenth to mid-seventeenth century.
15. Star Chamber minutes of 1554 STAC 4/6/77.

16. VCH Hunts. vol. iii, 154-58.
17. VCH Hunts. ii, 354.
18. BL Add Ms. 5834 f1. Coles Ms.
19. Cal. Pat. Roll 1549-1551, 402.
20. PRO C123/31/1 no. 6.
21. It has been suggested by Palmer and Fox, on the basis of plough acreage, that in fact the park at Castle Camps was present in 1086 but was not recorded in Domesday (Palmer and Fox 1924).
22. Cal. Inq. pm. viii 1331, 271; VCH Cambs. vi. 37-40.
23. Cal. Pat. Rolls 1343-1348, 168.
24. Rot. Hund. ii, 610-33.
25. E.g. 1533, item 14; 1594, item 4 and 5, the latter item making it clear that the hayward had responsibility for this "common park".
26. Hunts. Eyre Rolls, 1286, 449; in de Windt 1981, 333.
27. Cal. Pat. Rolls. 4 July 1334, p. 581.
28. Or, rather, the established process for recovery.

References

Astill, G. and Grant, A. (eds) 1988. *The Countryside of Medieval England.* Oxford, Blackwell.

Barnes, T. G. 1962. Due process and slow process in the late Elizabethan-early Stuart Star Chamber. *American Journal of Legal History* 6, 221-49.

Bellamy, J. G. 1973. *Crime and Public Order in England in the Later Middle Ages.* London, Routledge and Kegan Paul.

Bellamy, J. G. 1964. The Coterel gang: an anatomy of a band of fourteenth-century criminals. *English Historical Review* 79, 698-717.

Birrell, J. 1982. Who poached the kings deer? A study in thirteenth century crime. *Midland History* 7, 9-25.

Bushaway, R. W. 1992. Rite, legitimation and community. In B. Stapleton (ed.), *Conflict and Community in Southern England,* 110-34. Stroud, Alan Sutton.

Cockburn, J. S. (ed.) 1977. *Crime in England 1550-1800.* London, Methuen.

Coleman, M. C. 1984. *Downham in the Isle: A Study of an Ecclesiastical Manor in the Thirteenth and Fourteenth Centuries.* Woodbridge, Suffolk, The Boydell Press.

Emmison, F. G. 1970. *Elizabethan Life; Disorder.* Essex County Council (Essex Record Office Publication no. 56).

Hanawalt, B. A. 1974. Economic influences on the pattern of crime in England 1300-1348. *The American Journal of Legal History* 18, 281-97.

Hanawalt, B. A. 1975. Fur-collar crime: the pattern of crime among the fourteenth century English nobility. *Journal of Social History* 8, 1-17.

Hanawalt, B. A. 1979. *Crime and Conflict in English Communities 1300-1348.* Cambridge, Mass., Harvard Univ. Press.

Hare, J. N. 1992. The lords and their tenants: conflict and stability in fifteenth century Wiltshire. In B. Stapleton (ed.), *Conflict and Community in Southern England,* 16-34. Stroud, Alan Sutton.

Hilton, R. 1990. *Class Conflict and the Crisis of Feudalism,* 2nd ed. London, Verso.

Hobsbawn, E. J. 1972. Distinction between socio-political and other forms of crime. *Society for the Study of Labour History Bulletin* 25, 5–6.

Kaeuper, R. W. 1979. Law and order in fourteenth century England: the evidence of special commissions of oyer and terminer. *Speculum* 54, 734–84.

King, W. J. 1982. Untapped resources for social historians: court leet records. *Journal of Social History* 15, 699–705.

Maitland, F. W. and Bailden, W. P. (eds) 1891. *The Court Baron and the Court Rolls of Littleport*. London, Seldon Society (iv).

Miller, E. and Hatcher, J. 1978. *Medieval England – Rural Society and Economic Change 1086–1348*. London, Longman.

Munsche, P. B. 1981. *Gentlemen and Poachers: The English Game Laws 1671–1831*. Cambridge, University Press.

Neave, S. 1991. *Medieval Parks of East Yorkshire*. Hull, Hutton Press (Centre for Regional and Local History, University of Hull).

Palmer, W. M. and Fox, C. 1924. *Shudy Camps, Castle Camps and Waltons Park, Ashdon*. Reprinted from the Cambridge Chronicle. Held at CRO.

Parsons, C. E. 1914. A poaching affray at Castle Camps in 1556. *Transactions of the Cambridgeshire and Hunts. Archaeological Society* 3, 1–22.

Pred, A. 1985. The social becomes the spatial, the spatial becomes the social: enclosures, social change and the becoming of places in Skåne. In D. Gregory and J. Urry (eds), *Social Relations and Spatial Structures*, 338–65. Basingstoke, Macmillan.

Roberts, B. K. 1985. Village patterns and forms. In D. Hooke (ed.), *Medieval Villages*, 7–25. Oxford, Oxford University Committee for Archaeology (Monograph no. 5).

Sharpe, J. A. 1984. *Crime in Early Modern England 1550–1750*. London, Longman.

Stamper, P. 1988. Woods and parks. In G. Astill and A. Grant (eds), *The Countryside of Medieval England*, 128–48. Oxford, Blackwell.

Stapleton, B. (ed.) 1992. *Conflict and Community in Southern England*. Stroud, Alan Sutton.

Stone, L. 1967. *The Crisis of the Aristocracy 1558–1641*, abridged edition. Oxford, University Press.

Stones, E. L. G. 1957. The Folvilles of Ashby Folville, Leicestershire and their associates in crime. *Transactions of the Royal Historical Society* 5th series 7, 117–36.

Thompson, E. P. 1975. *Whigs and Hunters: The Origin of the Black Act*. London, Allen Lane.

Turner, G. J. 1901. *Select Pleas of the Forest*. London, Selden Society.

Watts, D. G. 1992. Popular disorder in southern England 1250–1450. In B. Stapleton (ed.), *Conflict and Community in Southern England*, 1–13. Stroud, Alan Sutton.

Way, T. 1994. Parks, Pales and Privatisation. Unpublished PhD dissertation, University of Cambridge.

Williamson, T. and Bellamy, L. 1987. *Property and the Landscape*. London, George Philip.

de Windt, A. R. and de Windt, E. B. 1981. *Royal Justice and the Medieval English Countryside*. Toronto, Pontifical Institute of Medieval Studies.

de Windt, E. B. (ed. and trans.) 1990. *The Court Rolls of Ramsey, Hepmangrove and Bury 1268–1600*. Toronto, Pontifical Institute of Medieval Studies.

8

Violence and the Face

Carmen Lange

According to II Kings 15: 19–20, the king of Israel, Menahem, "gave Pul [Tiglath-Pileser III] a thousand talents of silver . . . to confirm the kingdom in his hand. . . . Menahem exacted the money of Israel, even of all the mighty men of wealth, of each man fifty shekels of silver to give to the King of Assyria. So the king of Assyria turned back, and stayed not there in the land." When Tiglath-Pileser III (king of Assyria 747–727 BC) left Israel, his face was picked out and destroyed from the Dolomite relief (now in the Israel Museum, Jerusalem) left behind in the Zagros mountains as a symbol of his passage.

The Assyrian king Sennacherib recorded his total annihilation of Babylon with the words (quoted by L. Mumford 1961):

> The city and [its] houses from its foundation to its top, I destroyed, I devastated, I burned with fire. The wall and the outer wall, temple and gods, temple towers of bricks and earth as many as they were, I razed and dumped them into the Arakhtu Canal. Through the midst of that city I dug canals, I flooded its site with water, and the very foundation of it I destroyed. I made its destruction more complete than that by a flood.

After Sennacherib was assassinated by two of his sons, who fled to Ararat to escape reprisals (II Kings 19: 37) and were pursued there by Esarhaddon the heir apparent, the opportunity was taken to pick out his face, destroying it utterly, even though the image was on the palace wall reliefs (currently in the British Museum, London), thus supposedly "secure" rather than in a public place – as was the relief of Tiglath-Pileser III.

The bronze mask sometimes attributed as a likeness of Naram Sin, and currently in the Baghdad Museum, had one eye gouged out. Common theory holds this was to get at the purported "jewelled" eyes, but is nothing more than supposition, and does not explain the continued existence of the head at a time when metal was a valuable commodity, recycled for weaponry and other statuary.

The failure of a leader to provide what the people wants leads to anger, based upon humiliation and the shame at having somehow been "duped". History records that when the Italian Fascist leader, Mussolini, committed suicide his corpse was hung upside down from a gibbet. Mobbed, it was cut down and abused: men kicked and spat on it, women lifted their skirts and urinated on his face. In the case of the Assyrians, the only records currently available to us are the faces damaged by those whose anger led to acts of aggression against the only objects available to them: the stelae; the reliefs. These were images of the "god-king" – kings who, by reasons of power, politics and personal aggrandisement, proclaimed themselves as working solely on the gods' behalf while pursuing their own aims. Therefore, when the king fell, the god had been failed and the people, to dissociate themselves, reviled their ruler to regain the merit of their gods.

Defacements such as these were deliberate and directed against the ruler personally rather than the palace as an emblem of rule since many instances exist of accompanying "winged Genii" and other attendants remaining unscathed while the face of the king has been systematically "picked out" with a stone or other tool.

Objects are safer and easier to destroy than authority figures. To destroy the evidence of a person's existence is to symbolically wipe out that person. Beliefs in ancient Egypt, for example, included that destruction of all physical evidence, including references, to a person would obliterate them from memory, thus "destroying" the soul. It is possible that defacing Assyrian kings worked on a similar premise, using a ritual "magic" no longer available or understood by the modern world.

Archaeologically, little evidence exists to study the sociological effects of ancient warfare on the population involved, although a great deal has been written by and about the kings who led them, the armies they fought in and the commanders who ordered them to combat. While it is possible to recover evidence of destruction (siege ramps and arrow heads at Lachish) and to find evidence of the human activities involved (corpses clasping booty; Assyrian reliefs of families hiding to avoid capture), little notice has been taken by archaeologists of the impact on the ordinary population by warfare of the past. "Battles are deliberate, not chance, happenings" (Keegan 1976, 42) and "most wars are begun for reasons which have nothing to do with justice, have results quite different from those proclaimed as their objects, if indeed they have any clear-cut result at all, and visit during their course a great deal of casual suffering on the innocent" (Keegan 1976, 52).

Battles were a constant Assyrian threat. The Assyrians were expansionists whose empire, at its height, reached from Turkey almost to the borders of Egypt. For the Assyrian state, warfare was a necessity as long as it maintained its expansionist policies. As Tainter (1988) points out, once a conquest has been made there is a need to maintain and govern a captured society, which requires more wealth after the initial claim for booty than can be supplied by either the conquered or ruling society. This leads to the need for further warfare. Ultimately, war has to be taken into regions far distant from the homeland: this results in longer absences by the armies involved, with attendant resentments.

The Assyrians relied upon a force which was backed by those who could be called on as the need arose. These latter men, in exchange for what was termed an *"Ilku"* (a plot of land comprising house, garden and orchard), undertook to be available for military service when needed, and laws were formulated covering every possible eventuality from capture, to desertion, to death for both *Ilku*-holders and the families who remained on the land during the absence of the father or, in some case, eldest son. This suggests that *Ilku*-holders were of particular importance in Assyrian policy-making and war.

On the other hand, *Ilku*-holders were part of what Keegan (1976, 31) has termed "the almost universal illiteracy . . . of the common soldier of any century before the nineteenth." *Ilku*-holders, then, were in a similar position to the "modern" soldier: aware of the theory of their being called to fight, but not necessarily conversant with the practical aspects of leaving home and family, risking death, and facing the thought of their families becoming destitute without them. I believe these *Ilku*-holders, like volunteers of the First World ["Great"] War, were victims of state propaganda and, using S. L. A. Marshall's work with infantrymen fresh from combat which revealed that "even in 'highly motivated' units, and even when hard pressed, no more than about a quarter of all 'fighting' soldiers will use their weapons against the enemy" (Keegan 1976, 63), I believe *Ilku*-holders, where possible, undertook petty acts of revenge when they discovered war was not going to lead to the solutions and riches proposed by those who led them. Some of these acts of revenge can be seen in defaced monuments of rulers; their own or those of the opposition, for while "battle finds out the real strengths of individuals", the question remains – "How do you get subordinates to stand and fight when their instincts scream at them to run away?" (Keegan 1976, 10). The answer is that you do not, that resentment builds up until it explodes – in benign or malignant aggression depending on circumstances and personality.

Social psychologists and psychopathologists have long studied the causes and effects of violence among humans. Experiments with violence effectively demonstrate that (Aronson 1980, 173):

> when people are made angry, they frequently engage in overkill. ... The overkill produces dissonance ... there is a discrepancy between what the person did to you and the force of your retaliation. That discrepancy must be justified – and, just as in the "innocent victim" experiments, the justification takes the form of derogating the object of your wrath after you have hurt him.

This is what happened in the case of Assyrian images of the king.

Aronson (1980, 100) goes on to point out that "most people are motivated to justify their own actions, beliefs and feelings. When a person does something, he or she will try, if at all possible, to convince himself or herself (and others) that it was a logical, reasonable thing to do" and that "retaliation can reduce the need for aggression if something akin to equity has been restored" (p. 174). Destroying the image of a king can go a long way towards redressing the balance within a person's own conscience, while obviating the need to physically destroy another human being. It can also be a way to deal with unresolved "justification" when personal conscience clashes with political propaganda.

I believe the time is right for archaeologists to study the findings of other disciplines in order to more fully understand the effects of their physical findings. For example, a psychologist points out that "most human and animal actions are directed ... we walk and reach toward some objects, shrink and flee away from others" (Cleitman 1992, 47) and this might be borne in mind when considering the direction imposed onto the general populace by kings, military commanders and priests; all of whom have been responsible for causing wars. Invariably, however, as now, they relied on propagandist messages to incite the aggression of human beings.

The extent to which this aggression is, or has to be, expressed "depends very much on environmental conditions" (Scharfetter 1980, 207) rather than being innate and this understanding is echoed by Fromm (1973, 251), who concluded that only "defensive aggressiveness is 'built in' to the animal and human brain, and serves the function of defence against threats to vital interests." Fromm (1973, 224) further states the belief that

> War as an institution was a new invention, like kingdom or bureaucracy, made around 3000 BC. Then as now, it was not caused by psychological factors, such as human aggression, but, aside from the wishes for power and glory of kings and their bureaucracy, was the result of objective conditions that made war useful and which, as a consequence, tended to generate and increase human destructiveness and cruelty.

In this, he followed the views of V. G. Childe, who suggested that, when the need for more land arose, old settlers had to be taken away, replaced or dominated by the conquering group. Hence some sort of warfare must have been waged before the urban revolution had even begun. This, Childe (1936, 36) stated, could not be demonstrated by archaeological evidence: taking instead the position that in the prelude to the urban revolution, after 6000 BC "warfare has to be admitted, though only on a small scale and of a spasmodic kind." I, however, believe archaeology can demonstrate such theories, if we only know where to look, and learn to interpret the evidence correctly.

For example, the American army historical service during the Second World War undertook the first systematic study of human behaviour in combat, yielding (Keegan 1976, 46–47)

> remarkable results. Foremost . . . was the revelation that ordinary soldiers do not think of themselves, in life-and-death situations, as subordinate members of whatever formal military organisation it is to which authority has assigned them, but as equals within a very tiny group – perhaps no more than six or seven men. They are not exactly equals . . . because at least one of them will hold junior military rank and he – through perhaps another, naturally stronger character – will be looked to for leadership. But it will not be because of his or anyone else's leadership that the group members will begin to fight and continue to fight. It will be, on the one hand, for personal survival, which individuals will recognise to be bound up with group

survival, and on the other for fear of incurring by cowardly conduct the group's contempt.

This might go far in explaining the lack of physical evidence of individual violence, since much of this destruction would take place against individuals perceived as more helpless than themselves, such as women and children, or against inanimate, unprotected property such as statuary, wall reliefs and other immobile artefacts, many of which were utterly destroyed.

However, the American study does not account for the likelihood of disillusionment among individuals or groups if their original reason for engaging in conflict is betrayed: if persuaded to undertake a "Holy War", only to discover there are financial, rather than religious, reasons behind the decision; or a promise of booty is withheld. This, Philip Zimbardo (1969, 13) suggests, is a principle that "beliefs change following a commitment to behaviour discrepant with the original beliefs".

It is difficult to understand the minds and mentalities of social groups as long extinct as the ancient Assyrians, though we might attempt to do so through reading the available texts, although always remembering they were produced by an elite group instructed in the art of writing and dedicated to maintaining a social order of benefit to themselves.

> Before . . . changing attitudes . . . you would have to become acquainted with culture bound ways of perceiving and reacting. Certain attitudes and values are so often widely accepted in a given culture that they are virtually truisms for all members of that culture and rarely, if ever, are contrary points of view presented (Zimbardo 1969, 14).

It is, however, possible to make a few educated guesses based on the material available to us. The first of these are the law codes widely translated and transcribed. In comparing the law codes of Hammurabi and of the Hittite empire, a major difference can be immediately perceived. The Hammurabi Code deals in the first instance with crimes against property, while the initial Hittite laws deal with crimes against the person. These suggest very different social and political outlooks amongst these nations. Where property is considered more important than people, any rebellion is far more likely to be shown in acts of violence against that property than against individuals, and might be behind the destruction of facial images of Assyrians.

Given that "young men forget . . . the pity of war, its harshness and its bitter legacy" (Keegan 1976, 12) and "the effect of [such] amnesia" (p. 13) on warring nations, it is equally likely that anything which happens now – in the context of personality at least – has happened before; and modern studies of sociology, psychology, and warfare can lead to searches for answers in the past, and greater understanding of the behaviour patterns which led to violence to the face.

REFERENCES

Aronson, E. 1980. *The Social Animal*, reprint of 1972 edition. London, W. H. Freeman.

Aronson, E. and Helmreich, R. (eds) 1973. *Social Psychology*. New York, D. van Nostrand Co.

Childe, V. G. 1936. *Man Makes Himself*. London, Watts.

Fromm, E. 1973. *The Anatomy of Human Destructiveness*. London, Penguin.

Gleitman, H. 1992. *Basic Psychology*. New York, W. W. Norton.

Keegan, J. 1976. *The Face of Battle*. London, Barrie & Jenkins.

Meissner, W. W. 1971. *The Assault on Authority*. New York, Orbis.

Mumford, L. 1966. *The City in History*. London, Penguin.

Reeves, R. and Humber, W. J. 1966. *An Introduction to Social Psychology*. London, Macmillan.

Tainter, G. 1988. *The Collapse of Complex Societies*. Cambridge, Cambridge University Press.

Scharfetter, C. 1980. *General Psychopathology: an introduction*, reprint of 1976 edition. Cambridge, Cambridge University Press.

Zimbardo, P. G. 1969. *Influencing Attitudes and Changing Behaviour*. Reading, Mass., Addison-Wesley.

The Symbolism of Violence in Late Bronze Age Palatial Societies of the Aegean: a Gender Approach

Marianna Nikolaidou & Dimitra Kokkinidou

> When a boy finally enters the world of men, he does so by confronting death
> – Burkert (1983, 18)

Violence signifies the intentional rendering of physical or moral hurt exercised either directly or symbolically by human beings. From a gender point of view, such a behaviour appears as a widespread male attitude aiming at female oppression by means of violation of women's personal autonomy. Post-Freudian psychology has stressed men's fear and envy of women as resulting from the "psycho-sexual frailty" of the former (e.g. Money and Erhardt 1972, 117; cf. Paglia 1991, 19–20). In other words, aggressive and dominating attitudes in men are enhanced by male fears and envies for the more even physical maturation of women, their maternal ability, and their greater ease in sexual performance. Thus, in a number of pre-industrial cultures men tend to compensate by inventing painful rites of passage which are symbolic equivalents of the functions of the female body, involving bloodletting, scarification, the courageous bearing of pain, or acts imitating pregnancy and childbirth (e.g. Bettelheim 1962, Tester, König, Jonas and Jonas 1984, 207–08). The biological and psychological development of human beings appears to have different implications for the two sexes, and may partly underlie men's tendency to restrict and devalue women (e.g. Chodorow 1978, 183; Horney 1973, 117–18). It is in this tendency that the origins of warfare may be traced; among other social and environmental reasons, hand-to-hand fighting is likely to have emerged in an attempt to prove male supremacy. In most societies military training is primarily a male pursuit. Male involvement in knowledge and use of martial equipment can lead to female oppression, either through action or simply through the threat of force (e.g. Gough 1975, 69).

According to theories arguing for an innate capacity of human beings for violence (e.g. Ardrey 1977; Lorenz 1966; Storr 1968), male violence has often been described as normal and as being derived from some genetic predisposition, sparked by an uncontrollable drive. To explain the origins of gender asymmetry in terms of men's innate aggressiveness and their greater physical strength has been a favourite hypothesis in the social sciences (see, for instance, review articles by Quinn 1977; Mukhopadhyay and Higgins 1988). However, violent behaviour is best perceived within the context of human relations in a certain society (e.g. Ferguson 1984; Haas 1990; Riches 1986), given that it manifests itself in a variety of ways and is characterised by a multiplicity of meanings and purposes that can be explained only be reference to a specific cultural discourse. Therefore, in order to understand male intimidation and violence we must see through the ways in which society allows for, and on many levels encourages, such behaviour (e.g. Hunter 1991; Tsalikoglou 1989).

This paper explores the relationship between the culturally defined behaviour of the sexes and the symbolic manifestation of violence as seen in the archaeological record. It focuses on ritual behaviour and cult practices, religious iconography, burial customs, precious weaponry, and epigraphic evidence. Our goal is to draw a picture of some of the processes which shaped gender identity in palatial Aegean societies of the Late Bronze Age. We argue that cultural transformation in late Aegean prehistory was closely connected with the protagonistic role of males in an intensified social hierarchy and stratification. The relevant archaeological data suggest that androcentrism and the symbolic legitimation of violence were two parallel phenomena, although linked by a set of complex and often cross-cutting relationships.

THE CASE STUDY

The social setting

Between c. 1700 and 1450 BC Minoan culture in Crete reached its climax. The foundation of new palaces ushered in the palatial system's most flourishing period, during which the Aegean was directly influenced by Minoan civilisation. Major aspects of social life, such as the economy, administration, ritual and art, were dependent upon the palaces or local centres of power. Matrifocal structures can be discerned mainly in the religious domain, whereas social hierarchies were based on the differentiated position of individuals within the palatial system. At the same time in mainland Greece the wealth of the shaft graves at Myceneae (seventeenth and sixteenth centuries BC) testifies to the presence of a military aristocracy. The period between 1450 and 1100 BC, and especially the fourteenth and thirteenth centuries, mark the heyday of the Mycenaean palatial civilisation not only in the mainland but also all over the Aegean. Social organisation in the Mycenaean kingdoms was permeated by some form of patriarchal structure, although matrocentric elements were strong in the religious sphere (for a discussion of Late Bronze Age Aegean societies from a gender perspective see Kokkinidou and Nikolaidou 1993, 96–123).

Hostility is documented by the remains of defensive works in the Cyclades, in mainland Greece, and possibly in Crete, as well as by the depiction of fortified towns in art (e.g. Boulotis 1990, 436–37). The imposing fortifications of the Mycenaean citadels (Iakovidis 1973) provide a striking example. A great deal of weaponry was manufactured in Minoan Crete (Hiller 1984, 28; Hood 1978, 175–83; Sakellariou 1988, 52) which had been an important military power in the Aegean (Hiller 1984, 28– 30; cf. Warren 1979, 125–29). Detailed description of military organisation and equipment occurs in Linear B texts from the late Mycenaean palaces (MacDonald 1987). Much of the wealth accumulated in the Mycenaean centres is thought to have derived from raids and military campaigns (Kilian-Dirlmeier 1988, 163; Mee and Cavanagh 1984, 49; Mylonas 1983, 58–59; Vermeule 1964, 133–36), indicated, for instance, by the miniature fresco from the West House of Akrotiri on Thera (Warren 1979). Martial activity of the Mycenaeans is further attested by heavily injured human bones from cemeteries at Mycenae (Mylonas 1983, 60).

Of direct relevance to war enterprises is the occurrence of slavery lists in Linear B tablets. The slaves, mostly women and children from Asia Minor, were dependent upon the palace, and had either been captured (Chadwick 1976, 76–83) or purchased (Killen 1979, 100). According to the Homeric epics, on capturing a place or conducting a raid, it was customary to kill all male adults, and to enslave the rest of the population. If this practice was already common in Mycenaean times, it may account for the limited number of male slaves mentioned in the

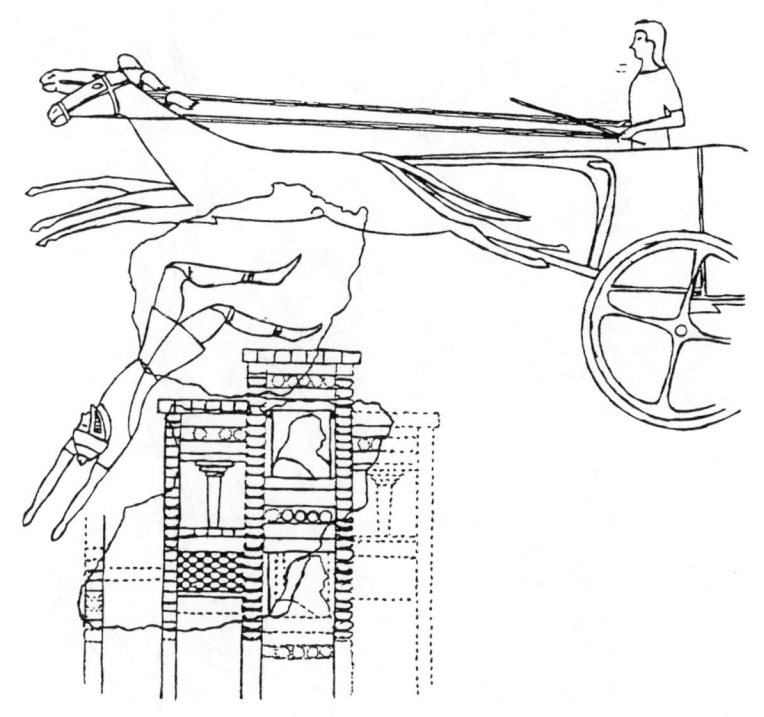

Figure 1. Siege scene on a fresco from the megaron of the palace at Mycenae (after Boulotis 1990).

documents. Female slaves would have been under complete control of their warrior masters. If, moreover, the female workers enumerated in the same documents were indeed slaves, and not free individuals as has been argued (Billigmeier and Turner 1981, 3–6; cf. Uchitel 1984, 278), this is then a further indication of a patriarchal society.

The presence of high-ranking warrior groups is attested archaeologically both in Crete and in mainland Greece. Apart from the shaft graves at Myceneae, richly furnished with precious weaponry of emblematic and ritual use, monumental tombs including similar offerings are known from Myceneae itself as well as from other sites in the Peloponnese (Dickinson 1989, 136; Graziadio 1991; Laffineur 1989b, 238; Vermeule 1964, 94–100 and 133–36; Wright 1987). War symbolism in the form of elaborate weaponry is also prominent in contemporary Minoan burials (Hood 1978, 173–74; Kilian-Dirlmeier 1988, 164–65; Matthäus 1983, 212). In many cases, skeletal analysis has identified the male sex of the dead. It seems plausible that the prestige of some male groups would have increased as a result of their involvement in military activities (Anderson and Zinsser 1988, 15; Thomas 1973,

Figure 2. Battle scene from a fresco at the palace at Pylos (after Xénaki-Sankellariou 1985).

172), which is further indicated by epigraphic evidence of Linear B tablets referring to military dignitaries (Chadwick 1976, 72–73 and 173–77).

The iconography of war

In Late Bronze Age art men play a protagonistic role in scenes which emphasise the elements of aggression and antagonism, whereas female figures, on the rare occasions that they occur in such contexts, are shown as mere spectators (Figure 1). Representations of this kind are quite popular and include armed figures; scenes of duelling on grave

Figure 3. Battle scene on a silver krater from Shaft Grave IV, Mycenae (after Xénaki-Sakellariou 1985).

stelae and on precious burial offerings from Mycenae; siege and battle scenes in frescoes (Figure 2) and on various elaborate artefacts, such as stone and metal vases (Figure 3), pottery, seals (Figure 4), metal and ivory objects from Knossos, Mycenae and Akrotiri (Goodison 1989, 106-08 and 113-15; Warren 1979, 125-29). War symbolism first appears in Minoan neo-palatial iconography (Hiller 1984, 8), but it becomes prominent in Mycenaean art (Hood 1978; Mylonas 1983), where it constitutes a favourite theme in the mural decoration of the palaces. It is worth noting the appearance of armed figures of both sexes, divine or priestly, for the first time in the religious iconography of the Late Bronze Age (Goodison 1989, 106-07; Säflund 1987, 228).

Attitudes toward nature

A spirit of aggression, dominance and violent control of the natural world permeates many aspects of Late Bronze Age art and ritual. Such attitudes are discernible in three interrelated practices and their respective symbolic manifestations, namely hunting, animal sacrifices, and bull-leaping.

Hunting seems to have been of particular significance for some high-standing groups in Mycenaean society where it would have been tantamount to an expression of strength and contending spirit (Boulotis 1988, 37-38; Morris 1990). References to hunters are found in Linear B texts (Chadwick 1976, 33). Hunting scenes, with male figures as the protagonists, are common on precious burial offerings from "princely"

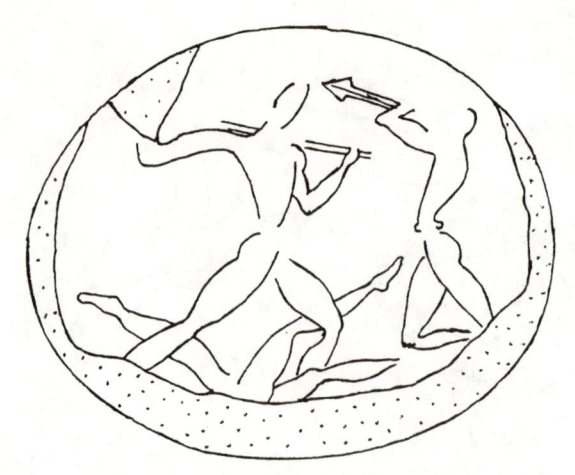

Figure 4. Combat scene on a seal from Zakros, eastern Crete (after Xénaki-Sakellariou 1985).

Mycenaean graves (Figure 5), as well as in mural paintings of the palaces at Pylos and Tiryns (on the iconography of hunting see Marinatos 1990; Morris 1990). On the other hand, there is a notable scarcity of females in such representations. In Crete depictions of the hunt are popular on *larnakes* (burial chests) of the fourteenth and thirteenth centuries BC (Figure 6), and have been interpreted as representations of desirable activities in a wished-for afterworld (Watrous 1991, 299). Would this then be a male afterworld? Unfortunately evidence on the sex of the dead buried in such coffins is lacking.

Other iconographic references to hunting in the Minoan and Mycenaean world include capturing or combat with animals (Figure 7), animals attacking each other, as well as wounded (Figure 8), mangled or dead animals, the latter occasionally being carried off by divine or priestly figures (Marinatos 1986, 34–35). Depictions of isolated animals' members, such as skulls and limbs, also abound. Characteristic are the themes of the "Master" (Figure 9) and the "Mistress of Animals" (Figure 10), that is divine figures taming or holding wild or mythical animals in a commanding posture (e.g. Goodison 1989, 114; Rutkowski 1981, fig. 30: 3, 5, 7–12); and figures of gods or priests as hunters (Marinatos 1986, 42–49). Hunting often ended with the sacrifice of the captured animal, so that hunting scenes have been interpreted as pictorial metaphors of sacrifice (Marinatos 1986, 42–49; for a penetrating discussion of the conceptual, symbolic and ritual links between hunting and sacrifice see Burkert 1983, 12–22).

Animal sacrifices seem to have constituted religious practices with a

Figure 5. Lion hunting scene on an inlaid dagger from Shaft Grave IV, Mycenae (after Marinatos 1986).

Figure 6. Hunting scene on a Late Minoan IIIA larnax from Armenoi, western Crete (after Betancourt 1985).

strong emotional and social impact, in that the natural forces released from the slaughtered victim were ritually "born anew" into elements benevolent for the community (Burkert 1983). Such rites would then have served as symbolic foci of social cohesion (Nikolaidou 1995). Sacrifices took place on such important occasions as agrarian and other fertility festivals, bull-games, funerals, foundation of prominent buildings, inauguration or renewal of the authority of high officials, and commemoration of important historical events (Marinatos 1986, 41–42). Although bloody sacrifices are not unknown from earlier

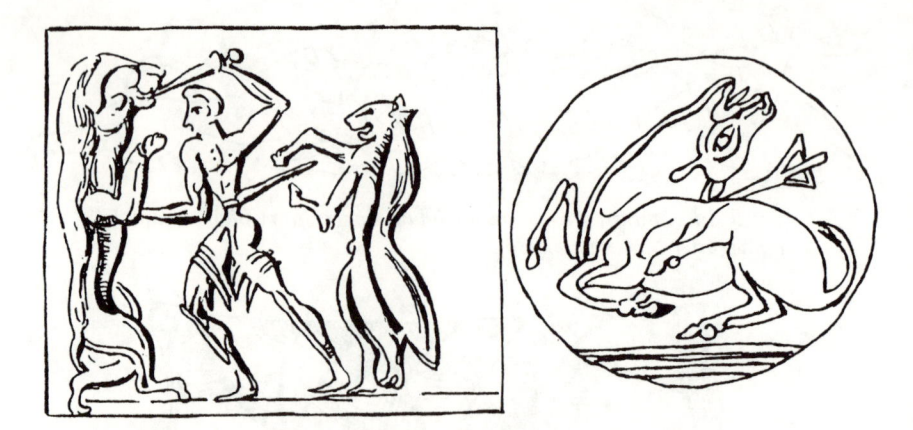

Figures 7 and 8. Left: hunter and theriomorphic demon attacking a lion on a seal from Kakovatos, Messenia (after Marinatos 1986); right: a calf in a contorted position with an arrow in its back on a seal from Mycenae (after Marinatos 1986).

Bronze Age phases, it is in the Late Bronze Age that such ritual events appear to have acquired major ideological significance. The iconographic celebration of sacrifice is attested in a variety of art forms, including seals (Figure 11), mural paintings, sarcophagi, and even pottery (Goodison 1989, 113; Hägg 1985, 120; Marinatos 1986; Nikolaidou 1995).

A usual theme is that of male figures pulling or standing beside sacrificial animals (Figure 12), and there is also the image of a priest examining the entrails. In sacrificial scenes it is men who perform the slaughtering of the victim or bear the killing instruments (knife and single-bladed axe) as their emblems (Figure 13) (Marinatos 1986, 35). Women, on the other hand, carry dead animals (Figure 14) or hold the double axe (Figure 10), a Minoan sacred symbol associated to ideas of renewal through death, and thus directly linked to sacrifice (Dietrich 1988). It is relevant to note here that the sacrificial symbolisms of the double axe are for the first time emphasised in Late Minoan art (Buchholz 1959; Nikolaidou 1995). It has been argued that priests were probably responsible for killing the animal, whereas priestesses would have been in charge of the climax point of the whole ritual, that is the consecration of the dead victim (Marinatos 1986, 35). This hypothesis is supported by a general tendency for role division between the sexes in Aegean religious practice (Marinatos 1987).

One category of libation vessels deserves special attention. They depict bulls with a net covering their back and with horns whose tips

Figures 9 and 10. Left: "Master of Animals" on a gold pendant from the so-called "Aegina Treasure" (after Rutkowski 1981); right: "Mistress of Animals" on a seal from Mycenae (after Rutkowski 1981).

have been cut (Figure 15). It has been suggested that the two iconographic elements of the net and the blunt horns are symbols of passivity, suggesting that the animal represented is not the wild bull but a sacrificial victim which has come under human control. Such zoomorphic vessels would have been used in bloody and other libations in the course of sacrificial ceremonies (Marinatos 1986, 31).

Closely connected with hunting and sacrifice was bull-leaping, a dangerous and often deadly game of possible initiatory character (Cameron 1987, 325; Eliade 1979, 134; Marinatos 1989; Säflund 1987, 231), whereby the element of violence was of primary psychological significance (Pinsent 1983). In Aegean societies bull-leaping would have served as a symbolic manifestation of human control over the wild forces of nature: the ferocious bull *Bos primigenius* (Dietrich 1988, 15), the sacrificial animal *par excellence*, must have been experienced as a quasi-human adversary (Marinatos 1989; cf. Burkert 1983, 20). Although it is generally assumed that women took equal part in these games, because fresco representations include figures in white skin that usually signifies females, women's participation in bull-leaping has recently been challenged on sound arguments (Damiani Indelicato 1988; cf. Marinatos 1989, 29). In such a case it is probably not accidental that only men took part in an event of social importance where the element of violence was prevalent.

[183]

Figure 11. Goat on a sacrificial table with a dagger in its neck on a seal from Mycenae (after Marinatos 1986).

Figure 12. Chariot procession and sacrificial (?) bull on a fresco at Knossos (after Marinatos 1986).

Other ritual and cult practices

Late Bronze Age religions combined matrifocal and physiocentric traditions with elements of aggression and violence, the latter occurring for the first time in the material symbolism of this period. It could be argued that violent trends in the religious domain were associated with the increasing participation of males, either as divine figures or priests and adorants, in cult activities and symbolism (Kokkinidou and Nikolaidou 1993, 110–11). A warlike character is also often attributed

Figures 13 and 14. Left: priest with an axe or mace on a seal from Crete (after Marinatos 1986); right: priestess carrying a sacrificed animal on a seal from Vapheio, Lakonia (after Marinatos 1986).

to the female image, deity or adorant, although she still maintained certain of her long-standing fertility aspects (e.g. Goodison 1989, 106). An armed female deity is likely to have been worshipped at the so-called Cult Centre of Mycenae, which yielded the "Palladium Tablet", a gypsum block depicting two women worshipping a figure-of-eight shield with a human head and limbs (Figure 16), and frescoes showing a "helmet-wearing goddess" and a sword-bearing woman (Marinatos 1988; Morris 1990, 155; Mylonas 1983, 162; Rehak 1984). The "Mistress of Animals" or "Lady of Horses" (*po-ti-ni-ja e-qu-e-ja*), who is mentioned on a Linear B tablet from Pylos (Chadwick 1976, 93; 1988, 98), seems to have been associated with the palatial weaponry workshop there (Tegyey 1984). Her martial nature is very likely, given that in Mycenaean times horses were mainly used in drawing battle chariots (Chadwick 1976, 126).

One of the most interesting features of the symbolic repertoire is the extended emblematic use of weaponry both in Minoan Crete and the Mycenean centres. Swords, helmets, daggers, spears, and figure-of-eight shields occur among the offerings at shrines (Rutkowski 1986) or are depicted as sacred insignia in palatial frescoes and in sanctuaries, as well as on ceramics, seals (Figure 17), precious weapons (Figure 18), and other pieces of minor arts (Cassola Guida 1975; Goodison 1989, 106; Hiller 1984, 28; Mylonas 1977, 56–62; Rehak 1984; 1992; Rutkowski

Figure 15. Bull-shaped rhyton *(libation vessel) with blunt horns and a net covering its back, from Akrotiri, Thera (after Marinatos 1986).*

Figure 16. The "Palladium Tablet" from the so-called Cult Centre at Mycenae (after Rutkowski 1981).

1981, 106). "Hoplolatry" or a weaponry cult may have been introduced as early as the Minoan neo-palatial period (Alexiou 1964, 101–03). As far as the figure-of-eight shield is concerned, recent studies have stressed its original magic and symbolic meaning, which subsequently acquired an emblematic value (Rutkowski 1981, 105–06). It is worth noting the changing meaning of this motif in Late Bronze Age iconography. In neo palatial times the figure-of-eight shield appears predominantly as a renewal symbol, probably connected with a fertility goddess, in the regeneration context of hunting and sacrificial practices (Figure 19) (Marinatos 1986, 57–58; Rehak 1992). In Mycenaean

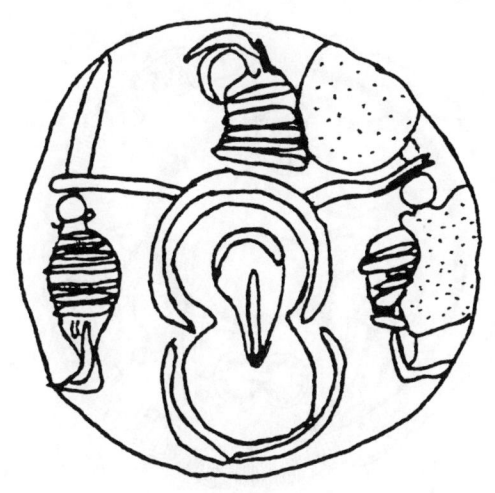

Figure 17. Panoply or divine (?) figure in military array on seal in the British Museum (after Younger 1988).

Figure 18. Double axe from Vorou, Crete, decorated on one side with a figure-of-eight shiled flanked by two sets of garments and swords (after Marinatos 1986).

iconography, however, it evolved into a sacred *insignium* of a female warlike deity (Rehak 1992; Rutkowski 1981, 106).

Indications for human sacrifices, as has been argued for the skeletal remains at the "Temple" of Archanes (Sakellarakis and Sapouna-Sakellaraki 1979; 1981) and in the North House of Knossos (Warren 1984; 1988, 28), reveal unprecedented aspects of Minoan religion (cf. Bintliff 1984, 37; Giesecke 1990). It might not be accidental that together with the human bones at the North House a cup-rhyton (libation vessel) was found decorated with a grotesque face and a frieze of helmets and figure-of-eight shields (Warren 1984; cf. Goodison 1989, 112–13, fig. 266a). Similar rites are suggested by Linear B documents which describe a number of individuals, both male and female, as

Figure 19. Bull (?), head of a goat, animal limb and two figure-of-eight shields on a seal from Mycenae (after Marinatos 1986).

divine "offerings", probably sacrificial (Chadwick 1976, 22; 1988, 200; but see objections by Uchitel 1984, 274).

There is, furthermore, iconographic evidence for dangerous initiation rites of boys such as combats, hunting and bull-leaping, all focusing on antagonism and violent control of nature or humans (Marinatos 1993, 212–20; Säflund 1987). Conversely, the equivalent ordeals of girls seem not to have laid much stress on aggression, but rather included games or mystic acts related to the element of fertility (Davis 1986, 403–06; Marinatos 1984, 73–84; 1993, 203–11; Säflund 1986). During the late Mycenaean phases, however, painful rites of passage, such as self-flagellation, would have been the lot for both boys and girls (Lebessi 1991, 111–13).

Discussion

The categories of material culture examined so far suggest that the phenomenon of violence, in its various manifestations, was of great concern to the people in Late Bronze Age Aegean societies. This may be interpreted in terms of cultural tensions and historical instability which partly determined developments in the Creto-Mycenaean world. To begin with, neo-palatial society in Crete was characterised by decentralising trends, which, along with sharp social divisions and antagonism, eventually resulted in the collapse of the palatial system itself (Cherry 1986, 23; Dabney and Wright 1990, 45–47; Hood 1983, 131). At the same time natural disasters, such as the eruption of the volcano at Thera, would have caused emotional and ideological anxiety (Castleden 1990, 158–68; Starr 1984; Waterhouse 1974, 154). Later on, in Mycenaean times, successive destructions of the palatial centres and other important sites attest to social and ethnic disruptions as part of the general turmoil in the whole eastern Mediterranean towards the end of the Bronze Age (e.g. Chadwick 1976, 188–93; Dickinson 1994, 303–09; Vermeule 1964, 254–77).

Related to these processes is the rearrangement of gender relationships, as can be traced in the archaeological record, which would have involved the prominence of androcentric tendencies of antagonism, aggression and individuality both in the social and symbolic discourse. These gender attitudes may have largely defined the profile of the Minoan and Mycenaean palatial systems, which were based on a stricter stratification than previous social hierarchical formations in the Aegean. In the Mycenaean kingdoms, specifically, textual evidence suggests that power was exercised by men (Chadwick 1976, 69–77; but see objections by Billigmeier and Turner 1981, 9–10). The leading part played by men in military affairs would have further enhanced their prestige. On the other hand, traditional matrifocal elements, such as collectivity and a strong ritual content of everyday life (e.g. Judd 1990), retained their significance mainly in the religious sphere (Kokkinidou and Nikolaidou 1993, 96–123).

The preoccupation with issues of violence that is indicated by the archaeological data hints at ideological changes, interwoven with the transformation of gender identity as has been outlined above. We must emphasise that male figures held a primary role in most representations of violent behaviour. Also important, this "iconography of violence", which had never before been so widespread, is seen mainly in palatial or ritual contexts, or on precious objects; we are probably dealing with a whole range of new aesthetics and cultural values, manifested in the artistic celebration of violence, which constituted an appropriate framework for the promotion of official ideology. We suggest that in the Aegean states of the Late Bronze Age the high-ranking groups were exalting an "ideal" of the male figure linked with certain status symbols, the notion of physical superiority, force and control over nature (cf. Laffineur 1985; Marinatos 1990). This type of iconography would have celebrated the prestige of a male "aristocracy" (Kilian-Dirlmeier 1990).

Within this historical context violent behaviour would have been most effectively dealt with when integrated in ritual discourse. The ritualisation of violence appears to have been a two-fold and highly ambiguous process, as indeed every ritual behaviour is, both supporting social order, that is "structure", and subverting it by creating an "anti-structure" in the "liminal zone" of the ceremony (for a discussion of "structure" and ritual "anti-structure" see Turner 1974, 50-54 and 272-98). To begin with, ritualised violent behaviour legitimised dominating ideology with the purpose of controlling natural and social surroundings. To give a characteristic example, hunting and its related iconography would have stressed, literally and symbolically, violent attitudes toward nature, which must have been interwoven with the possessive and competitive character of Mycenaean society (Goodison 1989, 113-15; Marinatos 1990; Morris 1990). It cannot be by chance that basic symbols of the "repertoire of violence", for example weaponry, occur both in the context of cult and as insignia of authority (e.g. Boulotis 1990, 454-57; Wright 1987, 177-84). This ideological framework may account for the integration of relevant scenes in ritual and religious contexts, obviously in an attempt to "sanctify" aggressive attitudes and violent behaviour (Marinatos 1986, 72). In other words, ritual manifestation of violence, in the form of bloody sacrifices, bull-leaping, painful initiation rites and the like, would have provided an archetypal example for the social status quo, the latter being permeated by androcentric values.

A "male" perspective might also be inferred from indications of sacred prostitution, as has been hypothesised with reference to the elegant women in the "Grand Stand" and "Temple" frescoes from the palace at Knossos (Platon 1970, 136) and other female figures from Mycenae (Evans 1964, 61). Even if we allow for the religious and mystic character of this practice (Lendakis 1986, 272-77; 1990, 15), we can still see in it devaluation and violation of at least some women's personal autonomy with the excuse of religious service. It has been claimed, for instance, that in Sumer sacred prostitution, as a means of control over women, was a process parallel with the institutionalisation of patriarchy (Rohrlich 1980, 90-92).

On the other hand, the ritualisation of violence may have functioned as an anti-stress mechanism for the control and elimination of violent attitudes of individuals and groups, and thus for the maintenance of social cohesion. As has been aptly noted, "it is precisely group demonstration of aggression . . . that creates a sense of close personal community" (Burkert 1983, 20). In the case of Minoan Crete, at least, it is worth noting the evidence for communal meals associated with sacrifices (Marinatos 1986, 37-39). The feeling of *"communitas"* (e.g.

Turner 1974, 50–54 and 272–78) reaffirmed in such ceremonies may be described as an "anti-structure" which cross-cuts the sharp divisions of social "structure".

Ritually encoded behaviour was a long-standing matrocentric tradition in Aegean societies where we observe the sacralisation of daily life, according to a female-centred archetype (Kokkinidou and Nikolaidou 1993, 70–96). For example, in proto-palatial Crete ceremonial practice rather than explicit force appears to have provided an effective means for the manipulation of social tensions (Warren 1987, 54). The prevalence of the female element in the religious domain during the Late Bronze Age would have created the proper background for the continuation of this tradition. The fact that the ritual manipulation of violence retained its ideological significance in Late Bronze Age palatial societies, despite the dynamic appearance of androcentric trends in this era, reveals the fundamental contribution of pre-existing matrifocal structures to contemporary developments. We see in the dialectics of violence imagery the symbolic negotiation of power between the two sexes aiming at a new social equilibrium.

Conclusion

The reinforcement of a patriarchal ethos affords a plausible explanation for the symbolic emphasis on violence in the Late Bronze Age Aegean. Nonetheless, women should not be viewed as passive receivers of but rather as active participants in the cultural discourse. Gender dynamics is vividly expressed in the ambiguous symbolic manipulation of violence, as has been traced in the archaeological record.

This paper has outlined a crucial social phenomenon from a gender perspective. In our case study we have approached violent behaviour as an amalgam of historical relationships and not as a biologically determined category which would apply universally when theorising about gender asymmetry. For this purpose we have set about a diachronic presentation of cultural trends throughout the Late Bronze Age, and applied a synchronic examination of archaeological data from different Aegean societies. The analysis has allowed us to focus on the active historical role of individuals, which can be illuminated by the social theory that gender archaeology introduces.

Acknowledgements

We would like to thank Professors Angeliki Pilali-Papasteriou and Stelios Andreou of Thessaloniki University, as well as Professor Joan Gero of the University of South Carolina for their constructive criticism. Our thanks also go to Dr Elli Philokyprou for commenting on an earlier version of this paper. Last but not least we are grateful to John Carman for his useful remarks and editorial assistance.

Bibliography

Alexiou, S. 1964. *Minoan Civilisation*. Herakleion, Sp. Alexiou and Sons (in Greek).

Anderson, B. S. and Zinsser, J. P. 1988. *A History of Their Own: Women in Europe from Prehistory to the Present.* vol. 1. Harmondsworth, Penguin.

Ardrey, R. 1977. *The Hunting Hypothesis*. New York, Bantam.

Betancourt, P. P. 1985. *The History of Minoan Pottery*. Princeton, N.J., Princeton University Press.

Bettelheim, B. 1962. *Symbolic Wounds: Puberty Rites and the Envious Male.* London, Thames and Hudson.

Billigmeier, J. C. and Turner, J. A. 1981. The socio-economic roles of women in Mycenaean Greece: a brief survey of Linear B tablets. In H. Foley (ed.), *Reflections of Women in Antiquity,* 1–18. London, Gordon and Breach Science Publishers.

Bintliff, J. L. 1984. Structuralism and myth in Minoan studies. *Antiquity* 58, 33–38.

Boulotis, Ch. 1988. Mycenaean frescoes. In *The Mycenaean World: Five centuries of early Greek civilisation. 1600–1100 B.C.,* 36–39. Athens, Ministry of Culture / ICOM-Greek Section (in Greek).

Boulotis, Ch. 1990. Villes et palais dans l'art égéen du IIe millénnaire av. J.-C. In P. Darque and R. Treuil (eds), *L'Habitat Egéen préhistorique: Actes de la Table Ronde Internationale organisée par le Centre National de la Recherche Scientifique. L'Université de Paris I et l'École Française d'Athènes (Athènes 23–25 Juin 1987),* 421–59. Athens, École Française d'Athènes (Bulletin de Correspondance Hellénique Supplément 19).

Buchholz, H. G. 1959. *Zur Herkunft der kretischen Doppelaxt: Geschichte und auswärtige Beziehungen eines minoischen Kultsymbols.* München, Kiefhaber, Kiefhaber und Eibl.

Burkert, W. 1983. *Homo Necans: The Anthropology of Ancient Greek Sacrificial Ritual and Myth.* Translated from the German by P. Bing. Berkeley, University of California Press.

Cameron, M. A. S. 1987. The "palatial" thematic system in the Knossos murals: last notes on the Knossos frescoes. In R. Hägg and N. Marinatos (eds), *Minoan Thalassocracy: Myth and Reality,* 320–28. Stockholm, Paul Åstrom.

Cassola Guida, P. 1975. Le armi nel culto dei Micenei. In *Studi Triestini di Antichità in onore di L.A. Stella,* 93–106. Trieste, Università degli Studi di Trieste, Facoltà di Lettere e Filosofia.

Castleden, R. 1990. *Minoans: Life in Bronze Age Crete.* London, Routledge and Kegan Paul.

Chadwick, J. 1976. *The Mycenaean World*. Cambridge, Cambridge University Press.

Chadwick, J. 1988. The women of Pylos. In J. P. Olivier and T. Palaima (eds), *Texts, Tablets and Scribes*, 43–95. Salamanca, Ediciones Universidad de Salamanca (Supplementos a Minos num 10).

Cherry, J. F. 1986. Polities and palaces: some problems in Minoan state formation. In C. Renfrew and J. F. Cherry (eds), *Peer Polity Interaction and Sociopolitical Change*, 19–45. Cambridge, Cambridge University Press.

Chodorow, N. 1978. *The Reproduction of Mothering: Psychoanalysis and the Sociology of Gender*. Berkeley and Los Angeles, University of California Press.

Dabney, M. K. and Wright, J. C. 1990. Mortuary customs, palatial society and state formation in the Aegean area: a comparative study. In R. Hägg and G. C. Nordquist (eds), *Celebrations of Death and Divinity in the Bronze Age Argolid*, 45–53. Stockhom, Paul Åstrom.

Damiani Indelicato, S. 1988. Were Cretan girls playing at bull-leaping? *Cretan Studies* 1, 39–47.

Darcque, P. and Poursat, J. C. (eds) 1985. *L'iconographie minoènne: Actes de la Table Ronde d'Athènes (21–22 Avril 1983)*. Athèns, École Française d' Athènes (Bulletin de Correspondance Hellénique Supplément 11).

Davis, E. N. 1986. Youth and age in the Thera frescoes. *American Journal of Archaeology* 90, 399–406.

Dickinson, O. 1989. "The origins of Mycenaean civilisation" revisited. In R. Laffineur (ed.), *Transition: Le monde égéen du bronze moyen au bronze récent*, 131–36. Université de Liège.

Dickinson, O. 1994. *The Aegean Bronze Age*. Cambridge, Cambridge University Press.

Dietrich, B. C. 1988. A Minoan symbol of renewal. *Journal of Prehistoric Religion* 2, 12–24.

Eliade, M. 1979. *A History of Religious Ideas: from the Stone Age to the Eleusinian mysteries*, vol. 1. Translated by W. R. Trask. London, Collins.

Evans, A. J. 1964. *The Palace of Minos*, vol. 3. New York, Biblo and Tannen.

Ferguson, B. R. (ed.) 1984. *Warfare, Culture and Environment*. Orlando, Academic Press.

Fester, R., König, M. E. P., Jonas, D. F. and Jonas, A. D. 1984. *Weib und Macht*. Translated into Greek by D. Kourtovik. Athens, Poreia.

French, E. B. and Wardle, K. A. (eds) 1988. *Problems in Greek Prehistory: papers presented at the Centenary Conference of the British School of Archaeology at Athens, Manchester, April 1986*. Bristol, Classical Press.

Giesecke, H. E. 1990. Menschenopfer. *Journal of Prehistoric Religion* 3–4, 45–47.

Goodison, L. 1989. *Death, Women and the Sun: symbolism of regeneration in early Aegean religion*. London, University of London Institute of Classical Studies (Bulletin Supplement 53).

Gough, K. 1975. The origin of the family. In R. R. Reiter (ed.), *Toward an Anthropology of Women*, 51–76. New York, Monthly Review Press.

Graziadio, G. 1991. The process of social stratification at Mycenae in the Shaft Gporave period: a comparative examination of the evidence. *American Journal of Archaeology* 95, 403–40.

Haas, J. (ed.) 1990. *The Anthropology of War*. Cambridge, Cambridge University Press.

Hägg, R. 1985. Mycenaean religion: the Helladic and Minoan components. In A. Morpurgo Davies and Y. Duhoux (eds), *Linear B: A 1984 Survey. Proceedings of the Mycenaean Colloquium of the Eighth Congress of the International Federation of the Society of Classical Studies, Dublin, 27 August – 1 September 1984*, 203–25. Louvain-la-Neuve, Cabay (Bibliothèque des Cahiers de l'Institut de Linguistique de Louvain. no. 26).

Hägg, R. and Marinatos, N. (eds) 1984. *Minoan Thalassocracy: Myth and Reality. Proceedings of the Third International Symposium at the Swedish Institute in Athens, 31 May – 5 June. 1982*. Stockholm, Paul Åstrom.

Hägg, R. and Marinatos, N. (eds) 1987. *The Function of the Minoan Palaces. Proceedings of the Fourth International Symposium at the Swedish Institute in Athens, 10–16 June 1984*. Stockholm, Paul Åstrom.

Hägg, R. and Nordquist, G. C. (eds) 1990. *Celebrations of Death and Divinity in the Bronze Age Argolid. Proceedings of the Sixth International Symposium at the Swedish Institute in Athens, 26–29 June 1988*. Stockhom, Paul Åstrom.

Hiller, S. 1984. "Pax minoica" versus Minoan thalassocrasy. In R. Hägg and N. Marinatos (eds), *Minoan Thalassocracy: Myth and Reality*, 27–30. Stockholm, Paul Åstrom.

Hood, S. 1978. *The Arts in Prehistoric Greece*. Harmondsworth, Penguin.

Hood, S. 1983. The "country house" and Minoan society. In O. Krzyszkowska and L. Nixon (eds), *Minoan Society: proceedings of the Cambridge Colloquium, 1981*, 129–35. Bristol, Classical Press.

Horney K. 1973. *Feminine Psychology*. New York, Norton.

Hunter, A. E. (ed.) 1991. *Genes and Gender VI. On Peace, War and Gender: A Challenge to Genetic Explanations*. New York, The City University of New York/The Feminist Press.

Iakovidis, S. 1973. *Mycenaean Citadels: University Lectures*. Athens, University of Athens (in Greek).

Judd, E. 1990. Myths of the golden age and the fall: from matriarchy to patriarchy. In F. R. Keller (ed.), *Views of Women's Lives in Western Tradition: frontiers of the past and the future*, 15–82. Lewiston, The Edwin Mellen Press.

Kilian-Dilmeier, I. 1988. Jewellery in Mycenaean and Minoan "warrior graves". In E. B. French and K. A. Wardle (eds), *Problems in Greek Prehistory: Papers Presented at the Centenary Conference of the British School of Archaeology at Athens, Manchester, April 1986*, 161–71. Bristol, Classical Press.

Kilian-Dilmeier, I. 1990. Remarks on the non-military functions of swords in the Mycenaean Agolid. In R. Hägg and G. C. Nordquist (eds), *Celebrations of Death and Divinity in the Bronze Age Argolid*, 157–66. Stockhom, Paul Åstrom.

Killen, J. T. 1979. The Linear B tablets and economic history: some problems. *University of London Bulletin of the Institute of Classical Studies* 26, 133–34.

Kokkinidou, D. and Nikolaidou, M. 1993. *Archaeology and Gender: Approaches to Aegean Prehistory*. Thessaloniki, Vanias (in Greek).

Krzyszkowska, O. and Nixon, L. (eds) 1983. *Minoan Society. Proceedings of the Cambridge Colloquium. 1981*. Bristol, Classical Press.

Laffineur, R. 1985. Iconographie minoènne et iconographie mycénienne à l'époque des tombes à fosse. In P. Darcque and J. C. Poursat (eds), *L'iconographie minoènne*, 245–66. Athens, École Française d' Athènes.

Laffineur, R. (ed.) 1987. *Thanatos: Les coutumes funéraires en Egée à l'age du bronze. Aegeum 1: Actes du Colloque de Liège (21–23 Avril 1986)*. Université de Liège, Histoire de l'art et l'archéologie de la Grèce antique (Annales d'Archéologie Égéenne de l'Université de Liège).

Laffineur, R. (ed.) 1989a. *Transition: Le monde égéen du bronze moyen au bronze recent. Aegeum 2: Actes de la deuxième Recontre internationale de l'Université de Liège (18–20 Avril 1988)*. Université de Liège (Histoire de l'art et archéologie de la Grèce antique).

Laffineur, R. 1989b. Mobilier funéraire et hierarchie sociale aux cercles des tombes de Mycenae. In R. Laffineur (ed.), *Transition: Le monde égéen du bronze moyen au bronze recent*, 227–38. Université de l'Etat de Liège.

Lebessi, A. 1991. Flagellation ou autoflagellation: Données iconographiques pour une tentative d' interprétation. *Bulletin de Correspondance Hellénique* 115, 99–123.

Lendakis, A. 1986. *Is Woman Inferior to Man? Or How Woman Is Constructed.* Athens, Dorikos (in Greek).

Lendakis A. 1990. *Sacred Prostitution*. Athens, Dorikos (in Greek).

Lorenz, K. 1966. *On Aggression*. New York, Harcourt, Brace and World.

MacDonald, C. 1987. A Knossian weapon workshop in Late Minoan II and IIIa. In R. Hägg and N. Marinatos (eds), *The Function of the Minoan Palaces*, 293–95. Stockholm, Paul Åstrom.

Marinatos, N. 1984. *Art and Religion in Thera: Reconstructing a Bronze Age Society*. Athens, D. and I. Mathioulakis.

Marinatos, N. 1986. *Minoan Sacrificial Ritual: Cult practice and symbolism*. Stockholm, Paul Åstrom (Skrifter Utgivna at Svenska Institutet i Athen 8° 9).

Marinatos, N. 1987. Role and sex division in ritual scenes of Aegean art. *Journal of Prehistoric Religion* 1, 23–34.

Marinatos, N. 1988. The fresco from room 31 at Mycenae: problems on method and interpretation. In E. B. French and K. A. Wardle (eds), *Problems in Greek Prehistory. Papers presented at the Centenary Conference of the British School of Archaeology at Athens, Manchester, April 1986*, 245–25. Bristol, Classical Press.

Marinatos, N. 1989. The bull as an adversary: some observations on bull-hunting and bull-leaping. *Ariadni: Annual of the Philosophical School of Crete University* 5, 23–32.

Marinatos, N. 1990. Celebrations of death and the symbolism of the lion hunt. In R. Hägg and G. C. Nordquist (eds), *Celebrations of Death and Divinity in the Bronze Age Argolid*, 143–48. Stockhom, Paul Åstrom.

Marinatos, N. 1993. *Minoan Religion: Ritual, Image and Symbol*. Columbia, University of South Carolina.

Matthäus, H. 1983. Minoische Kriegergräber. In O. Krzyszkowska and L. Nixon (eds), *Minoan Society. Proceedings of the Cambridge Colloquium, 1981*, 203–15. Bristol, Classical Press.

Mee, C. B. and Cavanagh, W. G. 1984. Mycenaean tombs as evidence for social and political organisation. *Oxford Journal of Archaeology* 3 (3), 45–64.

Money, J. and Ehrhardt, A. A. 1972. *Man and Woman. Boy and Girl: the Differentiation and Dimorphism of Gender Identity from Conception to Maturity*. Baltimore, Johns Hopkins University Press.

Morris, C. E. 1990. In pursuit of the white tusked boar: aspects of hunting in Mycenaean society. In R. Hägg and G. C. Nordquist (eds), *Celebrations of Death and Divinity in the Bronze Age Argolid*, 149–56. Stockhom, Paul Åstrom.

Mukhopadhyay, C. C. and Higgins, P. J. 1988. Anthropological studies of women's status revisited: 1977–1987. *Annual Review of Anthropology* 17, 461–95.

The Mycenaean World: Five centuries of early Greek civilisation. 1600–1100 B.C. 1988. Athens, Ministry of Culture / ICOM- Greek Section (in Greek).

Mylonas, G. E. 1977. *Mycenean Religion*. Athens, Athens Academy (Monographs of Athens Academy 39).

Mylonas, G. E. 1983. *Mycenae Rich in Gold*. Athens, Ekdotiki Athinon (in Greek).

Nikolaidou, M. 1994. The Double Axe in the Iconography of Minoan Vessels: Approaches to the Dynamics of Minoan Religious Symbolism. Doctoral dissertation, Aristotle University of Thessaloniki (in Greek).

Paglia, C. 1991. *Sexual Personae: Art and Decadance from Nefertiti to Emily Dickinson*. Harmondsworth, Penguin.

Pinsent, J. 1983. Bull-leaping. In O. Krzyszowska and L. Nixon (eds), *Minoan Society. Proceedings of the Cambridge Colloquium. 1981*, 259–71. Bristol, Classical Press.

Platon, N. 1970. *Creto-Mycenaean Religion: University Lectures*. Thessaloniki, Aristotle University of Thessaloniki (in Greek).

Quinn, N. 1977. Anthropological studies on women's status. *Annual Review of Anthropology* 6, 181–225.

Rehak, P. 1984. New observations on the Minoan "warrior goddess". *Archäologischer Anzeiger*, 535–45.

Rehak, P. 1992. Minoan vessels with figure-eight shields: antecedents to the Knossos throneroom alabastra. *Opuscula Atheniensia* 19 (9), 115–24.

Riches, D. (ed.) 1986. *The Anthropology of Violence*. Oxford, Basil Blackwell.

Rohrlich, R. 1980. State formation and the subjugation of women. *Feminist Studies* 6 (1), 76–102.

Rutkowski, B. 1981. *Frühgriechische Kultdarstellungen*. Berlin, Gebr. Mann.

Rutkowski, B. 1986. *The Cult Places of the Aegean*. New Haven and London, Yale University Press.

Saflund, G. 1986. Girls and gazelles: reflections on Theran fresco imagery. In *Philia Epi in Honour of Georgios Mylonas on the Occasion of the 60th Anniversary of His Excavation Work*, vol. 1, 185–90. Athens, (Archaeological Society Library no. 103).

Saflund, G. 1987. The "agoge" of the Minoan youth as reflected by palatial iconography. In R. Hägg and N. Marinatos (eds), *The Function of the Minoan Palaces*, 227–33. Stockholm, Paul Åstrom.

Sakellarakis, I. A. and Sapouna-Sakellaraki, E. 1979. Excavation at Archanes. *Praktika tis en Athinais Archaiologikis Etaireias*, 331–92 (in Greek).

Sakellarakis, I. A. and Sapouna-Sakellaraki, E. 1981. Drama of death in a Minoan temple. *National Geographic* 159, 205–22.

Sakellariou, A. 1988. Mycenaean metal-work. In *The Mycenaean World: Five centuries of early Greek civilisation. 1600–1100 B.C.*, 52–55. Athens, Ministry of Culture/ICOM-Greek Section (in Greek).

Starr, C. G. 1984. Minoan flower lovers. In R. Hägg and N. Marinatos (eds), *Minoan Thalassocracy: Myth and Reality*, 9–12. Stockholm, Paul Åstrom.

Storr, A. 1968. *Human Aggression*. New York, Atheneum.

Tegyey, I. 1984. The northeast workshop at Pylos. In T. G. Palaima and C. W. Shelmerdine (eds), *Pylos Comes Alive: Industry and Administration in a Mycenaean Palace. A Symposium of the New York Society of the Archaeological*

Institute of America and Fordham University in memory of Claivere Grandjiouan, 65-79. New York, Fordham University/Lincoln Center.

Thomas, C. G. 1973. Matriarchy in early Greece: the Bronze and Dark Ages. *Arethusa* 6, 173-95.

Tsalikoglou, F. 1989. *Mythologies of Violence and Repression*. Athens, Papazisis (in Greek).

Turner, V. 1974. *Dramas, Fields and Metaphors: Symbolic action in human society*. Ithaca, Cornell University Press.

Uchitel, A. 1984. Women at work: Pylos and Knossos, Lagash and Ur. *Historia* 33, 257-82.

Vermeule, E. 1964. *Greece in the Bronze Age*. Chicago, University of Chicago Press.

Warren, P. 1979. The miniature fresco from the W. House at Akrotiri, Thera, and its Aegean setting. *Journal of Hellenic Studies* 99, 115-29.

Warren, P. 1984. Knossos: new excavations and discoveries. *Archaeology* 34 (7), 48-57.

Warren, P. 1987. The genesis of the Minoan palace. In R. Hägg and N. Marinatos (eds), *The Function of the Minoan Palaces*, 47-56. Stockholm, Paul Åstrom.

Warren, P. 1988. *Minoan Religion as Ritual Action*. Göteborg, University of Göteborg.

Waterhouse, H. 1974. Priest-kings? *University of London Bulletin of the Institute of Classical Studies* 21, 153-55.

Watrous, L. V. 1991. The origin and iconography of the Late Minoan painted larnax. *Hesperia* 90, 285-307.

Wright, J. C. 1987. Death and power at Mycenae: changing symbols in mortuary practices. In R. Laffineur (ed.), *Thanatos: Les coutumes funéraires en Égée à l'âge du bronze*, 171-84. Université de Liège.

Xénaki-Sakellariou, A. 1985. Identité minoènne et identité mycénienne à travers les compositions figuratives. In P. Darcque and J. C. Poursat (eds), *L'iconographie minoènne*, 293-309. Athens, École Française d'Athènes.

Younger, J. G. 1988. *The Iconography of Late Minoan and Mycenaean Sealstones and Finger Rings*. Bristol, Classical Press.

Fighters and Foragers: Warfare and the Spread of Agriculture in Borneo

Paul Beavitt

Most studies of the relationships between agriculture and warfare examine the manner in which warfare may be seen as a response to population pressure within a given territory. Warfare is frequently seen as a means whereby a more satisfactory balance between the available land and the numbers of mouths to feed may be achieved. Marvin Harris provides one of the clearest discussions of some of these relationships (Harris 1975; see also Zimmerman, this volume). Harris writes: "primitive peoples go to war because they lack alternative solutions to certain problems – alternative solutions that would involve less suffering and fewer premature deaths".

Yet the emphasis need not always be one-way. Indeed, in this paper I would like to explore a different perspective, that is, to examine the extent to which the spread of agriculture itself could be seen to have been stimulated by warfare. The empirical context within which I intend to consider this problem is Borneo, which has yielded evidence for the earliest presence of rice in Island South-East Asia. However, whilst Sarawak demonstrated very early rice availability, a major problem which will be addressed concerns some of the reasons why this early availability had so little impact on many of the societies within Borneo. Indeed it is only over the last few hundred years that rice cultivation moved from Zvelebil's (1984) availability phase to that of consolidation and it is the case that many up-river societies have only become significantly dependent on rice cultivation since the 1940s and 1950s (Tuton Kaboy, Sarawak Museum, pers. comm.). The first part of this article will present and discuss the data related to the early occurrence of rice cultivation in Borneo.

In the second part of the paper I will examine in detail the part warfare may have played in stimulating a commitment to practising agriculture. Briefly, however, my argument will be that hunting and gathering, which had previously provided a long-term and relatively stable means by which most interior societies gained a livelihood, became undermined by the spread of warfare which was practised by societies in which farming was developing. Most of these hunter-gatherer groups themselves were then forced to become farmers and fighters in response to this advance.

In my examination of the relationship between agriculture and warfare I will consider the mechanisms by which I believe it can be argued that war and agriculture reinforced each other to create a series of new relations both between and within societies, between war leaders and followers, and between males and females. War effectively became a celebration of agricultural success, and agriculture spread over large tracts of land as farmers sought out good farming lands, wild foods to supplement rice, forest products to trade, and victims to fight.

Cultivation in Borneo

The archaeological evidence for the earliest settlement in Borneo (Palaeolithic and Mesolithic) occurs either on the edge of the coastal area (for example Gua Sireh) or within isolated mountain and cave complexes close to the coast (e.g. Niah) (for a good summary of this evidence see King 1993). Much of the Neolithic and Iron Age evidence derives from similar locations although some from inland caves (e.g. Mulu and Gua Kakus). There is one significant inland site, namely Putai, where a number of quadrangular stone axes have been found and dated to the Sarawak Neolithic (c. 2500 BC). However, rather more problematic to the argument here is that no archaeological evidence yet exists for early hunter-gatherers in the interior forests. Our evidence for their presence instead comes from the oral literature of the present agriculturalists.

There are three main sources of evidence for the spread of Neolithic societies in Island South-East Asia and Oceania. These are linguistic, archaeological and anthropological. Peter Bellwood and Robert Blust have been the major contributors to the debate, and many of their arguments are concisely summarised by King (1993). The Austronesian expansion is thought to have begun in southern mainland China; it had reached Taiwan by about 4000 BC, the Philippines by 3000 BC, and northern Borneo by 2500 BC. It had spread to south-western Borneo by about 500 BC. Blust (1988) suggests that the language he calls "Proto-Northwest Borneo" and which was spoken from about 2000 BC, split several centuries later into one group which gave rise to the languages of Sabah and another to the lower Baram, Kenyah and Kelabit languages of northern Sarawak. The Malay Iban language groups, he suggests, developed considerably later (third to fourth century BC) when the Austronesian expansion had been consolidated in south-western Borneo and was spreading to eastern Sumatra and the Malay peninsula. King summarises from Bellwood and others a number of characteristics of this Austronesian population, which include rectangular dwellings and frequently multi-family longhouses raised on piles with hearths inside the house; pottery; bark cloth; textile weaving; tattooing; domestication of pigs and fowls; boats; the cultivation of rice, millet, sago, yams, tubers, vegetables, and betel nut. However, a number of writers suggest that the expansion of this population throughout Borneo was not dependent upon shifting cultivation and possibly not on cultivation at all. Bellwood (quoted in King 1993, 98) suggests wet rice and taro could have been major crops, whilst Avé and King (1986) suggest sago (*Metroxylon* in coastal districts and *Eugeissona* inland). Gua Sireh provides the only evidence for rice at this early date (c. 4000 BP), and at a date well in keeping with the general arguments for the spread of Austronesian settlement (Ipoi Datan 1990). It can, however, also be noted that many of the techniques which must have been familiar to the Austronesian ancestors appear not to have been practised where abundant sources of wild foods were available.

EARLY EVIDENCE FOR RICE IN BORNEO – GUA SIREH

Glover (1979) has highlighted the importance of studies of plant remains in South-East Asia, particularly in the context of the debate as to whether rice domestication was preceded by root crops or alternatively that rice and root crops were "sister domesticates" (Gorman 1974: 55–59). In his own excavations at Ulu Leang, in South Sulawesi, Glover (1979: 24) has suggested a preliminary date for domesticated rice (*Oryza sativa* L.) of about 4000 BC – a higher level in the trench was dated 4172±90 BP (HAR-1734). In Sarawak, however, work on plant remains has not yet been carried out to any significant extent. Solheim

(1983) points to this in his review of Sarawak archaeology, indicating that with the exception of Majid (1982) few have collected soil samples, and none have been subjected to flotation. Instead, firm evidence for rice comes from a different source, namely pottery studies.

Gua Sireh is a limestone cave near the town of Serian in the Samarahan Division of Sarawak. It is some 40–50 metres above the valley floor and is approached by a steep and slippery path. The main opening is approximately 12 metres wide and the main chamber in which the excavations have been carried out, is 20 metres wide and about 30 metres deep – dimensions that are very small by Borneo standards. The cave was partially excavated in 1959 by Solheim and Harrison, but most of this work was never published and Ipoi Datan (1990) was unable to locate their field notes for his Australia National University M.A. thesis. He did, however, locate their trenches on his plan and the finds are still in the Museum. Zuraina Majid also excavated in Gua Sireh in 1977 but Ipoi Datan reports that she found little of significance; the same was true of the small-scale trial excavation carried out by Edmund Kurui of the Sarawak Museum in 1980.

It was against this rather unpromising background that Bellwood of the Australia National University and Ipoi Datan of the Sarawak Museum carried out their 1989 excavations. Two main areas were opened at Gua Sireh. The main findings reported by Ipoi Datan (1990) indicate the earliest evidence of human habitation can be set to some 20,000 years ago (ANU 7048, 21,630±80 bp). However, this date may be questionable because of the nature of the material dated, namely freshwater shell. Indeed Spriggs (1989, 598) has indicated that errors of up to 15,000 years are possible in the case of freshwater shell dates. Furthermore, Bellwood (1990) suggests that at the proposed date the site would have been some 500 kilometres inland. At present it is only about 50 km from the sea. Material found in these early layers suggests that both terrestrial and aquatic animals were hunted and freshwater shell fish and wild plant foods were gathered from the vicinity of the cave. Remains indicate that species taken include pigs, monkeys, freshwater turtles, snakes and lizards. Some chert and quartz flakes were also found in these layers. In the layers deposited more recently large amounts of pottery were found. During microscopic examination of the fabric of a number of pottery sherds from these layers, Peter Bellwood and Ipoi Datan observed indications of rice husk which had been used as a temper. This work was followed up by myself, Ipoi Datan and Edmund Kurui in Kuching in 1992, when a number of sherds revealed both the impressions of husk in the fabric and in some cases carbonised remains of husks were included within the sherd. These could clearly be seen at a magnification of about x 10.

The sherds discussed by Datan indicating rice temper (21 in all) are predominantly grey rim sherds, although decorated pieces with at least four different designs and decorative techniques were observed to contain rice temper. The lowest levels at which sherds containing rice temper were found were 20–25 cm in EFG8; charcoal pieces drawn from this layer provided a calibrated date of 4835–4096 BP (ANU 7049: Charcoal G8N). An AMS date from rice husk in pottery from F8 suggests a date of manufacture of about 4283 BP. Potentially, therefore, these offer the earliest evidence yet for the presence of rice in Sarawak, assuming of course that the pottery was made there (although even if not it would still suggest familiarity with rice through whatever contacts were necessary to obtain the pottery).

There is, though, every indication that hunting remained important in the local economy. Pig, monkey, barking deer, mouse deer, porcupine, rat, squirrel, tree shrew, cave swiftlet, bat, soft-shelled turtle, hard-shelled tortoise, monitor lizard and snake bones were all found, and most of the animals, it is presumed, were eaten. Dog bones were also present (Medway 1959) as were crocodile bones. However, Medway (1959) suggests that on the basis of modern ethnographic evidence these bones indicate medicinal rather than food use. Whilst botanical remains were not observed, Ipoi Datan (1990) by using modern parallels suggests that gathered foods could have included ferns, (*Nephrolepsis biserrata* and *Anthrium esculentum*), the tubers of wild swamp taro (*Cyrtosperma*) and a number of varieties of mushrooms and fungi.

A number of other excavated sites likewise indicate a more recent contact with rice-growing societies (Solheim 1983) (Figure 1). The distribution of these sites shows that there is good evidence for contact with mainland Asia at Santabong in the Sarawak River delta. At Sungei Jaong, about two miles from Santabong village, Tang dynasty stoneware (around 1000 AD) was found associated with iron slag and gold. At Bongkissan, close to Santabong, is the Tantric shrine, possibly associated with Kedah on the Malay peninsula, and dated between AD 1000 and 1350.

In addition to these coastal sites, we know that the Chinese traded with Borneo for forest products from at least the eleventh century AD, and that this trade was well established by the fifteenth century (Beavitt 1992). It may be concluded therefore that rice has long been

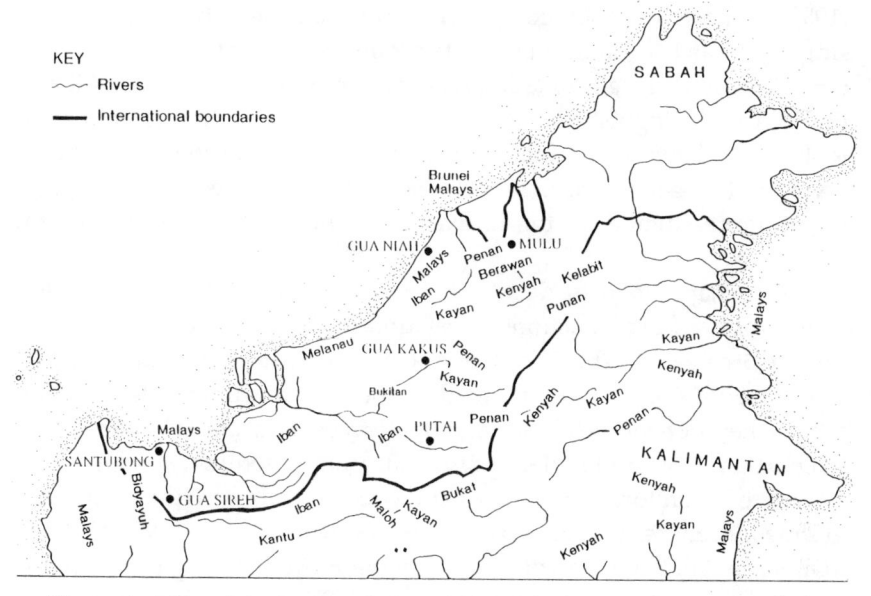

Figure 1. Map of Sarawak showing present-day distribution of the societies referred to in the text (drawing by Deborah Miles).

known in Borneo. However, it appears highly likely that while population had increased throughout Borneo by the time of Christ much of this population would have been made up of foragers, rather than farmers. The next section will consider some of the reasons for the very slow adoption of rice as the major staple for the majority of the population. These reasons include firstly the availability of alternatives to rice, and secondly the social relationship of interdependence between hunter-gatherers and farmers.

ALTERNATIVES TO RICE

In his study of rice domestication in South-East Asia, Glover (1979) summarises Sauer's (1952) argument that agriculture first developed on areas of plenty rather than scarcity. He thought that South-East Asia best met the requirements which he believed would have provided the preconditions for agriculture. These included sedentism in hilly country near rivers and lakes, well supplied with fish and shell fish and where there was a long history of vegetative propagation of roots and tubers. Yet there is a great problem in finding evidence for vegeculture in order to establish dates for its commencement. It is, after all, a very small step to cultivate wild plants: for example, Brosius

(1992a) reports how settled Penan do not plant fruit trees, but in fact simply discard seeds of wild fruits around their settlements and then tender (*molong*) the germinating seedlings to produce fruit trees. Glover (1979, 10) distinguishes between "cultivation" as human effort to look after plants, including wild plants, and "domestication" which involves the genetic and morphological changes required to make plants more suitable to the human environment than to the natural ones.

It is perhaps open to debate as to whether the term "cultivation" could apply to Penan actions in relation to "wild" sago. The implication of Brosius (1992b, 7) is that it would; he uses the term *"molong"* "to preserve" or "to foster" to describe Penan attitudes to trees on which they depend, such as sago, fruit trees, and the *tajem* tree from which they derive blowdart poison. Brosius describes *"molong"* as a system of monitoring resources, in which the Penan think of their grandchildren as potential beneficiaries. He recounts (1992, 112) the manner in which Penan will often thin out a clump of sago palm stems in order to encourage future starch production, even if they are not harvesting it on that occasion. Penan also take leaf buds, which will then not develop into starch bearing trunks, however, they are careful not to remove so many buds that trunk formation is seriously depleted. Perhaps, however, "cultivation" is too rigid; a term such as "manipulation" of nature may be more accurate.

Penan reliance on wild sago when their environment is being destroyed through tropical hardwood-logging has made them famous throughout the world as a hunter-gatherer society under threat. What is less well known is that most Penan are not nomadic although most are heavily dependent on "wild" sago, and furthermore that many other "settled" peoples are, or at least were until recently, heavily dependent upon sago. Rice for these groups does not provide year-round subsistence requirements. The simplistic analytical categories hunter-gatherer and farmer do not in fact accurately describe many of the interior peoples. Indeed one of the major coastal peoples, the Melanau, do not fit neatly into the farmer category: they are long settled, converted to either Islam or Christianity, and are cultivators of sago, although growing mainly domesticated varieties (*Metroxylon*) which grow in swamp lands – this contrasts with the hill sago (*Eugeissona*) of the interior peoples. It is noteworthy that Melanau oral accounts (Kurui, pers. comm.) describe how a mythical ancestor collected sago plants which they then cultivated from small plants which had grown from sago seeds which had floated down a river, and then germinated on the bank. It is interesting that these plants are described as having originally grown from seeds, because if the seeds of swamp sago are planted now they usually rot. Present-day propagation is through the vegetative planting of suckers.

FORAGERS AND FARMERS – PENAN RELATIONS WITH SETTLED SOCIETIES

Most Penan are no longer fully nomadic. Brosius (1992, 61), following Needham (1972), classifies Penan as eastern, numbering some 4294 and western numbering some 2221 (from a census of 1987). The nomadic Penan are all eastern and in 1987 were counted as 360. All of these Penan are to some extent connected with the outside world, and most depend on it for salt, iron and cloth. In return they exchange jungle produce, now notably rattan goods – baskets, mats – and in the past a variety of exotic animal products – gallstones, hornbill casque and rhinoceros horn (Beavitt 1992). There has been some debate concerning the extent to which this trade dominates the raison d'être of Penan society. Carl Hoffman (1981, 4) argues that "the Penan of Borneo derive from settled groups and they are simply the descendants of people who at different times and in different places, opted to specialise in exploitation of deep forest resources."

Solheim (1983) supports this view of Borneo and extends it in space to most countries in South-East Asia and in time "thousands of years into prehistory" (p. 45). Hoffman had speculated that the process could have started with, or almost certainly been accelerated by, links with Chinese traders from the Ming period onwards. He describes the manner in which this trade was controlled by settled people who acted as middlemen between nomadic forest collectors and the Chinese traders. He suggests that the former knew little of the price paid by the Chinese, or the purpose for which the goods were required.

Brosius (1992) rejects the extreme position adopted by Hoffman that the Penan have adapted to occupy an ecological niche, on the grounds that such a view suggests that the Penan could not be considered as a viable society in its own right. Instead, his view of the relationship between Penan and settled peoples stresses their interdependence. Indeed, Brosius emphasises the manner in which the settled peoples would not reveal the location of the Penan to outsiders who might attack them and the generally mutually supportive obligations which were a part of the Sebila relationship cemented through the act of smoking tobacco to which had been added drops of blood of both the forager and farmer who made the alliance with each other.

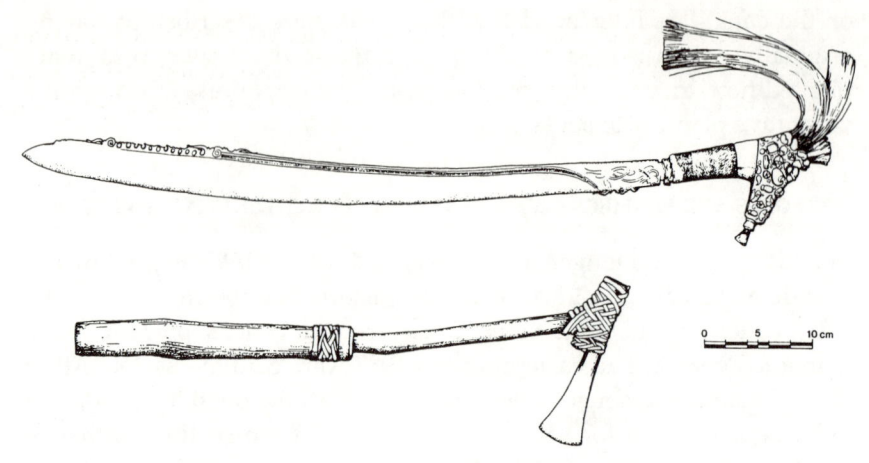

Figure 2. Iban fighting sword (parang) *and axe* (bliong) *(drawing by Alison Ingram).*

Relations between settled peoples and foragers such as those described above are now exceptional and confined to the remotest interior areas. As suggested above, one of the obligations of the settled peoples is not to reveal to outsiders the location of the foragers because they would then be vulnerable to attack. Such attacks and warfare in general have been widespread in north-western Borneo over the last four to five hundred years with major episodes of fighting taking place well into this century. I will argue below that it was this warfare which played a significant part in encouraging the adoption of rice cultivation – a crop which seems to have been available for three to four thousand years and yet was not taken up by many interior peoples until fairly late in the second millennium AD.

THE EXPANSION OF WARFARE AND THE SPREAD OF IBAN AGRICULTURISTS

It has been suggested that the name "Iban" means "roving stranger", deriving from the fact that they pushed other groups out as they advanced, (Richards 1981). The aggressive Iban expansion is well documented in a number of modern works – notably Pringle (1970), Sandin (1967), and Morgan (1968) – although explanations of their warfare have been offered by other writers without first-hand fieldwork experience, such as Vayda (1976) and Wagner (1972). Such explanations have often had ecological underpinnings such as the suggestion that warfare may have been an attempt to obtain secondary forest land in order to avoid the onerous task of cutting down the tropical hardwoods in primary forest with the rather small axes (*bliong*) available to the Iban (Figure 2). However, all the available evidence shows that historically the Iban expansions were directed towards uncleared forest, while ethnographic evidence suggests that the Iban probably had an efficient means of clearing large tracts of forest. Such means include co-operative labour systems (*bedurok*), enthusiasm on the part of young men to demonstrate their strength and skills, and felling techniques in which trees lower down slopes are only partially severed to be toppled by the final felling of a strategically selected tree at the top of the hillside which is being cleared.

Stone axes have been found in areas now occupied by Iban but there is no evidence for an Iban Neolithic phase nor mention of stone tools in their oral traditions (Freeman 1970). For the Iban the use of iron for axes and weapons (Figure 2) was fundamental to their expansion. Low (1948, 210) described the blacksmith as "the only person in the village with the exception of the '*manang*' or doctor whose time is solely occupied by a profession or trade." An important use of iron in relation to warfare was in the construction of warboats (*bankong*), which were made out of planks sometimes up to seventy feet long tied together with rattan and caulked with resin. These boats were regularly taken apart and the planks conserved during the rainy season, and rebuilt for the next year's raiding activities. These boats regularly held fifty to one hundred warriors, and often many more. The European name for the Iban – "Sea Dayaks" – derives from their activities as sea-going raiders of the coastal peoples.

Ecological explanations of Iban warfare are very effectively argued against by King (1976), who shows how many assumptions are based on an inaccurate reading of ethnography. King also shows how the Iban who live closest to the Maloh in the Kapuas did not compete with them for land, but rather engaged in trade and intermarried with them. Iban farmed the hill land and Maloh the lowlands near the river valleys. Other Iban who were settled on the Sarawak side of the border attacked the Maloh, particularly during the nineteenth century. The lowland Maloh settlements were usually avoided by the Iban expansion from the upper Batang Lupar to the Rejang and Baleh rivers (Figure 3).

Nineteenth century accounts clearly indicate that Iban warfare was dependent upon rice cultivation, and took the form of expeditions to enemy territory for days or weeks at a time, usually after the trees had been cleared and rice planted. Women, children and old men would be

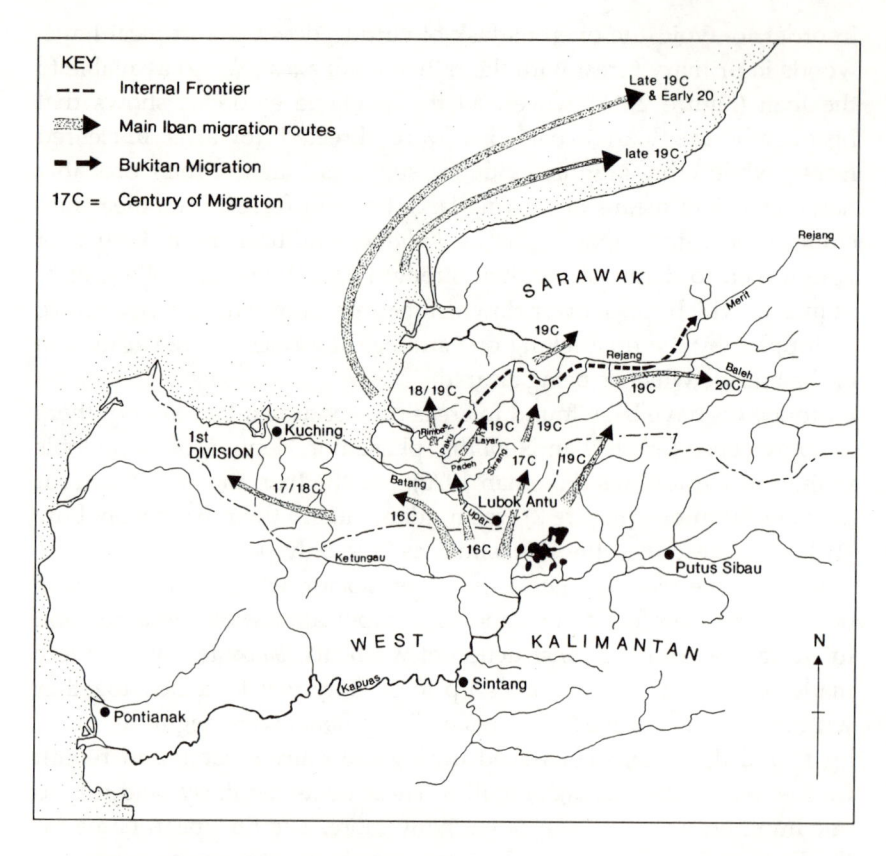

Figure 3. Map showing main routes of Iban expansion and Bukitan migration (drawing by Deborah Miles).

left to cultivate the rice. Young men might make no contribution to farming beyond cutting down trees and carrying rice from the swiddens to the longhouses, but these activities alone served to demonstrate their strength and agility. The value of rice as a staple is shown by Low (1848, 224) who described how five Iban starved through returning home after a raid on foot, through enemy territory, when their boat had capsized, and with it had gone their supply of rice.

However, the account also reveals the manner in which agriculture spread, as does Sandin's (1967a) account based on oral history of Iban expansion. The groups of hunter-gatherers which occupied the land into which the Iban moved were either wiped out by them (e.g. the Seru or Beliun) or learned to farm. In the latter case (e.g. the Bukitan) they either became Iban and lost their old identity or learned to confront the Iban on their own terms. The Iban expansion also accelerated the rate of agricultural commitment on the part of other farmers, such as Kayan or Kenyah, who were part farmer, part forager, but who had to compete with the encroaching Iban for hunting and farming territories. Furthermore, as warfare between Iban and these groups increased they were forced to settle in more substantial and defensible houses and to ensure their own supplies of rice to survive Iban attack.

The Iban oral accounts, as recorded by Sandin (1967a) or Henry Gana (pers. comm.), provide good illustrations of this process of Iban expansion. These suggest that there were a number of groups which became defined as enemies of the Iban and were pushed to the edge of the Iban territories (*menoa*). According to Iban sources one of these groups – the Beliun – are now extinct, having become Islamised by Sarikei Malays. There may well have been some intermarriage with Iban, although the Iban accounts stress the hostility between Iban and Beliun. The Seru were another group where hostility prevailed; they were described by Charles Brooke as "all but extinct" in 1886 (vol. 2, 335) comprising not more than thirty or forty families. Brooke suggests that one of the reasons for their extinction may have been inbreeding. However, many must have been absorbed into Malay society. Sandin (1967a) further helps record the manner in which Iban sold captives of many groups to Malay chiefs, and how in return Iban were given titles by these down-river Malays. The same accounts mention the conversion of many Seru to Islam, and whilst it seems clear that the last remaining culturally distinct Seru died at the end of the last century, many are the ancestors of the Kalaka Malays, who are now rice growers.

TRIBAL RELATIONS: IBAN AND BUKITAN

The Iban oral accounts associated with genealogies (*tusut*) which are still regularly recited at weddings and funerals, provide information on the relations between the Iban and the Bukitan. The Bukitan are the best example of a hunter-gatherer group providing clear evidence of their having to accommodate Iban and to some extent become assimilated into Iban society. Iban expansion was far more than a process of slow encroachment into the edges of the previously settled lands. Rather it was a dramatic, long-distance movement of pioneers into new territories (*menoa*) which sought uncleared land for rice cultivation, animals to be hunted, fruit trees and other wild foods to be exploited, and hardwoods and rattan for building and handicrafts. If there were victims who might fall prey to Iban head-hunting so much the better. These territories would provide all of the prerequisites for the display of Iban leadership.

The Bukitan inhabited the watershed between the Skrang River and the upper tributaries of the Saribas. They were hunters and gatherers, and some were renowned blacksmiths, such as Ginyum, who, according to Iban sources, was killed and whose head was taken when he had been tricked into making a knife for Braugh Ngumpang (some 18 generations from the present). If we accept 25 years per generation, this episode took place about 450 years ago. From another account, offered by Sandin (1967b), we learn of Tindin whose life history involved migrations from the Skrang, along the Padeh and Layar rivers and finally to the Paku where he met and fought with Entingi, the Bukitan leader. A peace accord was established in which Tindin's daughter, Rinda, married Entingi's son, Demong. Entingi is said to have given Tindin a padi bin full of newly taken heads and a brass gong as a dowry. Sandin (1967a) provides one tantalising reference to agriculture in suggesting that Entingi and his followers were different from the other Bukitan of the Paku who were nomads wandering in the forest. Entingi is said to have planted some crops; we do not know which, although tapioca (*ubi kayu*) and sugar cane (*tebu*) are possibilities. It is unlikely that they were rice planters, as we hear in many of the oral accounts that Bukitan learned to plant rice from the Iban. Furthermore, they are generally thought by the Iban to be poor rice growers.

After this noted marriage alliance there were undoubtedly other Bukitan who married Iban and so "became" Iban, while others retained a Bukitan identity which was characterised by a commitment to hunting and gathering as a major element of diet. Entingi's son, Demong, erected a stone boundary marker on the watershed between the Paku and Julau rivers. Those descendants from Demong's first marriage to Rinda who were Iban retained an Iban identity and stayed in the Paku, whereas descendants of this second marriage to a Bukitan woman, Lemia, were not allowed to return. Bukitan oral literature (Sandin 1967b) charts the course of their movement through the Julau and other Rejang tributaries to their present location just above the Pelagus rapids (Figure 3). These accounts indicate that they were largely uninterested in rice cultivation until thirty or forty years ago, moving only when forest products were exhausted. At present there are some 60 Bukitan living in four longhouses in the lower Merit area above the Pelagus rapids. They have a reputation as excellent sawmillers providing the building materials which are used by the neighbouring peoples. They have learned their rice cultivation from the Iban and follow mainly Iban farming methods and festivals (*gawai*). For example, they weed the growing rice in the Iban way, whereas their Kayan neighbours further up the Rejang do not. The Iban aggressive expansion from the Kapuas into Sarawak from the fifteenth and sixteenth centuries encouraged the spread of agriculture in several ways. It was not a process of continuous forest clearance, but rather a process within which islands of rice growing enclaves were created. These enclaves changed the societies on their boundaries. Some hunter-gatherers were absorbed and others were pushed out of the way. They went either to the Islamic rice growers near the coast or towards the less densely inhabited areas to the north and north-east. In the latter case the transition to agriculture, or at least to rice cultivation, did not take place until the twentieth century.

HEAD-HUNTING AND IBAN SOCIETY

Blust (1976), in describing some of the characteristics of an expanding Austronesian population, suggests that head-hunting may have been established by 2000 BC, along with secondary treatment of the dead. Iban explain the origins of head-hunting as a part of the requirements of despatching the souls of the dead to the afterworld. Their myth describes an ancestor, Serapoh, who was told by a member of the spirit world that the plagues which were then affecting the living world were a consequence of the fact that the Iban had no proper burial customs. Serapoh was told he needed a human head to end the period of mourning for the dead. He could find no one to fight with him and obtained the head by killing a Kantu boy whom he bought as a servant. When the Kantu discovered the murder they killed Serapoh's sons and warfare and head-hunting between the two groups became institutionalised. Head-hunting was thus primarily, in Iban eyes, a means of showing respect for family members, but became a means by which the living showed their bravery and skills in warfare. The newly taken heads (*antu pala*) (Figure 4) were brought to the home village with much celebration, ceremony and respect; they were given offerings of food, tobacco and betel nut and welcomed as members of the societies (Figure 5) which had taken them. In Low's (1848, 207) words, the purpose of these ceremonies was "to propitiate the spirit by kindness, and to procure its good wishes for the tribe, of whom it is now supposed to have become a member." The *antu pala* were dried in the smoke of a fire and placed in the longhouse suspended in rattan baskets in a circular arrangement. The first stage (*enchaboh arong*) of the

Figure 4. Newly taken heads (Hose and MacDougal 1912, reproduced by permission of Frank Cass).

celebratory festival for war (*gawai burong*) should be performed soon after the head had been taken, because of the danger of the unappeased victim to the soul of the head taker. The heads were displayed in the open and public part of the house and can still be seen in many longhouses. At a later stage (often many years later) the dried skin, hair and lower jaw would be removed and a new basket constructed (Figure 6). These skulls (*kabak*) would be suspended on a straight pole. Sandin (1967, 68–69) provides a graphic description of Iban recollections of a head-hunting episode:

> It was during this attack that Chulo (Tarang), a leading warrior of Linggir (Mali Lebu), received his nickname (*ensumbar*). In the heat of the battle he jumped from the high open platform (*tanju*) of one of the Banting longhouses, carrying two valuable jars which he had looted, one over each arm, and holding a head which he had just taken in his mouth. "I am Chulo," he called out, "my name is now
>
> Tarang mandang Banting, Tarang mandang Lingga
> Tarang mandang langit, Tarang mandang dunya."
>
> (Light flashing over Banting, light flashing over Lingga
> Light shining in the heavens, light over the whole world.)

Figure 5. Placating the spirit of a head (kabak) after removal of skin (photograph by P. Beavitt).

WARFARE AND SOCIAL STRUCTURE

Having considered the manner in which Iban interacted with hunter-gatherer societies, we need to examine what it was about the structure of Iban society which rewarded warfare and encouraged the spread of a population which was both expanding through reproduction and through the incorporation of hunter-gatherers. As noted, this expansion of the Iban seems to have commenced in the fifteenth and sixteenth centuries and spread to cover approximately one half of the land within the present state of Sarawak (Sandin, 1967).

The early development of coastal states such as Brunei or Santubong in Borneo left the interior relatively untouched. It is suggested (King 1993, 119) that even iron, which was to be so necessary for the Iban expansion, was probably scarcely available in the interior before the fourteenth century. The states were based on trade and commerce rather than agricultural development. Since much of the coastal plain of Borneo is covered with mangrove and nipah swamp, it was not easily cultivable with the slash-and-burn methods available in the past, and even now with modern technology much remains in its natural state. The early states thus depended on the trade of forest pro-

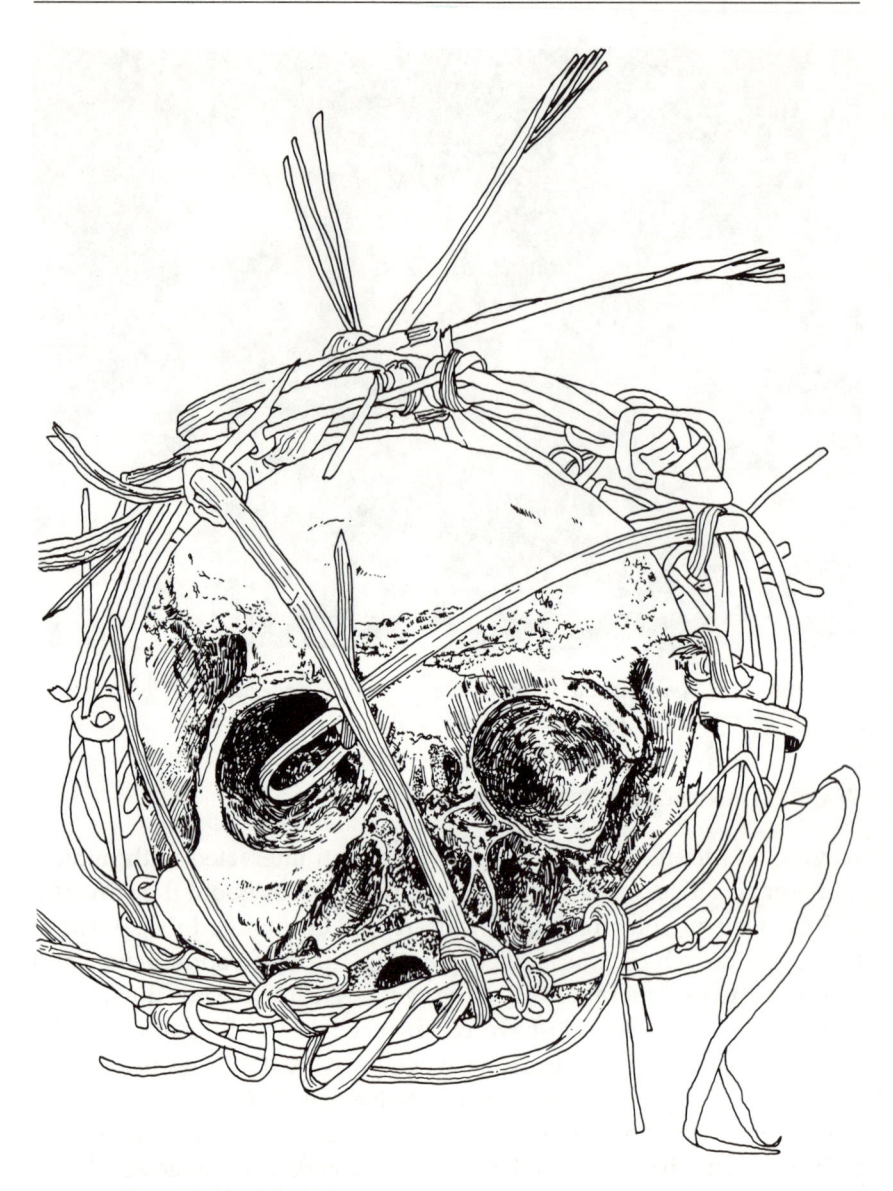

Figure 6. Skull (kabak) *prepared for suspension on a straight pole.*

ducts from the interior. We have evidence from sixteenth-century European visitors to South-East Asia and from Chinese sources of trade between Borneo, India and China in which gold, birds nests, animal gall stones, rhinoceros horn and other animal products, gem stones, camphor, aromatic woods, wild latex, canes, and vegetable tallow were traded for cloth and ceramics. However, whilst the early states had contact with the interior peoples they had very limited influence over them. The interior areas had very low population densities until the expansion from the Kapuas of the Iban peoples in the sixteenth and seventeenth centuries and of the Kayan from central Borneo in the seventeenth and eighteenth centuries.

It is probable that the establishment of Islam in some of the coastal settlements played a major role in driving some peoples up river to escape its influence. Many of these coastal states (e.g. Brunei) embraced Islam in the early sixteenth century, probably through Indian traders (King 1993). These Islamic states varied in size, although most were small-scale trading posts on which interior peoples depended for salt, tobacco, iron as well as brassware and ceramics, which were adopted as prestige property. However, there was a tension between the interior peoples and these states stemming from various taxes and trade levies. Indeed, the interior peoples were also sometimes captured as slaves or became debtor slaves. The prime means of escape from these arrangements was to move up-river, and the Iban were up-river peoples who seem to have avoided becoming enslaved by the coastal Malay states. They must have nevertheless come under pressure from other peoples who began moving into their hunting and farming territories.

There were at this time three major types of society in Borneo. The coastal states were often small scale with more of the trappings of statehood than real political muscle. Their small income was derived from trade in such items as birds nests. Few had standing armies or the ability to enforce their rule or taxation over the area they controlled but rather depended on native allies to enhance the force at their disposal. The Iban frequently became such allies subsequent to their expansion into Sarawak in order to obtain the heads of enemies; in return they would support the Malays in their acquisition of slaves and plunder.

The second type of society comprised the stratified interior societies, and of these the Kayan and Kenyah are major examples. These societies are described by Rousseau (1978) as containing three main classes: aristocrats, commoners and slaves. Commoners were the most populous group and were free agriculturalists, although they were obliged to provide some labour services for the aristocrats; slaves were owned by the aristocrats, and worked in their households and farms. The aristocratic group controlled membership of the community, migration to new areas, head-hunting and raiding parties. Longhouses were large substantial structures, built largely of hardwoods. They were not easily moved, nor were they easily added to because they were organised according to status and new households could not usually be accommodated unless the house was being totally rebuilt. Marriage was a relatively complex affair, involving discussions of rank, bride wealth exchanges and the formation of political alliances.

In contrast, the third type of society consisted of egalitarian groups. These were structurally much more flexible and their communities were far more loosely organised. They could easily absorb new members, particularly if they could claim some affiliation through kinship or marriage ties, but also even if they were unrelated. New families could join the end of a longhouse community. Furthermore, families could leave longhouse communities if they chose and move elsewhere. Houses were traditionally much less elaborate than those of most of the hierarchical peoples and could be moved easily or abandoned in the search for new lands. Leadership was largely based on personal qualities and the role of the leader was to arbitrate between disputants through reference to *adat* (customary law), and to lead migrations and war parties. Within this egalitarian society, leadership of migration was open to all and families could leave one longhouse and form another. Movement was, however, not uncontrolled or haphazard. Members of a longhouse community were united by their adherence to the *adat*, and were collectively responsible for the maintenance of the spiritual balance on which the well being of all depended. The founder of a new house had to have the necessary charms to ward off evil forces. These could be obtained by an aspiring leader and if confirmed by the correct dreams could provide the basis to persuade others of the legitimacy of the claims of leadership. In pioneering days the migration leader (*tuai mindah*) would need to be war leaders (*tuai ngayau*). Freeman (1981) calls such leaders *pun mubok menoa* (originator of the opening up of the land). He also records the manner in which the cognatic kinship of the Iban facilitated the formation of large fighting groups in which an other male in "the interlocking aggregation of kindreds" that made up the tribe of this *pun ngayau*, or of any other friendly Iban tribe, could join such a fighting group if he so chose. He describes the expedition of 1863 led by Charles Brooke which started with a force of 2,400: five days and some fifty miles distant it had grown to 3,500 and three weeks later, at the height of the campaign, it had grown to 15,000. The overwhelming majority of such war and migration leaders were men although there are accounts of women in the *tusut*. For example, in the settlement of the Paku (Figure 3) Tindin is remembered as the *pun mubok menoa*.

Some 15–16 generations (= c. 400 years) ago he moved from the lower Skrang, fought with the Bukitan in the Padeh area and established his home in the lower Paku. The process of forest clearance, fighting with Bukitan and population expansion continued and by 7–8 generations ago a woman, Nasa, is credited as the migration leader to the mid-Paku, some 10 miles up-river.

In general, however, warfare set up different career paths for men and women. Males would advance in status through the taking up of heads and carrying out festivals associated with warfare. For women, status centred on the weaving of textiles, in which prestige was associated with particular designs, and the ability to weave these designs had to be confirmed in dreams. Warfare also became of significance in making successful head-hunters more eligible in marriage. Hose and McDougall (1912) reported how "the Iban women urge on the men to the taking of heads; they make much of those who bring them home, and sometimes a girl will taunt her suitor by saying that he has not been brave enough to take a head".

The development of warfare thus played a critical role in the formation of Iban culture and society. It seems highly likely that as a part of the Iban expansion some hunter-gatherer societies came to be aggregated around a core of advancing agriculturalists. These groups then became Iban through their adherence to Iban techniques of rice cultivation and its associated *padi* cult and through the adoption of head-hunting which was primarily justified in Iban customary law (*adat*) as providing the means by which the souls of the dead could be safely despatched to the afterworld. Here the souls would facilitate the work of the living as rice cultivators. Lingering and malcontent souls are thought by the Iban to become *antu rua* – spirits of waste – whose presence is most clearly manifested in the harvested and stored padi becoming used up too quickly. Life and death, fighting and food, are thus all inter-linked elements in the dramatic expansion of the Iban. The celebration of head-hunting was fundamental to the nature of Iban society and the spread of agriculture across Sarawak was to a significant extent a consequence of a quest for victims.

Acknowledgements

With thanks to Sarah Beauchamp for typing an illegible script and to Neil Christie for valuable comments on a legible text. Figure 4 is reproduced by kind permission of Frank Cass.

REFERENCES

Ave, J. B. and King, V. T. 1986. *The Peoples of Weeping Forest: Tradition and Change in Borneo*. Leiden, National Museum of Ethnology.

Beavitt, P. 1992. Exotic animal products and Chinese trade with Borneo. *Anthropozoologica* 16, 181–88.

Bellwood, P. 1990. *The Prehistory of Borneo*. Paris, Autrement.

Brooke, C. 1866. *Ten Years in Sarawak*. London, Tinsley Bros.

Brosius, J. P. 1992a. The Axiological Presence of Death Penan G@ng Death Names. Unpublished PhD. Thesis, University of Michigan.

Brosius J. P. 1992b. Perspectives on Penan development in Sarawak. *Sarawak Gazette* 119 no. 1519, April 1992.

Freeman, J. Derek, 1953. Family and Kin among the Iban of Sarawak. Unpublished PhD Thesis, University of Cambridge.

Freeman, J. D. 1970. *Report on the Iban*. London, Athlone Press.

Freeman, J. D. 1981. *Some Reflections on the Nature of Iban Society*. Canberra, Australian National University.

Glover, I. C. 1979. Prehistoric plant remains from southeast Asia, with special reference to rice. In *South Asian Archaeology 1977*. Naples (Papers from the Fourth International Conference of South Asian Archaeologists in Western Europe).

Gorman, G. F. 1974. Modèles apriori et préhistoire de la Thailande: à propos des débuts de l'agriculture en Asia du Sud-Est. *Etudes Rurales* 52–56, 41–71.

Harris, M. 1975. *Cows, Pigs, Wars and Witches*. London, Hutchinson.

Hoffman, Carl, L. 1981. Some notes on the origins of the "Punan" of Borneo. *Borneo Research Bulletin* 13 (2), 71–75.

Hose, C. and McDougall, W. 1912. *The Pagan Tribes of Borneo*. London, Frank Cass.

Ipoi Datan 1990. Archaeological Excavations at Gua Sireh (Serian) and Lubang Angin for Gunong Mulu National Park, Sarawak, Malaysia. Unpublished M.A. Thesis, Canberra, Australian National University.

King, V. T. 1976. Migration, warfare and culture contact in Borneo: a critique of ecological analysis. *Oceania* 46 (4), 306–27.

King, V. T. 1993. *The Peoples of Borneo*. Oxford, Blackwell.

Low, H. 1848. *Sarawak; its Inhabitants and Productions*. Richard Bentley 1848.

Medway 1959. Niah animal bone: II. *Sarawak Museum Journal* 9 (13–14), 151–63.

Morgan, S. 1968. The Iban aggressive expansion: some background factors. *Sarawak Museum Journal* 16, 141–85.

Needham, R. 1982. Penan, Punan. In F. M. Lebar (ed.), *Ethnic Groups of Insular South East Asia*, vol. 1, 176–80. New Haven, H.R.A.F. Press.

Pringle, R. 1970. *Rajahs and Rebels*. London, MacMillan.

Richards, A. J. N. 1981. *An Iban – English Dictionary*. Oxford, University Press.

Rousseau, J. 1978. The Kayan. In V. T. King (ed.), *Essays on Borneo Societies*, 78–91. Oxford, University Press.

Rousseau, J. 1990. *Central Borneo*. Oxford, University Press.

Sandin, B. 1967. *The Sea Dayak of Borneo*. London, MacMillan.

Sandin, B. 1967b. The Baketans. *Sarawak Museum Journal* 15 (30–31), 228–42.

Sauer, C. O. 1952. *Agricultural Origins and Dispersals*. New York, American Geographical Society (Bowman Memorial Lectures Ser. 2).

Solheim, 1983. Wilhelm G. II, archaeological research in Sarawak, past and future. *Sarawak Museum Journal* 32 (53), 35–58.

Solheim, Wilhelm, G. II, 1983. Remarks on some notes on the origins of the "Punan" of Borneo. *Borneo Research Bulletin* 15 (1), 45–46.

Spriggs, M. J. T. 1989. The dating of the Island Southeast Asian Neolithic: an attempt at chronometric hygiene and linguistic correlation. *Antiquity* 63, 587–613.

Vayda, A. P. 1968a. Foreword. In R. Rappaport (ed.), *Pigs for the Ancestors*, vii–xi. New Haven, Yale University Press.

Vayda, A. P. 1968b. Hypotheses about functions of war and general discussion. In M. Fried, M. Harris and R. Murphy (eds), *War: the anthropology of armed conflict and aggression*, 85–91, 102–05. New York, Natural History Press.

Vayda, A. P. 1969a. Introduction and expansion and warfare among swidden agriculturalists. In A. P. Vayda (ed.), *Environment, Culture and Behaviour*, vii–xi, 202–20. New York.

Vayda, A. P. 1969b. The study of the causes of war with special reference to head-hunting raids in Borneo. *Ethnohistory* 16, 211–24.

Vayda, A. P. 1971. Phases of the process of war and peace among the Marings of New Guinea. *Oceania* 42, 1–24.

Wagner, U. 1972. *Colonialism and Iban Warfare*. Stockholm, OBE-Tryck Stockholm.

Zvelebil, M. and Rowley-Conwy, P. 1984. Transitions to farming in northern Europe: a hunter gather perspective. *Norwegian Archaeological Review* 17, 104–28.

Giving Archaeology a Moral Voice

John Carman

The aim of this book – as set out in the preface and the introduction – is to contribute towards the development of a "voice" for archaeology in the important debates of our time. For this purpose, the social sciences (including archaeology) can be seen as moral sciences, since they concern not simply the brute material circumstances of human existence but also how human beings understand and manipulate those circumstances. In trying to construct a "moral" archaeology, the aim is not to impose either on people in the past or on people in the present a particular moral order (i.e. a set of prescriptions on how people ought to behave or think) but to add to our understanding of how people have behaved and thought at different times and places in the past, how they behave and think now, and why this should be so. The issues of violence and war – the twin themes of this book – are, as indicated in the introduction, of contemporary concern to a number of branches of the social sciences. It is time for archaeology to start making its own contribution to these debates.

THE ARCHAEOLOGY OF VIOLENCE

The papers in this book have considered the phenomenon of violence from a number of archaeological perspectives reflecting the areas contributors were initially invited to consider. These were: the definition of – and archaeological correlates for – violence; the circumstances (including the extra-personal causes) of violence; sanctioned versus non-sanctioned violence; "levels" of violence – interpersonal, intra-societal, inter-societal – and the boundaries between them; moral versus physical violence; violence towards objects rather than people; the phenomenon of war (and its distinction – if valid – from warfare, the making of war); ethical and moral aspects of the uses of violence.

In general, archaeologists have taken a relatively unsophisticated approach to the study of violence and war. They have usually drawn on *a priori* assumptions and knowledge to interpret their material, either by concentrating study on objects classed as "weapons" (Oakeshott 1960; Scottish Art Review 1965; Snodgrass 1964) or by making studies of previously known military organisations by reference to material remains (Webster 1969; Dixon and Southern 1992). This is not to deny the usefulness of such approaches, but they have failed to provide much more than illustrations and examples of things already known from other classes of evidence.

A more sophisticated approach is conventionally taken in the field of "forensic archaeology" (Boddington et al. 1987; Davis 1992; Iscan 1988), where the concern is to discover the precise cause and circumstances of death. In the case of Lindow Man (Stead et al. 1987) detailed dating, medical and environmental study complemented by a consideration of folklore and other finds at the same location led to the conclusion that "Lindow Man was executed" rather than murdered (Stead 1986, 178). On the day he died, the victim ate a meal washed down with water, and was then (p. 177)

> stripped naked, apart from a fox-fur band on his left arm. . . . While standing or kneeling he was struck from behind [with an axe]. . . . Perhaps at the same time he received a vicious blow in the back...which broke one of his ribs. Then a cord was tied tightly round his neck. . . . A stick inserted into the cord . . . was used to twist it tighter and tighter. Unconscious . . . Lindow Man was now strangled and his neck was broken by the garrotte. That was the moment of death – but the executioners had not yet finished with their victim. They slit his throat. . . . At the end of this gruesome sequence the body was dropped face downwards into . . . the bog.

Where attempts are made to do more than simply catalogue the material remains of warfare, anthropological theory is usually drawn upon to construct a model of what war by the community under study would be like, and the archaeological material is then interpreted in the light of that model. Halsall (1989, fig. 11.1) constructed a model of "warfare and society" from anthropological sources which he used to understand Anglo-Saxon warfare. This comprised lists of the levels of violence (from brawls through feud to warfare), scales of warfare (frequent and small-scale versus periodic and serious), and distinguished the reasons for and the effects of making war between small-scale "ritual" war and large-scale "non-ritual" war. This, he argued, overcame the problems of the ambiguity of the evidence for warfare in England before the Norman conquest (AD 1066) by allowing the recognition of at least two kinds of warfare operating concurrently. Similarly, Mercer (1989; 1989b) draws on anthropological insights to understand violence in the British Neolithic, distinguishing various kinds of warfare by reference to their causes and their relative frequency among types of society as measured by economic subsistence. On this basis, he infers from the evidence of defensive sites and their destruction, together with evidence for contemporary economic activity, that in Britain by about 3000 bc "a currency of warfare" was established, fuelled by economic rivalry and taking the form of cattle-raiding (Mercer 1989b, 11). Elsewhere, research has led to the identification of war as one of the causes of "tribalization" (itself an anthropological concept rather than an archaeological one) among the Kayenta Anasazi in the twelfth and thirteenth centuries AD (Haas and Creamer 1993; Haas 1990).

This kind of approach – in which anthropological understandings are thrown "forward" onto archaeological evidence – was supported by Darvill (1989) in his review of a Prehistoric Society conference on prehistoric warfare. Such approaches can be criticised, however, on the grounds that they too are based on *a priori* assumptions about the nature of the evidence, the meaning of that evidence and what was happening in the past society under study. In this case, perhaps the archaeological evidence is not so much seen against an anthropological background (which is perhaps what is thought to happen) but instead is perceived through the filter of anthropological assumptions. If so, the anthropological perspectives used may mask rather than highlight the contribution archaeological study may make to human knowledge. Accordingly, this paper advocates a different approach, one that invites archaeologists to examine past violence along a number of different "dimensions" evident from their material. Those evident from the contributions to this book constitute its themes.

MATERIAL EVIDENCE FOR VIOLENCE

Archaeologists usually have a reasonably clear idea of what constitutes evidence for war and violence in the past. "A strongly defended hillfort implies two things: coercive power in the hands of society's leaders and the need to protect the community from attack" (Cunliffe 1974, 262). Similarly, "evidence of defence prompts us to look for evidence of attack" (Cunliffe 1974, 63), which Cunliffe finds in war cemeteries and the destroyed entrances to hillforts, coin evidence of political unrest among the Atrebates (p. 68), weaponry (p. 65) and occasional warrior burials (p. 65). Here the question is begged that the existence of war cemeteries and warrior burials and the meanings of numismatic evidence are not self-evident but the result of interpretation; here, as elsewhere, violence is assumed rather than proved.

Hawkes' (1989) edited volume, *Weapons and Warfare in Anglo-Saxon England*, draws on a wide range of types of evidence: literature (for military training and organisation), weapon burials, weapon studies, injuries (from which is derived information about fighting styles), place-name evidence (for fortified centres), and (like Cunliffe) numismatics. Mercer's (1989a; 1989b) evidence is more limited: the existence of fortifications, their destruction and burning, and the discovery of corpses containing arrowheads (as at Carn Brea, Cornwall, England – Mercer 1989b, 4).

Haas and Creamer (1993, 25) have a longer list of evidence for war in the south-western United States. They look for "signs that a prehistoric tribal group was either engaged in some form of conflict with foreign groups or was at least concerned about potential conflict." They find this "objectified in the construction of defensive features [at specific places] . . . or the deliberate selection of defensible site locations" (Haas and Creamer 1993, 25–26). On the other hand, there may be defensible "central places", where common goods could be stored [and] to which the population could retreat" (p. 26). Alliances appear as "joint regional defensive systems" and the "increased exchange of resources between allied villages" (p. 27). An increase in the burning of structures provides evidence for actual fighting, especially "a pattern of burned storage rooms as opposed to living rooms" (p. 27), as does "significant numbers of broken forearms . . . among the population, skull fractures, marks of scalping, and the taking of trophy heads. [In addition], the frequency of deaths of young adult males . . . should be higher in the presence of tribal warfare" and "there should be an overall increase in the frequency of weapons" (p. 27). Against all this, however, they level the caveat that "it is necessary to distinguish the possible archaeological manifestations of warfare from the material consequences of . . . responding to the stress . . . imposed by the degrading environment" (p. 27).

The contributions to this book represent between them a particularly wide range of material: skeletal remains (especially – but not exclusively – skull damage) (Wakely, Filer, Zimmerman, Nikolaidou and Kokkinidou, Lange, Tarlow); textual evidence (Filer, Way, Nikolaidou and Kokkinidou, Lange, Tarlow); iconography and art (Filer, Oosterbeek, Nikolaidou and Kokkinidou, Lange); subsistence data (Beavitt, Zimmerman); ethnographic evidence (Beavitt); monuments and fortification (Oosterbeek, Way, Zimmerman, Nikolaidou and Kokkinidou); destruction (Oosterbeek, Zimmerman, Lange); weaponry (Bridgford; Nikolaidou and Kokkinidou); and context of deposition (all, but especially Wakely, Filer, Zimmerman, Oosterbeek, Bridgford, Tarlow). The wide range of material is perhaps to be expected, but the manner of use by contributors to this volume is particularly exciting. None employs a single body of evidence; and even where a single class of material is under examination (Wakely, Bridgford) it is studied from a range of perspectives. Thus, Wakely distinguishes skull-damage caused by violence from that resulting from medical treatment. Similarly, in her study of swords, Bridgford looks at them from the point of view of their design, manufacture, use (the degree of notching on the blade) and their context of deposition, all of which can contribute to understanding.

The use of the evidence is uniformly sophisticated, with no simple assumptions being made. Thus, unlike some of the examples cited above, evidence such as fortification, skull damage or the presence of weapons is not immediately taken to "mean" warfare or violence. Some contributors are concerned to challenge the assumption of violence as a general causal explanation for archaeological phenomena: Wakely provides a methodology for the distinction of non-violent injury from violent injury, Bridgford seeks among other things to discover if Bronze Age swords were really used in combat, and Oosterbeek challenges the assumption that the Iberian Chalcolithic hillforts indicate extensive warfare in this period. Others seek to find violence where it has previously been assumed away: Zimmerman indicates the different interpretations that can be based on the evidence from Crow Creek, Way challenges any assumption that lack of material evidence for conflict over parkland indicates lack of conflict, Lange provides an explanation for the incidence of smashed facial representations in eighth century BC Assyria, and Tarlow reinterprets the "re-use" of burial grounds in one part of medieval Britain. The use of ethnographic, textual and iconographic evidence (especially by Filer, Beavitt, and Nikolaidou and Kokkinidou) serves to place the archaeological material they consider in its wider social context, a second major theme of this book.

THE CONTEXT OF VIOLENCE

Violent acts do not take place in a vacuum. They are directed against people or things by other people and arise in each case out of particular sets of circumstances. In other words, all acts of violence have a context. Archaeology is the science of material culture in its context (Hodder 1986, 120):

> Archaeology is defined by its concern with context. To be interested in artefacts without any contextual information is antiquarianism, and is perhaps found in certain types of art history or the art market. Digging objects up out of their context, as is done by some metal detector users, is the antithesis in relation to which archaeology forms its identity. To reaffirm the importance of context thus includes reaffirming the importance of archaeology as archaeology.

This means making "abstractions from the associations and contrasts in the archaeological record" (Hodder 1986, 45), and in particular along the "temporal, spatial, depositional and typological" dimensions (pp. 128–34), all of these together constituting *"the totality of the relevant environment"* (p. 139, emphasis in original). This *archaeological* focus on context reflects the emphasis placed on appreciating the *social* context in understanding violence emphasised in the book's introduction.

Hodder's "contextual archaeology" is largely concerned with placing evidence in its particular context – as are Filer, Wakely and Tarlow here. In concentrating on particular archaeological phenomena, each refers to other evidence for that phenomenon, either to distinguish violence from non-violence (Wakely) or to identify similar phenomena and possibly explain them (Tarlow, Filer). Overall, the trend in this volume is to place the archaeological data in as broad a social context as possible. Way sees medieval and early modern imparkment in England as a factor increasing social conflict generally. Nikolaidou and Kokkinidou discuss the intensification in the representation of warfare in the context of an increasingly hierarchical political system, leading also to increased tension between social groups. Lange considers the social position of those she considers to be responsible for smashing the representations of the faces of rulers. Bridgford places swords in the context of their social production, use and deposition. Oosterbeek sees the construction of hillforts as central to an understanding of all aspects of Iberian Bronze Age society. Zimmerman seeks to explain a single violent event by placing it in its ecological and historical context. He and Beavitt possibly take the broadest approach, especially the latter in considering that in Borneo (Beavitt, this volume)

> war and agriculture reinforced each other to create a series of new relations both between and within societies, between war leaders and followers, and between males and females. War effectively became a celebration of agricultural success, and agriculture spread over large tracts of land as farmers sought good farming lands, wild foods to supplement rice, forest products to trade, and victims to fight.

Hodder's contextual archaeology emphasises the contemporary context of the material under study (and thereby the uniqueness of individual cultures). In studying a universal phenomenon such as violence, however, there is the suggestion in some papers here that there are things to be learnt from broadening one's approach. In a manner similar to Patricia Southern (1993, 154), who has suggested that for studying Roman military activity in Scotland it can be useful to examine the practice of other soldiers at different times in the same place or sometimes in different places (p. 150), so Bridgford draws on modern experience in sword-use and Lange on modern understandings of the attitudes of soldiers. Although taking a broadly contextual approach in his analysis of the Crow Creek data, Zimmerman is forced to confront the contemporary context in his interpretation by engaging with the attitudes of modern Native Americans and the responsibilities of the archaeologist in the modern world.

LEVELS OF VIOLENCE

Violence can take place in different degrees. Here, Beavitt and Oosterbeek specifically limit their attention to the most general level – that of war. Zimmerman distinguishes war and raiding although treating them as related phenomena with very similar forms and consequences – especially for those on the receiving end. Filer distinguishes military activity from other forms of violence – such as "mock fights". Similarly, Lange discusses war abroad and uprisings at home. Nikolaidou and Kokkinidou take the broadest range – from war, through human sacrifice and painful initiation rites, to forms of violent control over nature especially as animal sacrifice and bull-leaping. Wakely does not distinguish between wounds caused by interpersonal violence from those inflicted in war – thus emphasising the similarity of the physical consequences of both on the victim – but does distinguish medical treatment from deliberate injury.

"Non-violent" violence

Wakely and Filer provide fairly obvious examples of what may be termed "non-violent" violence. Wakely in particular discusses forms of medical treatment which break skin and bone but with the intent of repairing hurt rather than causing harm. Similarly, Filer's mention of "mock fights" in Egypt suggests the possibility of the pretence of violence without real harm coming to the participants; the reality of broken heads and possible drownings, however, seems to have been very little different from "real" fights.

Other examples of this occupy the realm of the symbolic. Oosterbeek sees hillforts as symbolic enforcers of inequality rather than the sites of warfare. In similar vein, Way sees imparkment as a means of asserting social and political control, but this is met by various forms of resistance: park-breaking and poaching, in particular, rarely result in physical harm to the park's owners and guardians. Grave violation, as suggested by Tarlow, carries an intimidatory message. So too did Lange's violence against representations of the ruler. This may apply also to Nikolaidou and Kokkinidou's discussion of the various means of violent control over nature: if we can do this to *nature* we can do it to *you*. The same can be said for the iconography of violence.

The symbolism of violence

The message that violence is possible and available to be used as a sanction can be carried by visual images, as in the growth of depictions of violence in the Aegean Bronze Age documented by Nikolaidou and Kokkinidou. Filer's Egyptian kings emphasise their capacity to use violence by their common depiction with an upraised arm, ready to strike down an opponent. The same message may be carried in Iberian Bronze Age rock art, and is for Oosterbeek the purpose of the construction of hillforts. The same suggestion can be carried by the active destruction of things. Lange's dissatisfied soldiers chose to destroy the face of their rulers rather than the rulers themselves. In the same way, incoming pagans to the medieval Isle of Man destroyed the cemetery of the present inhabitants. Less utilitarian swords were deposited in Ireland's rivers in the Bronze Age, leaving utilitarian ones for use on people.

Symbolic means can also be used to depict others as violent – as in Zimmerman's mention of the movie-maker's image of the American Indian. Words, too, are important here: as we all know, the cry "Indians!" indicates the imminence of attack by violent savages; but "Native Americans" live in harmony with nature and are victims of the white man's mistreatment. If Zimmerman has a message for us it is that neither picture is completely true: in the end, the victims and perpetrators at Crow Creek were just people.

Gender

Ethnic differences are not the only factors involved in violence, however. As discussed in the book's introduction and confirmed by Lange's discussion of eighth century BC warfare, violence is generally considered an almost entirely male preserve. Nikolaidou and Kokkinidou relate the rise in the legitimation of violence to the rise of androcentrism, and Beavitt takes gender relations into account in his consideration of the connection between warfare and the spread of agriculture in Borneo.

Filer's discussion of the skulls from Kerma invites us, however, to consider the potential differences in gender relations between the present and ancient Egypt. While violent harm tends to predominate amongst males – both as perpetrator and victim – in modern society, at Kerma damage was evident in approximately equal proportions to both males and females. Filer presents plausible explanations for this, but the possibility remains of a fundamentally different set of relations from that experienced today between men and women and especially in the realm of violent behaviour.

Sanctioned and Non-sanctioned Violence

As suggested by Riches (1986) and outlined in the introduction, all violence is sanctioned by someone, even if only by the perpetrator (although, as Riches makes clear, they may not be prepared to admit their actions as violent). Victims will, in general, take the position that violence is non-sanctioned and so may witnesses. Violence in the form of war is highly sanctioned, and may even be deemed to be necessary or even inevitable (thus lifting responsibility off fighters and their leaders and decision-makers altogether). Filer's mention of "mock fights" suggests that these were positively allowed in ancient Egypt, and may have been a normal and required part of professional and commercial life. Lange's face-smashers clearly thought their actions to be legitimate, but to smash the body of the living ruler illegitimate. On the other hand, the law of the time emphasised the wrongness of action against property, which would give moral force to the rebellion and make clear to rulers the anger of those involved. For Nikolaidou and Kokkinidou, the integration of an imagery of violence both legitimised violent attitudes and acted to symbolically control aggression.

WRITING A "MORAL" ARCHAEOLOGY OF VIOLENCE

The assumption behind this book stands at odds with the opening statement of a recent text concerned with archaeology as an interpretive process: "Archaeology is increasingly important in contemporary society" (Hodder et al. 1995, 1). This is not to say that this statement ought not to be true, but that, as things stand at present, archaeology is not especially significant as a contributor to debates about issues of serious concern as it may once have been (Carman 1993).

The findings of archaeology are often drawn upon by workers in other fields to give support to their own conclusions, but what they draw on is often a style of archaeology or an understanding of the past that has been surpassed or abandoned in archaeology, and often a reading of the past its proponent would not recognise. O'Keefe (1982, 349), for instance, cites Childe in attempting to build an interesting social theory of magic as the force which challenged collective religion in the Palaeolithic and thus shaped the emergence of the institution of the individual in the Neolithic (pp. 366–67). Here, concepts such as "band", "tribe" and "chiefdom" are uncritically lifted from archaeological (and other) texts and applied where a modern archaeologist would fear to tread. The theory of magic thus forged has many strengths, but fails in attempting to locate specific stages of religious, magical and human development in specific periods of prehistory where more recent archaeological work would challenge the conclusions drawn. Similarly, Donald's *Origins of the Human Mind* (1991) outlines a theoretical framework which is of particular relevance to Palaeolithic archaeologists since it incorporates both biological and technological factors (Lake 1992, 267). Lake's (1992, 268) review of Donald points out that "Donald is not an archaeologist" and accuses his "treatment of the archaeological record" of being "sometimes inadequate"; in particular, Donald's assertions about the archaeological record are unreferenced and the works cited are "dated and/or simplistic" (p. 268). Nevertheless, Donald has "challenged archaeologists to put their work in its proper context and make a contribution to the wider debate about what it is to be human – and how we came to be that way" (p. 270). The aim of this book echoes this appeal of Lake's so that Hodder et al.'s (1995, 1) statement quoted above can become true.

As stated at the beginning of the book's introduction, violence is not an easy subject to write about, and is problematic for individual contributors to this volume, its editor and no doubt readers too. The purpose of this final chapter nevertheless is to suggest ways in which archaeology can contribute towards contemporary moral debates. In arguing for archaeologists to take more seriously the study of gender, and to avoid imposing twentieth-century cultural constructions on Roman Britain, Eleanor Scott (1992, 89) makes a methodological distinction between the study of material remains and the reconstruction of meaning from those remains. This distinction can, for our purposes, perhaps be broadened into one between the specific type of content a "moral" archaeology might contain from the form in which it could be written. This distinction can then be broken down to show how the two elements support each other.

CONTENT: CONTEXT, MATERIALISM AND LONG-TERM DIFFERENCE

The review of the approaches taken towards violence in other fields in the introduction particularly emphasised three aspects, two of which have been reflected in the contributions to this book, and which may, when taken together, suggest ways forward.

Throughout, the *context* in which violent acts take place was considered crucial to any kind of understanding of the type of violence encountered, at whom or what it was directed and its causes. At the same time, a specifically *materialist* approach was advocated – one particularly apt for archaeologists, containing as it does the recognition that violence is a form of action in the world which leaves its traces upon that world (and all too often in the form of shattered flesh and bone and spilt human blood). These components of an approach require a lack of squeamishness on the part of archaeologists – a willingness to engage with and confront unpleasant things, and a preparedness to call things by their proper names. They also provide a hint as to another potentially very valuable contribution that archaeology can make: as a counter to the prevalence of individualistic explanations for acts of violence.

For a large part of the human past, the names and psychologies of individuals are unknown and will remain so. Accordingly, any understanding of phenomena derived from the content of the individual human psyche is closed to us. On that basis, and combining the materialist approach which is the only one open to the archaeologist with the focus on context (and especially social context) advocated here, archaeology is capable of producing a *social* understanding of violence for particular times and places. There is, however, one major danger with such an approach: that of producing a mechanistic, possibly deterministic, and consequently inhuman interpretation which contains little or no value for the contemporary situation. To prevent this, an additional component needs to be added from outside the discipline: Riches' (1986) anthropological recognition of the three-way relationship between victim, witness and perpetrator combines an abhorrence of the action with a simultaneous identity of the common humanity of all those involved.

The third aspect touched upon in the book's introduction is also particularly apt for an archaeological approach, although not well developed here: that of the *long term*. Over time, the construction of a society and the way things are viewed and understood by people will change. These changes are reflected in, and sometimes caused by, changes in the material record. They can therefore be traced archaeologically. Indeed, it is the process of change which frequently marks the passage of time: an unchanging world is also a "timeless" one (Fabian 1983, 52–69). Thus, the long term marks significant change, and change means the difference of the past from the present. The past, then, becomes a place where things are different from the way they are now: the past comes to represent an alternative way of being, a challenge to our present perceptions of the world.

The idea of the fundamental difference of the past from the present is one that is being actively investigated in so-called "archaeologies of the body" in which it is recognised that even the one thing we all share – our physical frame – is to some large extent culturally constructed. Three examples will serve to introduce the notion that an archaeology of violence can form part of this "archaeology of the body": one example comes from outside the discipline of archaeology, but constitutes a starting point for many contributions to it and is particularly relevant to our concerns; the other two are specifically archaeological but do not directly concern violence.

Foucault's *Discipline and Punish* charts the replacement of physical torture and public execution with incarceration as the means of treating criminals in European culture from the late eighteenth century to the mid-nineteenth and beyond to the present. This shift represents two simultaneous processes: "the disappearance of punishment as a spectacle" (Foucault 1977, 8); and "a slackening of hold on the body" (p. 10). As the process took place "the tortured body was avoided" (p. 14) and "the non-corporal nature of the penal system" became increasingly established (p. 16). This shift in methods of processing criminals is not simply the product of increasing humanity, but also marks a shift in the object of punitive operation, from the body of the criminal to the soul (p. 16). This in turn represents a greater change in the structures of Western thought (Foucault 1977, 23):

> [this] book is intended as a correlative history of the modern soul and of a new power to judge; a genealogy of the present scientifico-legal complex from which the power to punish derives its bases, justifications and rules, and from which it extends its effects and by which it marks its exhorbitant singularity.

This "exhorbitant singularity" epitomises our modern society, which is invested with identically-structured institutions performing varied functions so that "prisons resemble factories, schools, [military] barracks, hospitals, which all resemble prisons" (p. 228).

For Foucault (1977, 35), "in the 'excesses' of torture a whole economy of power is invested." The extreme horror of a public execution "has a juridico-political function. It is a ceremonial by which a momentarily injured sovereignty [of the state or monarch] is reconstituted" (p. 48). Here, then, we meet the symbolic power of violence commented upon by Riches (1986, 11). We in the West no longer condemn our criminals to horrible death by torture, and indeed by international law it is a crime to subject anyone to "cruel and unusual punishment". The kind of execution which was common in the eighteenth century and before would now be considered as cruel and unusual. It follows that this kind of punishment was not considered either as particularly cruel or unusual in its day. The change, then, represents not simply the rise of "humanitarianism" but also a shift in society's attitude towards the human body (Foucault 1977, 54):

> the existence of public tortures and executions were ... the effect of a system of production in which labour power, and therefore the human body, has neither the utility nor the commercial value that are conferred on them in an economy of the "industrial" type. Moreover, this "contempt" for the body is certainly related to a general attitude to death.

Here, in this modern historical account of penal practice, we find reflected several of the themes evident from contributions to this book: the materiality of violence (especially its effect on its victims); the context – political, social, ideological – in which it took place; the level at which violence took place – that of the state versus the individual; the symbolic power of the infliction of harm in public; and the manner in which such violence was expressly sanctioned by juridico-political authority.

Specifically archaeological texts suggest other changes in attitude towards the human body since the distant past. Yates' (1990) analysis of Bronze Age rock carvings at Bohüslan, Sweden present a challenge to the distinction between "sex" and "gender" (the one determined biologically, the other culturally) on the grounds that biologically-based "sex" distinctions between "male" and "female" do not take account of the third category of "abnormalities" recognised by medicine and students of physiology (Nordblah and Yates 1990, 224). Yates' analysis and interpretation of the carved images reveals evidence for further "abnormalities": people "becoming" boats and animals while boats and animals "become" people, among other strange things (Yates 1990, 175–87). The outcome is that "biological sex is a composite concept.... The two main classes male and female are not totally separated but rather two extremes on the same scale" (Nordblah and Yates 1990, 224) and thus "the binary biological structure with which our own culture is concerned is not the only possible one nor, indeed, one that can have claim to natural and therefore cross-cultural status" (p. 225).

By contrast with Yates, Barrett (1991; 1994) and Thomas (1991) construct a past that is different from the present, based upon a common understanding of the human scale across the millennia. Barrett's chosen focus is on human movement through space. Of prehistoric monuments in Wiltshire, England, he says (1994, 29):

> for the distinctions [between people] to have operated . . . it was necessary for people to move between these [architectural] regions; to enter and leave each other's presence, to observe passively or to act, to lead processions or to follow. The practice of social life is thus . . . performed.

This "archaeology of ritual" sees ritual activity as a form of objectified (through movement and performance) (textual) discourse (Barrett 1991, 5; see also Thomas 1991, 34), focusing on the physicality and "objectivity" of ritual acts (Barrett 1991, 4–6) wherein the "text of [collective Neolithic burial] ritual would have been written in the bodily

[233]

movement of those within the tomb" (p. 8) and where participants are guided through a series of specific signifiers, leading them to make the approved connections between them (Thomas 1991, 34). The focus of individual Beaker burials, for Thomas (1991, 34), was on the body of the deceased, and objects which were put into the ground "constituted material signifiers whose role was to ensure that the intended reading of the dead person was made by the audience within the temporally restricted conditions of the funeral." Mourners thus became active participants in the funerary ritual (Thomas 1991, 39) and the significance of the Beaker assemblage lay in the reading of the (dead) body (p. 40). Summing up this style of approach, Barrett's (1994, 73) "interpretive archaeology [is intended to achieve] . . . an understanding of what may have been possible within certain material conditions . . . It is an open-ended project in which we must re-evaluate the pasts which we have created" and to this end his overall project "is concerned with the creation of the human subject" (p. 155).

These two very different approaches to the difference of the past by Yates and by Barrett and Thomas – one specifically seeking out and defining difference, the other drawing on a common humanity to delineate difference – again emphasise the importance of context and of materiality in writing the past. They also reflect other themes of this collection: types of evidence, symbolism (as rock-carving images, of assemblages of objects or as movement through spaces); gender; and what is sanctioned and non-sanctioned. Although not specifically concerned with the issue of violence, both approaches nevertheless have a moral dimension to their work in the sense meant here.

Writing the Past a Different Way

Exploring new ways in which archaeology may be written has become something of a feature of contemporary archaeological texts, especially those written from a post-processual perspective. These generally fall into two kinds: discussion of what a new form of writing might be like; and attempts at producing new forms of archaeological text. This chapter is necessarily of the former kind.

Considerations of writing draw heavily on the realisation that archaeology is always written (Shanks and Tilley 1987, 16) – whether in the form of site reports and syntheses, or more metaphorically in museum displays and other forms of publication (Carman 1995). The mediating role of the text is emphasised, in that it transforms its object and thus "writing material culture is producing material culture"

(Tilley 1990, 332). Accordingly, the production of meaning is "an expressive and formative exercise" in which texts are fields of meanings which require on the part of the author an attention to detail, rather than the reduction of objects to tables of attributes, and the use of data as a means of clarification of an argument rather than its sole basis (Tilley 1990, 333-34). In attempting to produce his own "producer" rather than "consumer" text, Tilley (1991, 81) urges the building-in of contradictions to a text so that there are "cracks" in it where it is broken and becomes non-linear. In a similar way, he is self-reflexive throughout (see, for example, p. 183).

An alternative line taken in feminist archaeology (Spector 1991, 394) is to include others (women, indigenous peoples whose past is under study) in the practice of archaeology and thus into the written text. The result is an example of a writing form focused on a particular (and generally ignored) body of material described as *a time of loss one summer day at Little Rapids* (Spector 1991, 397-401). The tale is a simple human story, of interaction with white men, refusal to adopt new ways, individual growth (from girl- to woman-hood) and changing times. It contrasts with other styles of writing in that it concentrates on (native-made bone) awl-handles rather than (European-made metal) awl-tips, concentrates on people rather than abstract relations such as "trade", and places the emphasis on the domestic female sphere rather than the public male sphere (Spector 1991, 402-03).

While Tilley's new writing is constructed so as to be deliberately difficult to follow, and requires work on the part of the reader to gain from it all that is there, Spector's is deceptively and beguilingly simple to read and enjoy. They differ greatly in style and to some extent in the content they allow to enter their work, but their aims are similar: to open archaeological writing up to things previously excluded from it. Tilley (like Yates) deliberately seeks out the difference of the past, and makes us work to come to terms with it. Spector (like Barrett and Thomas) emphasises our common humanity with people in the past and tries to make them live for us. Either approach is perhaps appropriate for an archaeology which aims to contribute something to debates about the important issues of our times. Adopting an approach like that of Yates and Tilley, an archaeology of violence would identify and record changing social attitudes to the object of violence, changing understandings as to what was deemed "violent" and what was not, what was sanctioned and non-sanctioned. Adopting an approach like that of Barrett, Thomas and Spector, an archaeology of violence would emphasise the common humanity of victims, witnesses and perpetrators past and present, and the social conditions under which violence took place. Neither approach would make the subject of violence any easier to write about or face, and none of these particular writers may wish to write about it, but each form of content and style can contribute something which can be taken up and used in wider debates.

THE WAY FORWARD

Archaeology has yet to make a major contribution to contemporary debates of moral or ethical concern. The purpose of this collection of papers has been to open the way for such a contribution to be made and to suggest what form it might take. A number of the themes of the book are reflected in the contribution made by other social sciences, and archaeology can add weight to these aspects by providing a historical dimension to them. At the same time, archaeology can itself draw on these themes to make a distinctive contribution not available from elsewhere. This contribution lies in playing off two opposed approaches to the past: its sameness as the present and its difference from the present.

Drawing on its access to the long-term history of the human race, archaeology can demonstrate the universality of violence as an available human behaviour. This points us away from any notion of the capacity for violence as an "abnormal" trait (genetic or cultural) which can be "rooted out" of individuals or cultures to create a non-violent species. Violence may not always be inflicted on others, and may even be a rare phenomenon, but it is always present as a possibility and is simply part of being human. Such a view of the human capacity for violence does nothing to sanction the use of force on others, for at the same time archaeology emphasises the common humanity of all people in all places at all times and the effect violence has on the human frame. That effect is the same on you and me as it is on any other victim of hurt.

Specific archaeologies can also emphasise the specifics of individual times and places to reveal the context of violent acts. These will reveal the circumstances (individual and social) of violence, the causes of it, and distinctions between perpetrator, victim and witness. At the same time archaeology can demonstrate the different forms of violence apparent in differing contexts: war as opposed to individualised assault, symbolic or symbolised/"non-violent" violence and sanctioned versus non-sanctioned violence. From such analyses, constants may appear across time and space: violence as a male preserve, the effect of environmental conditions which may predispose towards war. Other assumed constants may be found not to be: violence may not be a male preserve, and environmental conditions may be of limited importance in leading peoples to war.

Recent developments in the way archaeologists think about the content and form of their written work provide models for a moral and contributing archaeology – an archaeology that makes a contribution on issues of importance to the people of the contemporary world. The aim of such an archaeology is not to impose prescriptions on others – neither in the present nor in the past – but to open us up to the alternatives available to us. Such an archaeology recognises the common humanity of all people in all times and places and challenges us to rethink and to remake our world in new – and maybe better – ways.

References

Barrett, J. 1991. Towards an archaeology of ritual. In P. Garwood, R. Skeates and J. Toms (eds), *Sacred and Profane: proceedings of a conference on archaeology, ritual and religion, Oxford 1989*, 1–9. Oxford, University Committee for Archaeology (Oxford University Committee for Archaeology Monograph 32).

Barrett, J. 1994. *Fragments from Antiquity: an archaeology of social life in Britain 2900–1200 BC*. Oxford, Basil Blackwell.

Boddington, A., Garland, A. N. and Janaway, R. C. (eds) 1987. *Death, Decay and Reconstruction: approaches to archaeology and forensic science*. Manchester, University Press.

Carman, J. 1993. The P is silent – as in archaeology. *Archaeological Review from Cambridge* 12 (1), 39–53.

Carman, J. 1995. Interpretation, writing and presenting the past. In I. Hodder, M. Shanks, A. Alexandri, V. Buchli, J. Carman, J. Last and G. Lucas (eds), *Interpreting Archaeology: finding meaning in the past*. London, Routledge.

Cunliffe, B. 1974. *Iron Age Communities in Britain: an account of England, Scotland and Wales from the seventh century BC until the Roman conquest*. London, RKP.

Davis, J. 1992. Forensic archaeology. *Archaeological Review from Cambridge* 11 (1), 151–56.

Dixon, K. R. and Southern, P. 1992. *Roman Cavalry*. London, Batsford.

Donald, M. 1991. *Origins of the Modern Mind: three stages in the evolution of culture and cognition*. Cambridge, Mass. and London, Harvard University Press.

Fabian, J. 1983. *Time and the Other: how anthropology makes its object*. Cambridge, University Press.

Foucault, M. 1977. *Discipline and Punish: Birth of the Prison*. Harmondsworth, Penguin. (Translated by Alan Sheridan from the French *Surveiller et punir: naissance de la prison*, Paris, Gallimard).

Haas, J. (ed.) 1990. *The Anthropology of War*. Cambridge, University Press.

Haas, J. and Creamer, W. 1993. Stress and warfare among the Kayenta Anasazi of the Thirteenth Century AD. *Fieldiana Anthropology*, n.s. 21. Chicago, Field Museum of Natural History.

Halsall, G. 1989. Anthropology and the study of pre-Conquest warfare and society: the ritual war in Anglo-Saxon England. In S. C. Hawkes (ed.), *Weapons and Warfare in Anglo-Saxon England*, 155–77. Oxford, University Committee for Archaeology (Oxford University Committee for Archaeology Monograph 21).

Hawkes, S. C. (ed.) 1989 *Weapons and Warfare in Anglo-Saxon England*. Oxford, University Committee for Archaeology (Oxford University Committee for Archaeology Monograph 21).

Hodder, I., Shanks, M., Alexandri, A., Buchli, V., Carman, J., Last, J. and Lucas, G. (eds), *Interpreting Archaeology: finding meaning in the past*. London, Routledge.

Iscan, M. Y. 1988. Rise of forensic anthropology. *Yearbook of Physical Anthropology* 31, 203–30.

Lake, M. 1992. Evolving thought. Review of *Origins of the Modern Mind: three stages in the evolution of culture and cognition* by Merlin Donald, 1991, Cambridge, Mass. and London: Harvard University Press. *Cambridge Archaeological Journal* 2 (2), 267–70.

Mercer, R. 1989a. The earliest defences in Western Europe. Part 1. *Fortress* 2, 16–22.

Mercer, R. 1989b. The earliest defences in Western Europe. Part 2. *Fortress* 3, 2–11.

Nordblah, J. and Yates, T. 1990. This perfect body, this virgin text: between sex and gender in archaeology. In I. Bapty and T. Yates (eds), *Archaeology after Structuralism: post-structuralism and the practice of archaeology*, 222–39. London, Routledge.

Oakeshott, R. E. 1960. *The Archaeology of Weapons: arms and armour from prehistory to the age of chivalry*. London, Lutterworth Press.

O'Keefe, D. 1982. *Stolen Lightning: the social theory of magic*. Oxford, Martin Robertson.

Riches, D. 1986. The phenomenon of violence. In D. Riches (ed.), *The Anthropology of Violence*, 1–27. Oxford, Basil Blackwell.

Scott, E. 1992. Images and contexts of infants and infant burials: some thoughts on some cross-cultural evidence. *Archaeological Review from Cambridge* 11 (1), 77–92.

Scottish Art Review 1965. *Special Number: Ancient Scottish Weapons*. Glasgow.

Shanks, M. and Tilley, C. 1987. *Reconstructing Archaeology: Theory and Practice*. Cambridge, University Press.

Snodgrass, A. 1964. *Early Greek Armour and Weapons from the Bronze Age to 600 b.c.* Edinburgh, Edinburgh University Press.

Southern. P. 1993. Comparative frontier studies. In E. Scott (ed.), *Theoretical Roman Archaeology: first conference proceedings*, 147–54. Aldershot, Avebury.

Spector, J. 1991. What this awl means: towards a feminist archaeology. In M. Gero and M. W. Conkey (eds), *Engendering Archaeology: women and prehistory*, 388–406. Oxford, Blackwell.

Stead, I. M. 1986. Summary and conclusion. In I. M. Stead, J. B. Bourke and D. Brothwell, *Lindow Man: the body in the bog*, 177–80. London, British Museum.

Stead, I. M., Bourke, J. B. and Brothwell, D. 1986. *Lindow Man: the body in the bog*. London, British Museum.

Thomas, J. 1991. Reading the body: beaker funerary practice in Britain. In P. Garwood, R. Skeates and J. Toms (eds), *Sacred and Profane: proceedings of a conference on archaeology, ritual and religion, Oxford 1989*, 33–42. Oxford, University Committee for Archaeology (Oxford University Committee for Archaeology Monograph 32).

Tilley, C. 1990. Foucault: towards an archaeology of archaeology. In C. Tilley (ed.), *Reading Material Culture: structuralism, hermeneutics and post-structuralism*, 281–347. Oxford, Blackwell.

Tilley, C. 1991. *Material Culture and Text: the art of ambiguity. Material Cultures.* London, Routledge.

Webster, G. 1969. *The Roman Imperial Army of the First and Second Centuries A.D.* London, A. & C. Black.

Yates, T. 1990. Archaeology through the looking-glass. In I. Bapty and T. Yates (eds), *Archaeology after Structuralism: post-structuralism and the practice of archaeology*, 154–204. London, Routledge.

INDEX

Abu Simbel (site) 56
Abydos (site) 58
accident 56, 60
Aegean 174-191
Africa 37, 38-39
age 84
aggression 4-5, 7, 8, 28, 139, 170-171, 174-175, 178, 183
agriculture 90-91, 114, 120, 123, 146-147, 181, 198-217
Akrotiri (site) 176
Alcala (site) 123
Amada and Elephantine stelae 53
Amenemhet I (King of Egypt) 52-53
Amenhotep II (King of Egypt) 53
Anasazi (people) 222
Annals of Thutmose III 53
Andes 37
Anglo-Saxons 37, 40, 41
animal-inflicted damage 27, 83, 87
anthropology 133-134, 199
 legal 16
 of violence 10-12, 221-222
 of war 6-10, 12
anti-semitism 133
appearance, of wounds 29-34
archaeology 143, 148, 163, 168-169
 defined 2, 20
 responsibility of 75, 92-93, 226
 of violence 6, 19-20, 191, 220-225
 of war 1-2, 221-225
archers, archery 55, 56, 61-62
armour 35
Asia 25, 38
assassination 18, 66, 167
assault 149, 157, 158-160, 161-162, 163
Assyria 167-173
Aswan Dam (site) 68
Australia 28, 38

Babylon (site) 167
balance (of sword) 104-105
Balearic Islands 118
Balladoole (site) 134-141
Ballintober (sword type) 97
Ballycroghan (site) 101
Baqt, tomb of (site) 55-56
battle, described 54-56
Baútas (site) 119
beakers 123-124

Beliun (people) 209
betony (herb) 41
Beverley (site) 154
Bilboa Park (site) 49
biological effects,
 of violence 11
 of war 8, 50, 169, 176
blade 99, 102-103, 106
boat burial 134-141
boatmen, fighting of 56
Bohovny (site) 101
Bohüslan (site) 233
Bongkissan (site) 202
Borneo 198-217
Boundary Stela of Sesostris III 54
Bousargues (site) 118
brain damage 35-36, 49, 69
Brazil 18
Breughel 41
briga (street-fight) 18
Britain 40
Bronze Age 37, 95-115, 118-119, 123, 124, 174-191, 233
Buckden (site) 161-162
Buckworth (site) 160
building techniques 120-121
Bukitan (people) 209-211, 216
bullfighting 18
bull-leaping 183, 190
bureaucracy 91, 171
Burke and Hare 40
burning 87
butchery 31-33, 40
Burrough Green (site) 161
Byzantine period 68, 69

Cahokia (site) 77
Cambridgeshire 143-164
Camp de Laure (site) 118
Campman (site) 118
Campos (site) 118
Canary Islands 28, 49
cannibalism 26, 139
capture 84
Carn Brea (site) 223
Carp's Tongue (sword type) 99
Carriceiras (site) 120
Castelo Velho de Freixo de Numão (site) 119
Castelos de S. Brás (site) 119
casting, of metal 101, 102, 110

INDEX

Castle Camps (site) 159–160
Celts (people) 134–141
central place 124, 223
Central Plains tradition (CPT) 77–78, 88
Cerro de las Canteras (site) 119
Cerro de los Castellones (site) 119
Cerro de Castrejón (site) 119
Cerro de la Virgen (site) 119
Chalandriani (site) 117
Chalcolithic 116–127
Chapel Hill, Balladoole (site) 134–141
Charnea do Fratel (site) 119
Chibanes (site) 119
children 187–188
China 200, 202, 205
Christianity 134, 136, 137–138, 139, 204
churches 145–146, 147
Cirencester 30
civil disorder 18, 143–164
civil war 6, 64
civilian injury 56, 61, 67
cleaning 96
Cloonlara (site) 113
Cold War 7
colonialism 10, 38
Columbureira (site) 119
combat 113–114, 171–172, 180, 187, 223
conquest 169, 206, 209–210
contact with Europeans 76
copper 99–100, 120, 123
Cornwall 99, 223
coup counting 76
Crete 174–191
criminality 18–19, 143–164, 231–232
crocodile 56
Crow Creek (site) 28, 75–94
Cullen, "Golden Hoard of" (site) 109
cultural resource management 91–93
Czechoslovakia 37

Dainton (site) 101
Dalkey Island (site) 101
damage 96, 106–107, 109–110, 135
Dani, Grand Valley (people) 90
dating 96, 134–135
dealers, of antiquities 95–96
decapitation 30, 86, 137
decoration (of swords) 107
defacement 167–173
Deir-el-Bahari (site) 61
demography 83–84, 90–91, 117, 124, 126
Den (site) 58
deposition 107, 108–113, 114
depressed fracture 25, 29–30
desecration of graves 105, 110
Deshasheh (site) 54–55
diffusion 117
directionality of wounds, blows 31

discourse 138–139, 140, 188–191, 233–234
discovery 75–76, 80–81
disease 34–35
disposal of dead 31, 109, 116, 118, 121, 123–124, 126, 133–142, 175, 176–177, 179–180, 211, 223
domestic violence 6, 17, 64, 65, 141
Downham (site) 161
drought 89

eating difficulties 49, 64
ecology 9, 114, 204, 205, 207
economics 10, 114, 124, 144, 146–147, 154–156, 160, 161, 162–163, 169, 222
Edwin Smith Papyrus 40, 50–52, 68
Egypt 40, 41, 47–71
El Magalon (site) 119
emotion 140–141
England 37, 40, 99, 221–222, 223
environment and warfare 9, 88–91, 114, 206–207, 223
epilepsy 39
Escoural (site) 119
ethnography 27, 28
Ets Antigors (site) 118, 120
Europe 25, 37, 40
    contact with 76
evidence 19–20, 48, 49, 70–71, 175, 199, 222–225
    art as 54–59, 116–117, 169, 175, 176, 178, 179–188, 189
    biological 59–70, 84–87, 120, 176, 221, 223
    textual 50–58, 143, 144–145, 148, 163, 172, 176, 178, 179–188, 189, 199
evolution, social 8, 9, 114, 116, 117, 120–124, 125–126, 213–215, 222, 227
excavation 80–83
experience 1, 11, 14–16, 139
Ewart Park (sword type) 97–98
eyesight loss 49, 62

face, image of 167–173
facial injury 49, 50, 62–69
famine 89
Fay Tolton (site) 76
feminism 235
fencing foil 103
flint 119–120, 122, 126
forensic science 27, 221
forgeries 95
Fórnea (site) 120
fortification 76, 77, 114, 117–127, 176, 111–113
fractures 25–46, 47–48, 51–52, 60–70, 85–86
France 37, 118

[242]

INDEX

gang war 17-18
Gebelin (site) 60
gender 17-18, 28, 49, 64-65, 84, 139, 174-191, 199, 228, 234
genes 4-5, 27, 28, 34, 42, 175
genocide 26
Giza (site) 66-68, 69
Glatton (site) 162
gout 36-37
grasp, of hilt 105
grave violation / desecration 133-142
Great Staughton (site) 155
Greece 38, 40, 41
Grundlingen (sword type) 98
Gua Kakuo (site) 199
Guanche (people) 28, 49
Gua Sireh (site) 199, 200-203
guns, introduction of 10, 76

Hallstatt 98
Hammurabi (King of Assyria) 172
hand, removal of 86-87
hand-to-hand combat 26, 27, 28
hardening, of bronze 100-101
Haughey's Fort (site) 114
headache 49, 64
head hunting 209-210, 211-212, 217
head injuries 24-46, 46-71, 84-86
healing, medical 35-42, 50-52, 226-227
   natural 33-34, 48, 61-70
hearing loss 49, 66-67
Hesa (site) 68
Hierakonapolis (site) 56
hillforts 114, 116-127, 222-223, 227
Hittites (people) 172
hoards 109
honour 18
horses 15-16, 76, 113, 135, 139
hunting 179-180, 189-190, 199, 201
Huntingdonshire 143-164
Hurtgen Forest (battle) 1-2, 20

Iban (people) 206-213
Iberia 116-127
iconoclasm 139
identification of violent injuries 27-28, 61
ideology 91, 117, 120, 121-127, 139, 147, 179-188, 189-191, 217
Ilku (people) 169-170
illness 68, 89-90
   mental 39
image 75-76, 91-93
indigenous peoples 10
Initial Coalescent tradition (ICT) 78, 88-89
Initial Middle Missouri (IMM) 77-78, 88
innate aggression 4-5, 174-175
insurrections 18
intentionality 31, 47, 69-70

interpersonal violence 10-12, 16-19
interpretation 75, 88-93, 117, 120-121, 147-148, 171, 173, 224-225, 229, 230
Inti, tomb of (site) 54-55
Ireland 95-115
Iron Age 37, 135, 199
Islam 204, 209, 214
Isle of Man 133-142

Japan 18

Kayan (people) 209, 211, 214-215
Kedah (site) 202
Kenyah (people) 209, 215
Kerma (site) 49, 62-65, 69
killing, defined 7
   numbers 223
kingship, violence an attribute of 59
Knossos (site) 186, 190

labour 120-121, 207
La Casulla (site) 117
Lachish (site) 168
landscape 118-119, 125-127, 136-137, 139-140, 143, 144, 146-147, 148
La Tailladette (site) 118
law 143-164, 172
Leaconfield Park (site) 154
lead (metal) 100-101
Lebous (site) 118, 126
Leccia (site) 119
legal anthropology 16
legitimacy 11, 228-229
Lexim (site) 119
Lindow Bog (site) 221
"Lindow Man" 221
linguistics 199-200
literary evidence (see also evidence, textual) 52-53
Littleton Bog (site) 109
location of wounds 27-29
Loma de Galera (site) 118
London (site) 27, 133
Los Castillejos (site) 119
Los Millares (site) 116, 118, 120, 126
Lough Eskrogh (site) 101
Lough Gur (site) 109, 113

Mafia 18
Malaya 200
Maldive Islands 41
malnutrition 89-90
Maloh (people) 207
manufacture, of swords 99-103
Marxism 10, 116-127
Matacães (site) 120
materialist approaches 9-10, 12, 14-20, 140-141, 229-237
Maxial (site) 119

[243]

INDEX

medieval 37, 41, 134–141, 143–164, 222
Megiddo (battle) 53
Melanau (people) 204
Memphis and Karnak Stelae 53
Menahem (King of Israel) 167
mental illness 39
Meri-Re-Hashetef, tomb of (site) 61
Mesolithic 199
metallurgy, metallographic analyis 95, 96, 100, 101, 102, 110, 116, 117, 121, 126, 207
metalwork 135, 207, 213
Methone, siege of (battle) 35
migraine 39
military,
  activity 174–191
  injuries 54–56, 61–62, 66–67
  studies 12–16, 221, 226
Minorca 37
mock fights 56, 61, 227
modelling 9–10, 90
modern period 133
Monte Claro (site) 118
Monte de Tumba (site) 119
monuments 2–3, 124, 135, 139–140
moulds for metal 96, 101
Mulu (site) 199
mummification 60
murder 90, 141, 221
Mussolini 168
mutilation 75, 76, 81, 84–87, 92, 133, 137
Mycenae (site) 176, 184, 190
My Lai (massacre) 92

Nabão Valley (site) 123
Naga-el-Der (site) 60–61, 70
Naram-Sin (King of Assyria), mask of 168
Narmer palette 53, 57–58
nasal injury 52, 68–69, 86
Native Americans 27, 28, 48–49, 75–94, 222, 226
nature, attitudes towards 179–183, 187, 189–190, 227
Navetas 118
Neanderthals 25, 26
Neolithic 37, 39, 120, 123, 124, 126, 199–200, 222, 226
Neo-Nazis 133
Niah (site) 199
non-surgical treatment 41, 51
Nubia 49–71
nuclear war 6, 7

occupational injury 56, 61
Odin (god) 139
Old Connaught (site) 101
Olelas (site) 119
oral tradition 199, 204, 208–209
organised crime 18–19

osteology 24–46, 83, 84–87, 176, 177, 186
Outeiro de Assenta (site) 119
Outeiro de S. Mamede (site) 119

Pacific Ocean region 38, 198–217
paganism 133–142
Palaeolithic 25, 123, 199, 229
palatial society 174–191
Papua New Guinea 10
paralysis 49
parks 143–164
park-breaking 143–164
Pecos Pueblo (site) 48–49
Pedra de Ouro (site) 119
Penan (people) 203–205
Penedo (site) 119
penetrating wounds 30, 117
Peru 49
Petraro de Melilli (site) 118
pharaoh 52–54, 56–59, 65–66, 71
Philippines 200
Philip II (King of Macedonia) 35–36
poaching 149, 152–153
politics 141, 144–147, 163
  of the past 75, 91–93
  and war 10
population 8, 83–84, 90–91, 117, 124, 126, 198, 200
Portugal 119, 124
post-cranial injury 69–70, 86–87
post-medieval 37, 40, 143–164, 214
preservation, of human remains 60
primates 27
primitive war 7–8
privatisation of land 144, 145–146
provenance 95–96, 108–113
psychology 5, 18–19
punishment 141, 231–232
Putai (site) 199
Pylos (site) 180, 185

Rameses II (King of Egypt) 56, 58
Ramsey (site) 162
rapier 105
Rathgall (site) 101, 109, 114
reburial 91
recruitment 8, 169–170
regulation, by government 91
relatives, violence by 90
Renaissance 40, 41
repair 96
  (for humans, see "healing")
respiratory problems 49
responsibilities of archaeologists 75, 92–93, 226
reuse 96
rice 198–199, 200–203
riotous assembly 149–150, 162
ritual 107, 108–113, 115, 175, 179–188, 189–191, 211–212, 221, 233–234

[244]

INDEX

rivers 107, 110, 112, 114, 119, 120, 207, 210, 215
rivets 101-102, 106
Romans 9-10, 30, 37, 38, 58
Rotura (site) 119
Rushoe and Whitley (site) 157, 158-159

sacrifice 139, 180-181, 186-187, 190, 221
sacrilege 139
sagas (Norse) 137-138
Santabong (site) 202
Santa Justa (site) 119
Sarawak 198, 199
Sardinia 118
scalping 75, 76, 81, 84, 91-92, 223
scanning electron microscopy 30
Scotland 226
sea, location by 120, 199, 213
self-inflicted injury 28-29
Sekhemet (King of Egypt) 58
Sennacherib (King of Assyria) 167
Sequenere Tao (King of Egypt) 59, 65-66
Seru (people) 209
Sesimbra (site) 119
Sesostris III (King of Egypt) 53-54
Seti I (King of Egypt) 58
sex differences 49, 64
sharpness, of blade 102-103, 110
shield 113, 135
Sicily 118
Sierra de la Pepa (site) 119
simulation 9-10, 90
Sinuhe, story of 52-53
size, of sword 107
skull damage 24-46, 47-71, 84-86
  by pharoah 52-54, 56-59, 65-66, 71
slavery 176-177, 215
smiting 52-54, 56-59, 65-66, 71
social context 75-76, 93, 114-117, 138-140, 143-144, 145, 146-147, 162-163, 175-178, 188-191, 199, 205-206, 209-217, 221-222, 225- 236
social evolution 8, 9, 114, 116, 117, 120-124, 125-126, 213-215, 222, 227
sociology 17
soldiers' graves 61-62
Somersham Park (site) 153-154
So'n Ferrendell (site) 118
So'n Oleza (site) 118
Spain 118-119
spearheads 107
speech difficulties 49, 86
spirits 39
state(s) 10, 124, 126, 213-215
stereotyping 75-76, 93
stone, tools and weapons 15, 31, 38, 62, 64, 66, 80, 83, 85, 168, 179, 199, 202, 207

suffering 49, 71
Sully (site) 76
Sumatra 200
Sumer (site) 190
Sungei Jong (site) 202
surgery 36-42, 51
S'Urecci (site) 118
Suthoe (site) 162
swastika 133
swords 95-115
symbolism 11, 12, 71, 107, 114, 117, 120, 125-127, 133, 138-140, 167-173, 174-191, 227-228

Taiwan 200
taphonomy 26-27, 31, 60, 83, 87
technology, effect of 15, 76, 125
teeth, removal of 86
Tenerife 49
terminology of violence 6
territorial imperative 5
theory, importance of 93
  of war 9, 175
Thera 176, 188
Thor (god) 139
Thutmose III (King of Egypt) 53
Tibet 41
Tiglath Pileser III (King of Assyria) 167
tin (metal) 99-101
Tiryns (site) 180
Tolton (Fay) Site 76
tongue, removal of 86
Torralba d'En Salord (site) 118
trade and exchange 12, 100, 117, 119-120, 123, 126, 141, 199, 202, 205, 213-214, 223
trampling 150
trepanation, trephination 34, 37-42
  defined 37
  techniques of 38
trespass 143, 150, 162
Trez Cabezos (site) 118
tribal zone 10
Troy (site) 117
true war 7
typology 96, 97-99, 117, 120, 125

Ukh-Hotp, tomb of (site) 56
Ulu Leang (site) 200
use, of sword 103-107, 110-112

vandalism 133
Vietnam War 7-8, 92
Vikings 134-141
Vila Nova de São Pedro (site) 118, 119, 120
violation, of grave 133-142
violence,
  anthropology of 10-12, 221-222
  archaeology of 6, 19-20, 191, 220-225

[245]

INDEX

attribute of royalty 59
biological effects of 11
defined 6, 11, 174
domestic 6, 17, 64, 65, 141
and gender 17-18, 174-191
interpersonal 10-12, 16-19
against objects 141, 167-173
properties of 11
relationships in 11, 90, 139, 143, 152-163, 199, 228-229, 231
scales of 6, 148, 226-227
studies of 3-20, 170, 173
terminology of 6
against women 17, 60
writing of 2, 140-141, 229-237

Wadi Maghara (site) 58
war 6, 12-16, 113-114, 167-173
anthropology of 6-10, 12
archaeology of 1-2, 221-225
biological effects of 8, 50, 169, 176
and disease 8
and economics 9
nuclear 6, 7
and politics 9, 10, 13
primitive 7-8
and social evolution 8, 9, 114, 116, 117, 124
and the state 10
theories of 9, 175
"true" 7

types of 15-16
warfare 139
perodicity of 85, 87
wealth 117, 126, 135, 175, 176, 177, 189
weapons 67-68, 85-86, 95-115, 117, 158, 175, 176-177, 185-186, 190, 221, 223
wet contexts (see also "rivers") 107-113
Whitepark Bay (site) 101
wife-battering 17
Wilstrup Park (site) 154
Wiltshire 233
Wisby (battle) 27-28
Witch of Magellen 41
women 17, 55, 60, 62-65, 67, 68, 84, 137, 174-191, 216-217
woodland (forest) 146-147, 160-162, 199, 207
Woodland tradition 77
Worb (site) 36-37
World War I 2-3
World War II 1-2
wounds 27-34, 117
writing 2, 140-141, 229-237

Yanomamo (people) 90
York (site) 27

Zambujal (site) 118, 119, 120, 126